To Ann,
who Has a
Meta - national Personality
Best Wishes
Ajay.
Sep 9, 2004.

From Global to Metanational

From Global to Metanational

How Companies Win in the Knowledge Economy

Yves Doz
José Santos
Peter Williamson

HARVARD BUSINESS SCHOOL PRESS
BOSTON, MASSACHUSETTS

05   04   03   02   01   5   4   3   2   1

Requests for permission to use or reproduce material from this book should be directed to permissions@hbsp.harvard.edu, or mailed to Permissions, Harvard Business School Publishing, 60 Harvard Way, Boston, Massachusetts 02163.

Library of Congress Cataloging-in-Publication Data

Doz, Yves L.
  From global to metanational : how companies win in the knowledge economy / Yves Doz, José Santos, Peter Williamson.
    p. cm.
  Includes bibliographical references and index.
  ISBN 0-87584-870-2 (alk. paper)
    1. International business enterprises—Management.   2. Knowledge management.   3. Organizational learning.   4. Technological innovations—Management.   I. Santos, José, 1951–   II. Williamson, Peter, 1957–   III. Title.

HD62.4 .D688 2001
658.4'038—dc21

                                                    2001024748

The paper used in this publication meets the requirements of the American National Standard for Permanence of Paper for Publications and Documents in Libraries and Archives Z39.48-1992.

Contents

Preface

WE BEGAN the journey that resulted in this book back in February 1995. It stemmed from a nagging doubt that what was known about the development and management of multinationals failed to address the new challenges that companies competing for global markets were beginning to face. CEOs were asking us what they should do when the critical technologies they needed were not to be found in their own backyard but halfway around the world; how to respond when the most demanding and sophisticated customers turned out to be in locations where their local subsidiaries where weak; and how to better mobilize and exploit the knowledge base that was fragmented across individual subsidiaries all over the globe.

We didn't have the answers. Worse still, when we looked at the performance of industry leaders that had seen the hotbeds of new technology and innovative consumer behavior migrate away from their headquarters, the results were alarming. Companies such as Digital Equipment Corporation, Wang, and IBM, which had seen the furnace of innovation in their industry move from East Coast to West, had basically lost the plot—their market shares and profitability had plummeted. In a world where geographic distance was supposedly becoming irrelevant in the face of improved communications and information technologies, why did location seem to matter so much? And if companies had such difficulty in coping with the axis of innovation shifting from one side of America to the other, what would they do if it shifted to the other side of the world or was fragmented across multiple locations as new hotbeds emerged?

We began to explore these problems in detail when Jorma Ollila, the CEO of Nokia, asked us to undertake some research on what a "new age multinational" would look like, so as to help him take Nokia from a company riding on its early development of mobile phones in its home country, Finland, to a global mobile communication equipment leader. A series of briefings on our initial findings and extended dialogues with Ollila and his team in the course of our research helped focus our efforts and sharpen our findings. Five years later, as we see the mobile telephony industry scrambling to understand the drivers of NTT DoCoMo's i-mode success, the first mass-market breakthrough for mobile data and video communications, the questions that prompted our research seem to be more relevant than ever.

In the course of our work, however, we came to recognize that the issue of how companies innovate by drawing on complex knowledge that is increasingly scattered in distant locales around the world has a relevance that extends far beyond the rarefied worlds of mobile telephony, semiconductors, or even high technology. The problem of how to learn from the world and then to exploit knowledge drawn from distant locations turned out to be just as relevant in industries as diverse as food, perfumes, music, auto manufacturing, industrial equipment, pharmaceuticals, and banking.

We started with two key questions in mind:

- How dispersed are the clusters of critical capabilities and markets that companies need to succeed?

- How can globally dispersed knowledge best be combined and leveraged?

Where could we find fertile ground to explore these questions? We examined new companies—the budding multinationals, often from unlikely origins—trying to discover innovative practices, and traditional multinationals with a strong innovative record that were trying to tap new knowledge and innovations from their far-flung operations.

Initially, we carried out interviews at thirty-six companies, a dozen each from America, Asia, and Europe—both incumbent multinationals, such as 3M, Hewlett-Packard, Whirlpool, ABB, Toyota, or Canon, and new globalizers, such as Acer, STMicroelectronics, or Business Objects. Rather than delving into the "usual suspects" of multinational management research—such as Ford, Unilever, or Sony, to name just a few—we looked for unlikely companies, such as PixTech, a global startup in flat-panel displays; surprising successes, such as Shiseido's in perfumes; unusual approaches, such as Acer's in brand building; unexpected knowledge sharing, such as between Affymax and Glaxo Wellcome; and demanding, nonobvious strategies, such as ST's putting a system on a chip.

To a respected colleague who queried, jokingly, about why we studied strange "anomalies," we retorted that this was precisely the point: We were trying to intercept and conceptualize the practices of innovative multinationals that did not rely on conventional wisdom about internationalization and global strategies.

We complemented the initial wave of interviews with a series of in-depth clinical studies on the more intriguing companies we identified, such as PixTech, Affymax, PolyGram, Nokia, ARM, Shiseido, Acer, and STMicroelectronics, some of which have been summarized and published as case studies.

Our emerging conceptual framework led us to revisit a number of well-documented early examples of cross-border innovation, such as the development of the IBM 360 or Nestlé's network of research companies or the Airbus 300. But it became clear that, in the past, the phenomenon of mobilizing globally dispersed knowledge to come up with innovative products and services was a rare exception; in tomorrow's global knowledge economy, it will have to become the norm.

From this work, our concept of a "metanational" emerged: a company that builds a new kind of competitive advantage by discovering, accessing, mobilizing, and leveraging knowledge from many locations around the world. Why another name? Aren't *global, multinational, multifocal, transnational,* and so on sufficient? Not really. We need a new name when we are trying to articulate a new model, a new paradigm. To the metanational, globalization is not about taking home-country know-how to new markets or projecting a formula it has developed in a single "center of excellence" around the globe. It is about efficiently fishing for knowledge in a global pool, harnessing that knowledge for innovation, and then harvesting its value for its stakeholders.

This book isn't about profiling successful companies as role models and entreating managers to replicate their formula. Instead, this book is a manifesto for managers who want to create a new kind of multinational corporation that is purpose-built to win in the global knowledge economy. We hope that this work begins a reevaluation of the theory of the multinational firm, and that our colleagues will accept the challenge of researching this new theoretical space and "make the mesh ever finer and finer."

In laying out this manifesto, we explain why traditional global strategies are no longer sufficient to differentiate leading competitors; we point out why the opportunities to leverage knowledge scattered around the world are growing; we explore the challenges that must be overcome in order to turn globally dispersed knowledge into innovations, profits, and shareholder value. We detail how today's multinationals can use their existing global networks to gain an important head start in the race to build tomorrow's metanationals. We also warn of some important traps that companies risk falling into as they embark on this transition. For startups and budding globalizers, we map out a way to leapfrog traditional competitors by rapidly building a new-style metanational corporation from a clean slate.

The emergence of metanational corporations seems set to change the nature of globalization and its impact on people and nation-states. In a world where companies compete on their ability to discover, mobilize, and leverage knowledge dispersed around the world, what matters is not where you are from but who you are. Countries, companies, and individuals that are small, or are isolated from the traditional "capitals" of global industries, will have new opportunities open to them by contributing a unique piece of the metanational jigsaw, rather than trying to be the best "all-rounder." Distinctiveness, not homogeneity, will be valued.

In expressing these ideas, we have been conscious that innovation is often an elusive concept, and so is the kind of knowledge you need to create it. In this book, we use many kinds of imagery to describe the metanational quest: You compete in *three* planes; you can prospect for nuggets of knowledge, fish in a global pool, cherry-pick the best ideas, or harvest the fruits of your search. We invite you to adopt whatever images make sense for you. Hunt, fish, seek, or sow the seeds of metanational innovation. Just be sure you do it.

Fontainebleau, France; Porto, Portugal; and London, United Kingdom
February 2001

Acknowledgments

SEVERAL of our colleagues were a source of inspiration and insight and this book would not exist without them. Most notably, Gary Hamel, contributed in a major way to the framing of the initial research questions. Conversations with many colleagues, in particular the late Gunnar Hedlund, helped us sharpen our questions and findings. The work of many others, such as Chris Bartlett, John Cantwell, Dick Caves, John Dunning, Sumantra Ghoshal, Bruce Kogut, Paul Krugman, Arnoud de Meyer, Michael Porter, CK Prahalad, John Stopford, and Eleanor Westney, also stimulated our enquiry. Kaz Asakawa's pioneering research on Japanese R&D labs in Europe, and on how they related to their mother companies, was a source of significant insights, so were subsequent interviews performed jointly with him among Japanese companies. Consultants from Strategos, in particular Pierre Loewe and Steve McGrath, contributed significantly to the first phase of the research. Researchers from INSEAD, in particular Jean Louis Barsoux and Marie-Aude Dalsace, also contributed to the work in important ways. We are also grateful to the anonymous reviewers who made important comments and suggestions in respect to an earlier draft.

Our greatest debt remains to the many managers who freely and openly contributed their time and shared their experience with us. We can't list all the ones we interviewed—special thanks are due to Alain, Aldo, Andrea, Carlo, David, Donald, Giuseppe, Jean-Philippe, Jorma, Matti, Pasquale, Philippe, Robin, Sari, and Stan.

Finally, our sincere thanks go to our editors, Colleen Kaftan, Marjorie Williams, and Lindsay Whitman who worked with us tirelessly to improve the exposition and clarity of the argument and through their sustained efforts and gentle prodding saw this project through to completion.

Despite the wonderful help we enjoyed from many quarters, shortcomings and deficiencies in the research reported here remain fully ours.

From Global to Metanational

Chapter 1

The Metanational Advantage

THE GLOBAL GAME has changed. Yesterday, becoming a global company meant building an efficient network of production, sales, and service subsidiaries capable of *penetrating markets around the world*. But the demands of the new knowledge economy are turning this strategy on its head. Today the challenge is to innovate by *learning from the world*. Tomorrow's winners will be companies that create value by searching out and mobilizing untapped pockets of technology and market intelligence that are scattered across the globe.

Consider the following examples:

A money-losing semiconductor firm in Southern Europe became a world leader by combining knowledge drawn from customers in places as diverse as San Jose, California; Tokyo; and Helsinki with pockets of technical expertise scattered from Grenoble to Milan, Noida (in Uttar Pradesh, India), Ang Mo Kio (in Singapore), and Carrolton (in Texas). With this unique combination of specialist knowledge, the firm was able to achieve something that eluded its competitors: It created tailored solutions for customer applications by incorporating dozens of specialized circuits on a single silicon chip. This breakthrough capability provided STMicroelectronics with the foundation for a semiconductor business that has created more than $50 billion in shareholder value and employs more than 40,000 people around the world.

A record company built an organization capable of identifying future global "hit artists" from local talent in the bars and clubs of cities like Sao Paolo, Reykjavik, Naples, Paris, Athens, and Hong Kong. By connecting this new talent with its own detailed knowledge of the international music markets and its global capabilities in creating, promoting, and distributing new albums, the company was able to sell millions of recordings by these new stars. This capability proved critical to building what was to become the world's largest record company: PolyGram netted its owners a sale price of more than $10 billion in 1998.

A startup flat-panel display company successfully entered an industry in which competitors have invested hundreds of millions of dollars to establish themselves. It did so by accessing capabilities it found inside institutions and companies including LETI (France), Motorola (USA), Raytheon (USA), Futaba (Japan), Rhône Poulenc (France), SAES Getters (Italy), Unipac (Taiwan), and Sumitomo (Japan) to create a new type of flat-panel display. This unorthodox strategy allowed PixTech to achieve the advantages of global scale overnight.

These are just three instances of a powerful new opportunity in the global corporate landscape: the chance to build new types of competitive advantage by connecting globally dispersed knowledge. Our examples are the forerunners of tomorrow's winners in the global game. The success stories of the future will be those firms that excel in sensing specialist knowledge about new technologies and emerging market needs that are scattered anywhere around the globe. They will mobilize this dispersed knowledge to create new products, services, processes, and business models. They will harvest value from those innovations in markets all over the world.

This new opportunity is being fueled by the emergence of a global knowledge economy, an environment in which:

• Competitive advantage is primarily based on knowledge.

• Not all the knowledge a global company needs to prosper is to be found in one place; instead, it is increasingly scattered around the world.

- The cost of distance is falling rapidly for commodities that are mobile—capital, goods, and information—so that they are readily accessible by all.

The rise of this global knowledge economy means that the opportunities and challenges of exploiting knowledge scattered around the world will become a key concern of senior managers across the spectrum of industries from mining to manufacturing and professional services. The impact won't be confined to a few sectors such as electronics or so-called knowledge-intensive industries. And mobilizing and leveraging globally dispersed knowledge will be just as vital to today's successful American multinationals (such as General Electric or Procter & Gamble) and Japanese giants (such as Matsushita and Toyota) as it is to European companies struggling to overcome Europe's fragmented markets or to Asian and Latin American corporations that have only recently joined the global game.

Of course, the idea of mobilizing globally dispersed knowledge is not entirely new. In fact, we found that it lay at the heart of some of the most powerful corporate innovations of the past—for instance, the IBM 360, the Airbus A-300, and Hewlett-Packard printers. To date, however, innovation based on accessing, mobilizing, and leveraging pockets of knowledge drawn from around the world has been the exception. In the global knowledge economy, it will be critical to success.

As companies begin to unlock the value of globally dispersed knowledge, they will no longer be captives of their geographic roots. Nor will they be accused of behaving like twenty-first century imperialists, imposing the exploits of their homeland on malleable markets worldwide. New multinational leaders will emerge from unlikely locations far away from the traditional "capitals" of their industries. Witness the fact that today such a high-tech industry as global mobile communications is being driven by such companies as Nokia and Ericsson, with roots on the edge of the Arctic, and NTT-DoCoMo of Japan; it is not under the sunshine of Silicon Valley.

The long-term challenge affects today's giants as well as their newly emerging competitors. For established multinationals, success in the future will increasingly depend on their ability to access knowledge from outside their existing subsidiaries and connect it with the skills that are scattered across their global operations network. This capability will allow them to create the innovative products, services, and processes they need in order to win in markets around the world. Building it will require that they dramatically improve their capacity to mobilize knowledge that languishes underexploited within their far-flung network of subsidiaries. But the problem goes far beyond knowing how to leverage knowledge from within an existing network of national subsidiaries. It will not be enough to designate existing countries or global business units as "centers of excellence" or "strategic leaders" for a business unit or product line. Winning in the knowledge economy demands a fundamental shake-up in the way traditional multinational organizations think and act.

Likewise, the emerging multinationals in the new economy will ultimately depend on their ability to innovate by drawing ideas, technologies, and market knowledge from a global pool. Ironically, revolutionaries such as Yahoo! and Amazon are proving to be conservative when it comes to globalization. In many ways, they are following in the footsteps of the early multinationals of the nineteenth century. Their globalization is achieved by moving sequentially, national market by national market, starting with those most similar to their home base. This strategy allows them to operate with minimal adaptation of their original formula. But the next breed of new economy winners will not blanket the world with a standard offering, projected from home base. Instead, they will succeed by learning from unique pockets of knowledge dotted all over the world and then using this knowledge to fuel a cycle of continuous innovation.

This book is a manifesto for managers of existing multinationals and budding "globalizers" who are together facing this coming sea change in the way we need to think about the advantages of becoming a world player in the knowledge economy.

In five years of research, we have seen many examples of companies from every continent—companies such as Acer, Airbus, Citibank, Glaxo Wellcome (now GlaxoSmithKline), Hewlett-Packard, IBM, Nokia, PolyGram (now part of Vivendi Universal), Procter & Gamble, SAP, Shiseido, STMicroelectronics, and Wipro—that are starting to create innovative products, services, and systems by building their capability to access, connect, and leverage knowledge from far-flung, nontraditional sources. The pattern is being repeated by startups like ARM, Logitech, PixTech, and Business Objects. The phenomenon is so striking that we invented a name for it. We call this new competitive capability *metanational advantage*.

We chose the prefix *meta*—from the Greek term for "beyond"—to emphasize a key point: Metanational companies do not draw their competitive advantage from their home country, nor even from a set of national subsidiaries. Metanationals view the world as a global canvas dotted with pockets of technology, market intelligence, and capabilities. They see untapped potential in these pockets of specialist knowledge scattered around the world. By sensing and mobilizing this scattered knowledge, they are able to innovate more effectively than their rivals.

The metanationals will therefore differ fundamentally from their multinational ancestors. Unlike most of today's multinationals, they won't try to prosper by spreading advantages learned in their American, German, or Japanese headquarters or subsidiaries across the world. Instead, metanationals will focus on prospecting for untapped pockets of knowledge around the world. They will build new types of advantage by connecting and leveraging dispersed pockets of knowledge.

The metanationals' key advantage won't come from crossing the borders between nation-states; it will come from transcending them. Their vision of economic paradise is not one of global homogeneity, in which it would be easy to deploy homegrown products, technologies, and systems to customers around the world. Quite the opposite is true. The metanationals will thrive on seeking out and exploiting uniqueness. They value geographic and cultural differences. And because they fish for knowledge in a global pond, they can potentially create new and better competencies than any multinational player's headquarters, national subsidiary, or center of excellence.

THREE LEVELS OF GLOBAL COMPETITION IN THE NEW KNOWLEDGE ECONOMY

The full-fledged metanational corporation does not yet exist. The challenge is to create it ahead of competitors. Some companies already have a head start in the race to build this new type of global advantage. But the challenge of sensing, connecting, and exploiting complex knowledge that is scattered around the world is clearly formidable. To meet this challenge, the winners in the knowledge economy must be able to outdistance their competitors at the three different levels depicted in figure 1-1.

The first level of competition is the race to identify and access new and relevant technologies, competencies, and knowledge of lead markets emerging in locations dotted around the world. Where, for example, is the next advance in biotechnology being hatched? Where are consumers experimenting with new uses for mobile phones?

The second level of competition is in the effectiveness and speed with which companies can connect these globally scattered pieces of knowledge and use them to create innovative products, services, and

Figure 1-1   The Three Levels of Competition in the Global Knowledge Economy

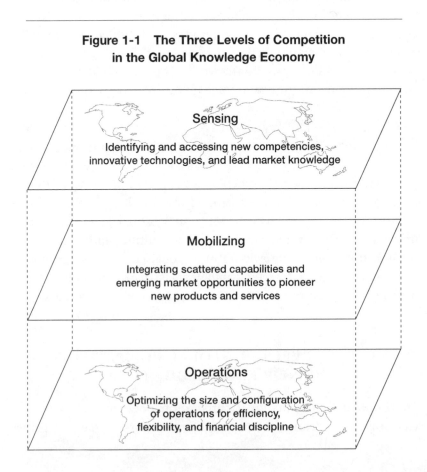

Sensing

Identifying and accessing new competencies, innovative technologies, and lead market knowledge

Mobilizing

Integrating scattered capabilities and emerging market opportunities to pioneer new products and services

Operations

Optimizing the size and configuration of operations for efficiency, flexibility, and financial discipline processes. How effectively, for example, can a semiconductor maker marshal technologies scattered around the world to serve a customer need emerging elsewhere, thus creating a radically new "system-on-a-chip"? Which record company is most capable of turning an unknown artist from an obscure location into a global star by fine-tuning her repertoire to the tastes of consumers in major international markets?

The third level of global competition is optimizing the efficiency of the global sales, distribution, marketing, and supply chain to leverage these product, service, and process innovations across global markets rapidly and cost-effectively. How efficiently can the record company, for example, gear up to promote, produce, and distribute its innovative album at the right price in the most markets? How efficiently can the semiconductor company adapt, produce, and sell its new chip to customers around the world?

BUILDING METANATIONAL ADVANTAGE REQUIRES THREE DISTINCT CAPABILITIES

To build metanational advantage, a company needs to extend its capabilities to compete at each of these three distinct levels. This means honing three distinct skill sets.

Sensing

To become a successful metanational, a company needs to extend its capabilities in identifying new sources of relevant technologies, competencies, and understanding about leading-edge customers. This means learning how to sense and process this complex knowledge into a form that the corporation can use efficiently. But identifying and accessing knowledge that rivals have already mastered will only bring competitive parity. Building new sources of competitive advantage requires a *sensing network* that can identify innovative technologies or emerging customer needs that competitors have overlooked—a network that preempts the global sources of new knowledge. We term this battle "competing on the sensing plane." The prevailing logic of sensing is *discovery and reconnaissance*.

Sensing—prospecting and accessing potentially valuable technologies and market knowledge from around the world—is one step toward creating new sources of competitive advantage. But concentrating on the sensing plane alone is not enough. A company that focuses only on sensing creates a well-informed global debating society: Everyone has a fascinating piece of knowledge about the latest technology or market opportunity discovered by his colleague somewhere across the globe. The organization is knowledgeable but impotent.

Mobilizing

A successful metanational therefore needs a set of structures (which may be virtual, temporary, or both) to translate new knowledge into innovative products or specific market opportunities. These new structures (the evidence suggests that existing operating units and systems will seldom do the job) need to mobilize knowledge that is scattered in pockets around the corporation and use it to pioneer new products and services, sometimes with the help of lead customers. PolyGram created such a structure—the international repertoire network—for unlocking the potential appeal of unknown global artists. This new structure enabled PolyGram to connect and mobilize a complex bundle of dispersed knowledge about new acts, international markets, and local capabilities to create international hits.

We call these structures "magnets." They attract dispersed, potentially relevant knowledge and use it to create innovative products, services, or processes, and they then facilitate the transfer of these innovations into the network of day-to-day operations. We term the battle to design and operate a better set of magnets than your competitors "competing on the mobilizing plane." The driving forces here are *entrepreneurship and mobilization.*

Operationalizing

Once a new product, service, or business model has been pioneered, its profit potential must be realized. This means scaling up the supply chain, improving efficiencies, making incremental improvements, and engineering local adaptations. Most multinationals are already proficient in this arena, which we call "competing on the operating plane." Like the traditional multinational, the metanational must configure and manage these operations for sales growth and profitability. The logic of the operating plane is *efficiency, flexibility, and financial discipline.*

THE TRADITIONAL VIEW OF GLOBAL ADVANTAGE

Compare these requirements with the capabilities and mindset of traditional multinationals. What gives a multinational company a competitive edge over a national champion? Most managers cite two key areas of advantage for the multinational:

- The multinational takes the products, services, technologies, systems, and know-how it has built in its home country and leverages this experience by selling, distributing, and producing around the world. This enables it to reap the benefits of global scale economies and cross-border arbitrage of goods, systems, and people. It also allows it to service multinational customers and attack national champions by using its global resources to bankroll forays into new markets.

- The multinational gains access to cheap labor and raw materials by moving its production or back-office functions to the developing world, leaving only the high value-added activities—for instance, R&D, product design, marketing, strategy, coordination, systems development, and finance—at home.

We call this two-pronged approach "projecting"—leading from the strength of the home base and seeking new market potential and cost advantages abroad. Nike, the global sports apparel giant, offers a prime example. Its headquarters (or "campus") in Beaverton, Oregon, is the nerve center of R&D, product design, brand concepts, quality control systems, finance, and related functions. Nike has a network of dedicated subcontractor production facilities in low-cost locations such as China, Indonesia, and Thailand. It maintains a quality-control and purchasing network throughout these Asian countries. It has built local marketing, sales, and distribution centers in its key markets around the globe.

This traditional "projection" model has driven the growth of huge multinational corporations—including Siemens, Procter & Gamble, General Motors, Microsoft, Sony, and Toyota. The most respected corporate executives of our day have refined and improved this model in myriad ways. International projectors learned to adapt their products, services, and systems in response to differences between national markets—an imperative championed by companies such as Unilever, "the multi-local multinational."[1] At the same time they sought to maintain the advantages of globally integrated strategies and operations—resulting in initiatives such as Ford's "world car" project. The combination of these advances led to the emergence of "glocal" strategies under such slogans as "think global, act local"; these strategies reached their zenith in the "transnational" model epitomized by organizations such as Percy Barnevik's ABB, with its "centers of excellence" and "entrepreneurial front-line managers."[2]

Despite these many important improvements, however, "projection" remained a hidden assumption at the very heart of multinational strategies. Globalization meant "teaching the world" from headquarters, or from subsidiaries in advantaged locations or dominant clusters (national "diamonds").[3] But the global competitive landscape is now changing in ways that will ultimately render the projection model obsolete.

NEW CHALLENGES, NEW OPPORTUNITIES

The new knowledge economy presents four fundamental challenges for traditional multinational companies:

- **Global spread is no longer a distinctive competitive advantage.** An efficient global network of production, distribution, and sales is necessary but no longer sufficient for competitive advantage. The leading competitors in most industries already know how to operate globally. Many companies embracing the digital revolution can now instantly project their standard offering around the world using the Internet.

- **A single national market no longer leads in most industries.** The "lead" customers, whose emerging needs drive innovation, are no longer in a single sophisticated market either. Often they appear in small markets on the periphery of most companies' global networks. A company that is unable to sense these dispersed and diverse market needs, and then leverage its knowledge globally, will not fare well against an organization that can.

- **Valuable knowledge is increasingly scattered.** The capabilities a multinational needs to outperform its competitors are increasingly spread in fragmented pockets of specialist expertise around the world. Today's winners understand how to identify and access new technologies, capabilities, and know-how that are dispersed around the world and combine them to create world-beating products and services.

- **Valuable knowledge is sophisticated and sticky.** Potentially valuable knowledge about technology and markets is often subtle, complex, and "sticky": That means it is deeply embedded in distant and unfamiliar environments. Understanding the emergence of the mobile telephone as a global fashion accessory, understanding the inner workings of a global customer headquartered on the other side of the world, or understanding the potential uses of advanced computer simulation techniques and robotics for drug development are three examples of such knowledge. Advanced telecommunications technology and the Internet may facilitate global interactions among individuals with this kind of complex knowledge, but they do not guarantee the transfer of true understanding. Companies need structures and processes to access, repackage, and mobilize this sophisticated, complex knowledge to reach those who can use it.

These four challenges threaten to undermine the advantages of existing multinational strategies. But they also open up powerful new sources of competitive advantage and growth—for both multinational incumbents and aspiring global startups. Consider the possibilities:

- **New sources of differentiation.** The fact that new technologies and competencies are emerging in nontraditional locations opens new sources of differentiation for companies able to discover, access, and leverage this knowledge ahead of their competitors. There are new opportunities to break out of head-to-head, "me-too" competition in which every competitor fishes for competencies in similar pools and ends up with indistinguishable offerings and identical costs. Moreover, the true breakthroughs in product performance, service value, and cost reduction come from *combining* technologies and competencies developed in different geographic environments, some of them from outside the industry. The real prize will go to companies that can leverage the resulting differentiation across the globe.

- **New opportunities to unlock global consumers' latent needs.** The fact that new lead markets are scattered outside the home base means that new customer needs and nontraditional uses for existing products or services are more likely to emerge. There is obvious profit potential in satisfying these peculiar local needs. But a much larger prize is available to the company that introduces these innovative uses to customers around the globe, tapping demand for needs that most consumers have not yet imagined.

- **New ways to create unique advantage.** The fact that new competencies and consumer needs emerge in complex, subtle bundles of knowledge means that the competitive advantages built using them will be difficult for competitors to copy. Therefore, multinationals that become successful international brokers of complex knowledge will enjoy robust and sustainable sources of advantage. Sensing and leveraging complex knowledge from multiple locations is often difficult and costly. But the rewards will be great for multinationals that overcome the difficulties and learn to broker complex knowledge efficiently.

- **Instant global reach and scale.** A company that can access dispersed knowledge and understand distant markets is poised for a fast, effective entry into a new international business. By connecting capabilities scattered around the world, the benefits of global scale in R&D and operations are available almost from Day 1.

HEEDING THE CALL

Many leading multinationals are starting to understand the fundamental significance of these global changes. Some are adjusting their strategies to enhance their ability to compete in the new knowledge economy. In its 1998 annual report, for example, U.S.-based General Electric stated:

> Market success is only part of globalization. We must globalize every activity in the Company. We've made some progress in sourcing products and components so critical to survive and win in a price-competitive and deflationary world, but our challenge is to go beyond that—*to capitalize on the vast intellectual capital available around the globe.* In 1999, we will move aggressively to broaden our definition of globalization by increasing the intensity of effort to search out and attract the unlimited pool of talent that is available in the countries in which we do business—from software designers in India to product engineers in Mexico, Eastern Europe and China. *The GE of the next century must provide high-value global products and services, designed by global talent, for global markets.* (italics added)

Like General Electric, your company needs to be asking how it will compete in the new global game, where the emphasis has shifted from penetrating new markets to learning from the world. The first step is to understand how you can turn dispersed knowledge to your advantage. To illustrate, we revisit two examples we used to open this book, each in very different industries.

STMicroelectronics: Mobilizing Complex Knowledge around the World

STMicroelectronics had an inauspicious beginning. The company was formed in 1987 through the merger of SGS Microelettronica of Italy and Thomson Semiconducteurs of France, both of which were indirectly owned by their national governments. ST lagged far behind other European semiconductor companies (namely, Siemens of Germany and Philips of the Netherlands) in a business in which many experts believed Europe had no future anyway, as it had already lost the chip race to the United States, Japan, and the Pacific Rim countries.

ST inherited a string of money-losing operations. Perhaps even more significant, very few of the lead customers in its industry were located in Europe. Moreover, many of the core technologies it needed were scattered around the world in its own far-flung operations and in global hotbeds of semiconductor technology and manufacturing expertise that were spread from California to Tokyo and Taipei.

ST proved the doubters wrong. By 2000, its net profits exceeded $1.4 billion on sales of $7.8 billion. Its share price soared after its 1994 flotation on the Paris and New York stock exchanges, reaching a market capitalization of more than $50 billion. Investment analysts at Morgan Stanley described ST as one of the world's best-managed companies. ST achieved this remarkable performance by unlocking the untapped potential of knowledge that was scattered around the world. It did so by sensing and mobilizing these isolated pockets of knowledge to innovate in ways its traditional multinational competitors could not.

Most competitors in the electronics industry typically focused on designing and producing specialized components in dedicated facilities. These components were then brought together by their customers in the form of a circuit board to do a particular job, such as control a hard-disk drive (HDD). But ST's worldview led it to the idea of connecting different specialist capabilities and knowledge to design a single chip that would perform all of the functions of a circuit board. If they could connect *knowledge* rather than *components*, they could design and manufacture a "system-on-a-chip"—replacing, for example, the usual soldered circuit board of electronic components that controls an HDD with just a few integrated circuit chips and, ultimately, a single chip.[4] The system-on-a-chip would allow customers (in this case HDD manufacturers) to reduce the size of their final products, to improve product performance, and to reduce manufacturing costs and reject rates.

To perform this feat, ST had to create a process that could integrate multiple specialized technologies for each of the requisite components into the design and manufacture of a single chip. At the same time, ST had to incorporate an intimate knowledge of the customer's complete application into every stage of the process. This integration challenge would be difficult enough for an experienced design team whose members had worked together in a single facility for years. But ST faced a situation in which the relevant specialist technologies were scattered all around the world, while customers with the potentially leading applications were dispersed throughout other, different locations.

Figure 1-2 illustrates how ST mobilized isolated pockets of technology, capabilities, and market intelligence to create a unique solution for the HDD application. Figure 1-2 is *not* a map of where ST sourced *components* or manufactured and sold its *products*. In sharp contrast to traditional diagrams of product and component flows, this map shows where ST sourced the *knowledge* it needed to fashion a world-beating solution to its customers' problems. It shows where ST accessed the process technologies, the product engineering and design skills, the detailed understanding of HDD applications, and the manufacturing capabilities necessary to create customized chips that would replace the component-laden circuit board in the traditional HDD controller.

By accessing and mobilizing this vast array of knowledge, ST learned to compress the entire HDD electronics system onto three chips, as compared with the older circuit boards that contained well over ten chips and more than one hundred electronic components. ST's sales of HDD chips passed the $500 million mark for the first time in 1996, capturing 27 percent of a world market dominated by American companies and outpacing the previous frontrunners. Not only had the company developed a huge new business from its modest beginnings with a few million dollars in annual sales in the late 1980s; even more important, it had also created a long-term competitive advantage with an approach to globalization that will be very hard for competitors to imitate.

ST replicated its new metanational strategy by mobilizing global knowledge for several new system-on-a-chip applications, including automotive applications, GPS and navigation systems, video monitors and TV set-top boxes, mobile phones, and xDSL communications. Implementing the metanational strategy was not always easy, but its advantages eventually became widely recognized within ST. It has proved the core engine driving the growth of ST's business and profitability.

PolyGram: Leveraging Talent Imprisoned in Scattered National Markets

The metanational advantage—the ability to access, mobilize, and leverage knowledge that is dispersed around the globe—is equally

Figure 1-2 Knowledge Dispersion Profile for STMicroelectronics in HDD Electronics

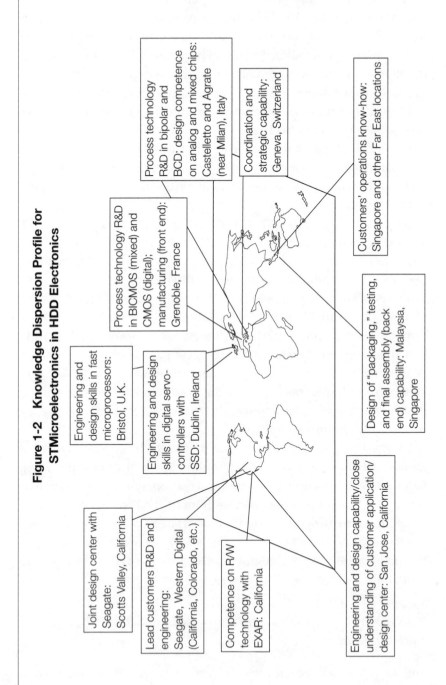

Engineering and design skills in fast microprocessors: Bristol, U.K.

Process technology R&D in BICMOS (mixed) and CMOS (digital); manufacturing (front end): Grenoble, France

Process technology R&D in bipolar and BCD; design competence on analog and mixed chips: Castelletto and Agrate (near Milan), Italy

Coordination and strategic capability: Geneva, Switzerland

Customers' operations know-how: Singapore and other Far East locations

Joint design center with Seagate: Scotts Valley, California

Lead customers R&D and engineering: Seagate, Western Digital (California, Colorado, etc.)

Engineering and design skills in digital servo-controllers with SSD: Dublin, Ireland

Competence on R/W technology with EXAR: California

Engineering and design capability/close understanding of customer application/design center: San Jose, California

Design of "packaging," testing, and final assembly (back end) capability: Malaysia, Singapore apparent outside the rarified world of semiconductors. Consider the experience of PolyGram in the recording industry.

Originally established as a small recording arm for Philips NV, PolyGram outpaced household names such as EMI and Sony to become the world's largest record company, worth a $10.4 billion takeover price paid by Seagram in 1998. It did so by finding a unique system allowing it to think outside national borders and turn selected local artists into international stars. Like ST, PolyGram illustrates several of the basic principles behind a successful metanational strategy. In PolyGram's case, the starting point was a loose confederation of individual record labels and national fiefdoms.

From its original base in the Netherlands and the United Kingdom, PolyGram built a formidable network that identified potential hit artists in more than forty countries around the world. PolyGram's artists and repertoire (A&R) staff made nightly forays to local bars, clubs, and concert halls, searching for the raw material for tomorrow's stars, the seeds of the next hit record. If the A&R staff found a promising act in Venezuela, for example, the local subsidiary geared up to produce a record and propel it to the top of the Venezuelan charts.

While a successful player in each of its national markets, PolyGram realized that it was missing out on the profit potential to make national stars into regional or even global stars. Some, but by no means all, of the hit performers in Venezuela, for example, might also succeed in the market for Hispanic music in the United States or throughout Latin America. In other cases, the same performer might even become an international star either in the local language or in English. If the company could identify and leverage those acts with international potential, it could earn very attractive returns. This was because most of PolyGram's competitors in the music business—such as EMI and Sony—sourced the vast majority of their international repertoire from just two countries: the United States and the United Kingdom. Intense competition for new talent inflated the cost of signing new artists in these well-known hotbeds of potential international hits.

It is still possible to make money by securing hit artists from the United States or the United Kingdom. But it was much more profitable to unlock the international potential of an artist or group popular in a national market outside the international music mainstream.

One notable example is the internationally famous pop star Bjork from Iceland. Not surprisingly, a record company can sign artists who are local stars in Iceland, or even in France, Italy, Venezuela, or Hong Kong, for example, at terms far more favorable to the company than the cost of securing a contract with a similar artist who has become a star in the United States.

For PolyGram's talent scouts in a large market like the United States, sifting through local records from subsidiaries all over the world in search of a new star was like looking for the proverbial needle in the haystack. Very few of the local recordings that piled up on their desks had international potential. Moreover, because Poly-Gram's marketing and sales staffs in the United States and at other corporate headquarters lacked the detailed, implicit understanding of what made each local act successful, it was extremely hard for them to judge which local acts could be "reformulated" to meet the needs of the global market. To learn how to create international hits from local artists, PolyGram needed to combine some rather complex knowledge bases. Specifically, it needed to find a way of linking its understanding of what made a local artist successful with its knowledge of whether this distinctiveness would sell records in other markets around the world. It would need to leverage the combined knowledge of talent spotters, producers, promotional specialists, and marketers all based in far-flung places around the globe.

PolyGram therefore decided to try a more radical approach by introducing a new structure: the International Repertoire Centres (IRCs). This network comprised a group of seventy-five professionals, located in twenty-one sourcing centers around the world—five in the United States, seven in the United Kingdom, and one each in Australia, Canada, France, Germany, Hong Kong, Italy, Japan, the Netherlands, and Switzerland. The people in this network had a single focus: to analyze repertoire sourced by their local colleagues and then identify and exploit those acts with international potential. They were measured and rewarded on the basis of their success in generating international sales from local acts.

PolyGram continued to build its position in national markets. But it is the metanational advantage—its ability to identify, source, and leverage local repertoire internationally through its network of IRCs—that propelled it to the top of the recording industry.

METANATIONAL UPSTARTS

Our first two examples moved toward a metanational strategy from an existing multinational base. But the advantages of tapping globally dispersed knowledge are available to other companies, too. For example, some smaller startups use a metanational strategy as a way to break into a global business. Two companies that have done so are Nokia and PixTech.

Starting as a Finnish mini-conglomerate dominated by stagnant businesses in rubber and paper, Nokia built a global leadership position in mobile phones in just over five years. It did so by accessing and leveraging valuable knowledge scattered across Europe, the United States, and Japan. PixTech, meanwhile, provides a dramatic example of a startup that was able to enter a global business in which formidable competitors such as Sharp and Toshiba had invested hundreds of millions of dollars and many years of R&D to establish themselves. Unlike the proverbial Silicon Valley entrepreneurs in a garage, these metanational startups built their launching pads on a foundation of the best capabilities available anywhere in the world.

PixTech: Using the Metanational Strategy to Achieve Instant Global Reach and Scale

PixTech, a company specializing in field emission displays (FED), harnessed metanational advantage to help build global reach and scale from a standing start in an unlikely location. FED is one of several technologies (such as liquid crystal and plasma) that compete to provide flat-panel displays in products ranging from laptops and handheld television sets to medical devices and high-definition television sets.

The risks were high for PixTech, a startup company based in Rousset, in the south of France. Players in the flat-panel display industry include such global household names as Sharp, NEC, Toshiba, Hitachi, IBM, and Motorola. Its humble local roots made PixTech an unlikely contender against established giants in Japan or other startups in the United States, both locations known for the best concentrations of flat-panel display technology in the world. The firm therefore devised a metanational strategy to beat its competitors by cherry-picking and then leveraging the best capabilities and knowledge it could find scattered throughout the world. Only by casting a global net could PixTech have a chance of succeeding.

PixTech began by signing an exclusive long-term licensing agreement with LETI, one of the research arms of the French Atomic Energy Commission, for the commercial rights to all of its accumulated research on FED technology. Based on the combined experience of PixTech's management team—many of whom had prior experience in multinational corporations such as Motorola and IBM—the company then set out to scout the world for complementary technologies and resources.

PixTech quickly incorporated itself in the United States to access the world's best pool of venture capital funding for high-tech startups. The initially French company formally became a subsidiary of an American corporation. It then established a series of technology alliances with Texas Instruments, Motorola, and Raytheon in the United States and with Futaba in Japan. All of these companies were committed to R&D in FED, were potential customers, or already had a substantial position in the flat-panel display industry. Motorola, for example, saw FEDs as key to developing its capabilities in video technologies and as a way to enhance the display performance of its end products. Beyond being a potential lead customer, Motorola provided knowledge of the manufacturing process technologies essential to successful design and planned to spend $150 million in developing manufacturing facilities for FED. PixTech also developed close working relationships with companies with specific competencies in key component areas, such as Rhône-Poulenc of France and Nichia of Japan in the field of phosphors.

PixTech acted as both the international knowledge broker and the "magnet" by which relevant technologies and know-how from around the globe could be connected and mobilized to design and prototype an effective FED flat screen. By 1995, PixTech had produced its first defect-free display in its own clean-room pilot facilities (leased from IBM in Montpellier, France). It then turned to the challenge of improving yields to permit high-volume, highly automated and efficient manufacturing. PixTech's management saw a delicate linkage between manufacturing and R&D in FED technology. "You can only learn about the limits of a technology by manufacturing," a senior manager explained.[5] This philosophy led to the next phase of global partnerships—this time to access knowledge of volume manufacturing processes using existing capital-intensive manufacturing facilities. By 1996, PixTech signed a manufacturing agreement with Unipac of Taiwan, an experienced, high-volume manufacturer of other types of flat-panel displays. Later it signed a distribution agreement with Sumitomo.

PixTech has since secured the position of its FED flat-panel displays in applications for the U.S. Army (with FED screens that can withstand a 50G shock impact and provide an instant image at any temperature) and in portable medical equipment (with screens that provide clear visibility from any angle). From a standing start, PixTech has effectively used the power of metanational advantage to break into a global industry that traditionally required huge investments in time and money. While the jury is still out on its long-term success (as is the case with all startups that have not attained "cruise speed" yet), PixTech was already able to launch an innovative line of products and enter an industry inhabited by powerful global rivals.

Nokia: A Metanational Market Leader

Back in the early 1990s, Nokia was focusing on mobile telephony and on globalization. It found that in order to ride the next wave of innovation and emerging customer needs, it could not simply rely on its Nordic home base, as it had historically done in other businesses. It would need to combine its existing Finnish culture and competency base with capabilities elsewhere in Europe—such as in its R&D lab in the United Kingdom. It would need advanced technologies and global marketing know-how from the United States—such as the design trends and skills in Los Angeles. It would seek out capabilities in miniaturization and data applications, as well as the leading "consumer electronics mentality" from Japan. It would look to Southeast Asia for management skills specific to low-cost manufacturing and low-margin businesses.

Nokia also sought capital in the United States. The American financial market context required a discipline and performance record that was not yet known in Europe. Nokia was to benefit from blending the objective, universal rules of success with its Northern European cultural heritage. Accessing capital in a distant and unfamiliar institutional setting is not merely a financial exercise; it is a humbling experience that forces corporate executives to see that the world cannot simply be mastered with familiar home rules. Again, in the case of Nokia (as well as for STMicroelectronics and PixTech), the difficulty of obtaining critical resources in its country of origin was a major blessing in disguise.

As it entered decisively in the mobile communications business, Nokia had to understand many things: emerging customer needs in lead markets around the globe, increased customization in Europe, new types of functionality in the United States and Japan, the emergence of the mobile phone as a fashion accessory in the United States and Asia, the substitution of mobile telephony for fixed lines in China and India, and the evolution of customer needs at high penetration rates—a trend that would happen first on Nokia's Nordic turf.

A Finnish cadre of managers dispatched to key locations around the world constituted a seamless network for knowledge sharing. Nokia developed its first digital mobile telephone from its U.K. R&D lab, not from Finland. Aiming at a phone that would be a global platform, Nokia had to understand the Japanese and the American markets, as well as the major European ones. It had to access different standards and technologies on the three continents. It had to gain experience of the leading Japanese market, where small phones were already half the size of its initial design. Nokia's efforts to understand Japan also showed the importance of a dramatically improved user interface. The resulting 2100 series became Nokia's "breakthrough product" and a global hit.

By 1998, five years later, Nokia was using its metanational capabilities to recognize that mobile phones were becoming a fashion accessory in California and Japan. The company set up a design pipeline that pumped out a new model every couple of months. Test marketing in Japan caught the attention of other fashion-conscious markets around the world, and a variety of chic new Nokia mobile phones became the hottest new accessory. Earlier than other competitors, Nokia also integrated email and other Internet capabilities into its phones. The benefits began to flow, catapulting the company to global first place in terms of mobile phone sales, growth, and return on capital employed.

Meanwhile, Motorola continued to develop its technologies and products based on the capabilities available in its own U.S. backyard.

Cellular telephony had been invented in America—at Bell Laboratories. Motorola was among the first to mass-produce mobile telephones and had been leading the world market by *projecting* from the original cellular technology home—but not for long. Fishing for innovation in a restricted, local pool, Motorola missed the shift to digital mobile telephony and the GSM standard—an outcome of European cooperation that would be the choice by many countries around the world, even in Asia. Motorola's mobile phone business was left in the dust as its smaller metanational competitor roared past on the sales curve.

THE INTUITIVE RESPONSE: SQUARE PEGS IN ROUND HOLES

Many forward-thinking multinationals recognize the opportunities and challenges that STMicroelectronics, PolyGram, PixTech, and Nokia have begun to address. They know that they must be able to access technologies, capabilities, know-how, and understanding of different types of lead customers that are dispersed around the world. They understand that to compete in the future they must be able to put this fragmented global knowledge to work to build world-beating product platforms, service systems, and marketing strategies that can then be tailored and adapted to the specifics of local markets.

Their response to the realization that they must compete in a new way is instinctive: Start from our existing multinational structure, add to it, and adjust it to suit the new realities. The evidence of this strategy is all around us. Companies spend millions on information technology and communications systems to share knowledge among existing subsidiaries. They appoint chief knowledge officers. They establish centers of excellence and business unit headquarters around the world with responsibility for innovation in particular products or processes.

In this book we explain why all of these worthy initiatives, while necessary, will not provide multinationals with the new sources of competitive advantage they are trying to create. The reason is simple but profound: They are trying to shoehorn a square peg into a round hole. The traditional projecting multinational was designed to leverage knowledge from headquarters and combine it with low-cost labor and raw materials from developing markets. Its beliefs, performance measures, incentive systems, decision-making processes, organization structures, information systems, and financial controls were all designed to achieve these objectives. And for the most part, the multinational systems and structures achieve these operating goals extremely well.

But ask the traditional multinational organization to leverage new capabilities, technologies, know-how, and understanding of lead customers when all of these different and specialized inputs are dispersed around the world—often on the periphery of the company's global network—and it will come to a creaking halt. Overhead and costs of coordination will rise, and the organization will become paralyzed with ambiguity.

We will see that building metanational advantage necessitates a highly interdependent organization. But it does not mean simply trying to "connect everyone to everyone else" in a massive internal market for knowledge and resources—such an organization would simply drown in its own overhead. Building an effective metanational requires management to establish a limited number of carefully selected connections and communication channels between specific sites, units, teams, partners, and customers, not just between national subsidiaries or global business units. The key roles within this network are no longer automatically allocated to the most important national subsidiaries or the units with the most resources, people, or even experience. In fact, we will see that, in a metanational, innovation and leadership are just as likely to come from the organization's periphery as from its headquarters, from large and powerful subsidiaries, or even from designated centers of excellence.

In a worst-case scenario, trying to force-fit an existing multinational organization and its people into a metanational mold will undermine its operational excellence and could imperil the company's very survival. Rather than delivering innovation by tapping into and mobilizing pockets of knowledge scattered around the world, the traditional multinational organization will end up in one or more of the following situations:

- Becoming a "global debating society" in which unguided networking and consultation undermines efficiency and rapid decision-making.

- Giving managers and staff ulcers and sleepless nights as they juggle a raft of new responsibilities on top of their operational "day jobs."

- Drowning in complexity and increased overhead.

Despite these risks, companies cannot ignore the emergence of a global knowledge economy in which the winners will need to tap the underexploited potential of pockets of technology, capabilities, and market understanding scattered around the world. In fact, the urgency of addressing these opportunities and threats is increasing daily. By adopting metanational strategies, new competitors are finding ways to achieve instant global scale and reach that they can use to leverage their innovations into every corner of the world, almost overnight. As was the case with the Japanese coming to America in the late 1970s, the most dangerous competition in the knowledge economy will come out of left field. But in a world where advantages are metanational, left field covers 360 degrees; powerful new competition can erupt from anywhere on the globe.

To move successfully from global to metanational in the new knowledge economy, companies must fundamentally augment their existing organizations or else build new ones that are much more than simply clones of today's multinationals.

Unlocking the potential of globally dispersed knowledge is by no means a straightforward task. Nor is it one that can be solved by investing in even the most sophisticated information and communications technologies and hardware and software. In fact, believing that information and communications technologies alone can harness the value of globally dispersed knowledge is a second trap we have observed many companies fall into. Companies make this mistake for two reasons:

- They underestimate the subtlety of what takes place when people with different pieces of the knowledge jigsaw work together in close proximity over an extended period.

- They assume that information is equivalent to knowledge.

Moving from global to metanational, therefore, also requires companies to become sophisticated managers of messy knowledge that is often imprisoned within a local context or only tacitly understood.

A ROADMAP FOR WINNING IN THE GLOBAL KNOWLEDGE ECONOMY

This book is about what companies can do to understand and then to meet the challenges of moving from global to metanational. First and foremost, this requires a fundamental change in strategy: They must relinquish their goal of projecting a homegrown formula and instead seek to build advantage by learning from the world. This new strategy must be backed by important changes in organizational culture, processes, structure, staffing, performance measurements, and incentives. Senior management will need to firmly embrace the metanational strategy. This means changing what they do and how they spend their time.

The good news is that many of today's multinationals have a powerful head start in becoming tomorrow's successful metanationals— provided they deploy and extend their existing capabilities and resources in the right way. At the same time, new players, be they startups or new divisions of existing corporations, also have an unprecedented opportunity to achieve global stature by embracing metanational principles.

In chapter 2, "Breaking Free of Geography," we explain why, as the time-honored strategy of international projection runs out of steam, there is a growing opportunity to innovate by tapping underexploited pockets of technology and market intelligence scattered around the world. To grasp this opportunity, however, companies need to break free of the legacies that their historic geographic roots and patterns of international expansion have left behind. We explain how these geographic legacies impede companies from building metanational advantage. Recognizing these impediments is the first stage to overcoming them.

Chapter 3, "Metanational Pioneers: The Benefits of Being Born in the 'Wrong' Place," draws out the lessons from companies that are beginning to exploit the potential for innovation based on learning from the world. It turns out that the companies that are farthest down the road are those that have had no choice but to look afar for technologies, capabilities, and market intelligence. These metanational trailblazers were born in the wrong place, in the sense that their home base does not provide the array of knowledge necessary to be globally competitive. Using these companies' experiences, we sketch a blueprint for the skills and structures that tomorrow's winners will need.

Chapter 4, "Shoehorning Won't Work," describes the pitfalls of trying to coax metanational innovation out of an organization that wasn't designed for the task. We explain the limitations of traditional multinational networks: They don't cover the right set of locations, and they don't have the full set of roles, responsibilities, and incentives to tap into the underexploited potential of knowledge scattered around the globe. Thus we begin to see how the structures, roles, and incentives in an existing multinational will need to be augmented to capture metanational advantage.

In chapter 5, "The Tyranny of Distance," we explore the trap of believing that information and communications technology, even if backed by a large investment budget, can eliminate the problems of mobilizing dispersed knowledge. We analyze the challenges that arise when relevant pieces of knowledge are imprisoned by their local context or remain only tacitly understood. This enables us to define the issues posed by distance as managers seek to unlock the innovation potential of specialist knowledge scattered around the world.

The next three chapters show managers how to augment their existing organizations or build new ones so as to avoid these costly traps while tapping the potential of globally dispersed knowledge.

In chapter 6, "Learning from the World," we explain how to build structures and processes that will enable a company to prospect for hotbeds of new knowledge that can differentiate it from competitors. We consider where to prospect, who will prospect, and how to access relevant knowledge in a distant location once it is identified.

When a company accesses a rich stock of new knowledge from different locations, it still faces the problem of creating value from this fragmented lode. Chapter 7, "Mobilizing Dispersed Knowledge," discusses how to recognize and exploit opportunities for creation of innovative products, services, processes, or business models based on global learning.

To extract the full value of metanational innovation, a company needs to make its discoveries operational. This means scaling up and leveraging the new opportunities through global sales, distribution, and marketing networks. It requires efficient and cost-effective production and delivery systems. The key task is relaying the innovation into the hands of the day-to-day operating network. This is the subject of chapter 8, "Harvesting Value from Metanational Innovation."

Finally, chapter 9, "From Global to Metanational," provides a practical blueprint for senior managers who are ready to move from global to metanational and eager to get under way on Monday morning.

Chapter 2

Breaking Free of Geography

FORD, GENERAL MOTORS, Intel, Cisco, Yahoo!, and eBay are companies that, to many, couldn't be more different. Some belong to the old economy, some to the new economy; others are part of the Internet revolution. They have been contrasted because of their different corporate cultures and management styles, their different structures and alternative business models. But all of these companies have at least one feature in common: They became global by projecting their homegrown formula into new markets around the world. The source of their strength was the homegrown advantage that they used to beat the national champions. For Ford and General Motors, Detroit was the wellspring of their competitive advantage. Cisco and Intel brought what they learned in Silicon Valley to the rest of the world. Yahoo! and eBay took a formula pioneered in California's Internet hotbed and projected it globally.

Multinational companies have long leveraged their geographic roots for competitive advantage. Many of today's giant "projectors" became great by bringing the distinct competencies and qualities of their home markets into the global arena. For example, German chemicals multinationals such as Hoechst, Bayer, and BASF initially grew strong by combining molecular chemistry—gleaned from the local textile industry's expertise in dyestuffs—with the bulk shipping capabilities developed on the nearby river Rhine. Over decades, they then leveraged this home-base knowledge to build global empires in the chemical industry.

Similarly, Silicon Valley firms like Yahoo!, Oracle, Sun, Intel, and Applied Materials gained competitive advantage through immediate and unparalleled access to emerging technologies. Their common home base permits frequent interaction with cutting-edge software and component and machinery developers—and they exploit this advantage to the fullest. Their location means that they can plug into the needs and trends of the world's most sophisticated electronics customers with a speed difficult to match by companies located elsewhere.

There are countless other examples of companies that have become global by projecting advantage honed in their home base: Louis Vuitton's travel goods empire flourished by tantalizing consumers around the world with a taste of French lavishness. Segafredo Zanetti became a multinational by personifying the warmth and joy of its Italian home in its espresso. Disney brought a piece of American fantasy to people around the world. IKEA built its international home furnishing business on Swedish woodworking and design. In every case, the geographic associations or advantages of a company's home base played a key role in the company's international success.

In many industries, however, multinational projectors are finding that this time-honored strategy is running out of steam. The cost of distance is falling dramatically as transport and communication technologies improve by leaps and bounds. So the ability to take a homegrown formula and successfully project it into new markets around the world no longer distinguishes one competitor from another. In a sector such as consumer goods, for example, all the major competitors—P&G, Unilever, Nestlé, Kraft, Sara Lee, and so on—have perfected the arts of global projection and local adaptation. Far from being a differentiator, these capabilities have become "table stakes" required simply to play the game. In many new economy industries, a strategy based on international projection simply isn't even viable. Before a new portal or e-business site can project a successful formula globally, a crop of local imitators have already copied its best features and incorporated them into their own domestic sites.

GLOBAL PROJECTION NO LONGER DIFFERENTIATES COMPETITORS

Thirty or forty years ago, global companies were uniquely positioned to move money, raw materials, and finished products around the world. Trading houses such as Japan's Mitsui or Britain's Inchcape prospered by exploiting this unique advantage. But as the ability to move these commodities became commonplace, margins declined to become razor thin.

Companies such as Ford or General Motors grew to be global giants by projecting their designs, manufacturing methods, or marketing procedures to the markets of Europe, Latin America, and Asia. But as almost every automobile company mastered the ability to project information and tightly specified systems globally, the margins earned from this kind of international arbitrage declined.

A decade ago, being able to transfer the technologies, systems, and procedures necessary to extract 6-sigma quality from an operation halfway around the world differentiated a multinational like Motorola from its international competitors. Quality was a form of magic known only to a few companies. Now, 6-sigma processes are well understood. They have been extensively codified. As a result, 6-sigma can be moved relatively freely around the world. The ability to project this advantage globally no longer acts as a source of competitive advantage. Today, 6-sigma quality is a "given" for most operations that are part of the global economy.

Today's multinationals need to create new sources of differentiation. Only by finding new sources of differentiation can the pressure on profit margins be stemmed.

One strategy is to stoke the fires of innovation back at home base: Use the advantages of Silicon Valley or Detroit to generate new products, services, technologies, and systems at an ever-faster pace and project these innovations across the world at blazing speed. For companies such as Intel, this kind of "global projection on steroids" seems to continue to deliver. But for those like Motorola, as we saw in chapter 1, it risks missing the next critical innovation, especially one that emerges in an unlikely location far away from headquarters.

Multinationals that adopt a strategy of global projection are missing a huge untapped opportunity: the opportunity to differentiate themselves through *learning from the world*.

UNTAPPED INNOVATION OPPORTUNITIES

The world is full of underexploited pockets of technology and market intelligence that are potentially valuable to a multinational's innovation processes. But many of these pockets remain underexploited because of any of the following reasons:

- They lie outside the classic hot spots where multinationals traditionally look for innovative technologies and emerging consumer trends.

- The technologies or market knowledge are imprisoned by their local context and therefore difficult for multinationals to use globally.

- They contain knowledge that is "tacit," including knowledge that exists in people's heads and has not been codified.

As we saw in chapter 1, a multinational able to successfully tap and connect these dispersed pockets of knowledge would have rich, new sources of innovation—innovation that could differentiate it from competitors and create fundamentally new types of competitive advantage. For example, as rivals reached technical parity with Nokia in mobile telephony, the new source of advantage came from connecting a deep understanding of the emerging "lifestyle" of mobile telephone users in California and Hong Kong with Nokia's technology skills.

In this chapter we explain why, in the global knowledge economy, the opportunities for exploiting untapped pockets of technology and market intelligence are now bigger than ever. We show why these underexploited opportunities continue to grow. We also discuss why geography's powerful role in creating competitive advantage blocks traditional multinationals from unlocking these new opportunities.

We argue that companies must break free of their geographic chains in order to unlock the potential of the new global knowledge economy. Companies need to go beyond being global to perfect the art of learning from wherever relevant knowledge is being generated, regardless of location. This means overcoming geographic myopia in order to become global knowledge *prospectors*. It entails sensing knowledge from around the world, using that knowledge to innovate, and leveraging the results across global markets.

This is not a simple process. It presents management with formidable challenges. The barriers derive from prejudices that are deeply ingrained in the organization. They permeate everything from the multinational's locations of assets and employees to its power structures, performance measurement systems, and corporate culture. The challenge is to overcome these barriers in a way that allows multinationals to *augment* their core geographic advantage with new sources of global learning—but without undermining their historic strengths. One of the toughest steps on the road to meeting this challenge is the very fact of recognizing it.

THE PRIMACY OF THE BIRTHPLACE

In the past, geography was destiny: If your company was founded or headquartered in the right place, your odds of global success were vastly increased. Firms from a privileged nation or region were able to create and sustain competitive advantage in a given field even against aggressive international competitors. In *The Competitive Advantage of Nations,* Michael Porter calls these privileged locations "diamond clusters."[1] Examples abound: Denmark in food additives and furniture, Germany in chemicals and optical instruments, Switzerland in watches and chocolates, Japan in facsimile machines and home audio equipment, Italy in ceramic tiles and ski boots, the United Kingdom in auctioneering and insurance, the United States in agricultural chemicals, computer software, and networking products. Silicon Valley is perhaps today's best-known example of a "diamond cluster."

Clusters as a Source of Global Advantage

These diamond clusters got their head start in global competition for a variety of reasons. Geographic or climatic conditions or nearby supplies of raw materials, for example, gave some locations a lead. Enckhuisen, a small town in northern Holland, dominates today's global market for seeds. Its geographic advantage in the seed business goes back to the 1600s. Ships' crews on long voyages then suffered from scurvy, a debilitating illness caused by lack of vitamin C. To counter this problem, ships stopped in Dutch ports to take on fresh vegetables, including large quantities of the local white cabbage known to be rich in vitamin C. Cabbage could not be stored at sea longer than five to ten weeks, so merchant ships took on further supplies in Cape Town, South Africa, where Dutch Boer farmers grew cabbage to supply their demand. Despite constant efforts, however, the cabbage plants would not produce seed in Cape Town. Seeding was sparked by the onset of frost, which was rare in the mild South African climate. Cabbage seeds therefore had to be continually imported from northern Holland towns like Enckhuisen.

The high added value of seeds captured the attention of local entrepreneurs, who focused their efforts on improving quality and yields. As their skills became known, Spanish and Portuguese merchants brought in potatoes and tomatoes for seeding. Turkish ships brought tulips. The world's seed and bulb capital was born.

In other cases, local technological breakthroughs sometimes kickstarted a cluster: The owner of a glass mold company in Marinha Grande, Portugal, learned about plastics during a trip abroad in the late 1940s. Back home, he used his glass mold skills to begin producing molds for plastic products. Thirty years later, Marinha Grande was the second largest supplier of such molds to the United States. More than 150 companies in the industry now call the region home.

More recently, a peculiarity of financial regulations has enabled the City of London to become the leading location for Euromarkets—the capital markets for currency deposits that accumulate outside their country of origin. For example, U.S. dollars in European or Middle Eastern hands are known as Eurodollars. If these dollars were repatriated into U.S. banks, they would fall under the U.S. interest rate controls prevailing in the 1970s. The controls, originally designed to keep home mortgage rates low, capped the rate that banks could offer on deposits. If the Eurodollars remained in London, however, the regulators treated them as being outside both the U.S. and British interest rate and foreign exchange controls. British and foreign banks in London quickly recognized the huge international credit potential in accumulating Eurodollars, and they began offering higher rates for the surplus dollars. The London Euromarkets, today among the largest financial markets in the world, thereby got under way.[2]

Sometimes clusters got their head start by pure chance, as was the case in the small Georgia city of Dalton, which in the early 1990s was home to six of the top twenty U.S. carpet-manufacturing firms. Dalton's preeminence as the U.S. "carpet capital" has lasted almost one hundred years. According to Paul Krugman, the local industry got its start when a teenage girl, Catherine Evans, made a tufted bedspread as a wedding gift. From this unexpected beginning, a local tufting handicraft industry sprang up. Surging demand in the 1920s led to semimechanization, and through successive improvements, a carpet-tufting machine was invented in Dalton just after World War II. In the face of competition from tufted carpets, many of the makers of woven carpets subsequently went bankrupt, or relocated to Dalton to establish tufting operations as the core of their businesses.[3] You had to be located in Dalton to have a chance of winning. Geography had become destiny.

Each of these examples shows the power of clusters as a source of competitive advantage for companies located within them. Being headquartered in one of these privileged locations gave budding global companies an advantage over competitors that were developing their products, services, and processes in less favorable places. It is therefore not surprising that most traditional multinationals looked to their home-base cluster as the primary fount of competitive advantages—advantages that they could then exploit by global projection.

Clusters as a Source of Innovation

Once a location gained leadership in a business, a virtuous cycle often became established. People would be attracted by the prospects of higher rewards in an area where their skills were in demand. The depth and quality of the local skill base would therefore increase. Companies that wished to compete in the business were attracted by this "honey pot" of skills. Initially this might drive up costs as companies competed for the best people. But higher salaries, in turn, would attract more individuals with the right skills.[4]

Such a location would also attract customers with its ready availability of quality products for volume purchasers. Buying at the "capital" of a particular industry reduces the costs of searching for the right supply. Over time, this virtuous cycle is propelled forward by the creation of new knowledge. Interaction with customers seeking sophisticated versions of the product or service gives local suppliers new insights about emerging applications and consumer needs. Suppliers develop new technologies, extending and improving their products and services. Local suppliers also learn from one another as employees move from company to company in search of higher rewards.

This process can be seen at work in Taiwan's high-technology cluster, Hsinchu Science–based Industry Park, an "industrial ecosystem" similar to Silicon Valley.[5] By bringing together semiconductor firms and venture capital organizations, and by fostering research partnerships between universities and the private sector, the park encouraged "flexible recycling" of skills and knowledge to form a virtuous, self-reinforcing cycle. Specialist suppliers of equipment, materials, and services soon started to locate there, adding further to the knowledge base.

By attracting people with relevant skills and sophisticated customers and suppliers, these clusters became rich pools of knowledge. The daily interactions among participants in the cluster, meanwhile, meant that new knowledge coming to the cluster was readily shared.

More than a century ago, the English economist Alfred Marshall noticed the benefits that individual firms derived from being part of "industrial districts" that specialized in a particular activity.[6] Marshall also observed that in a cluster or industrial district, "the mysteries of the trade become no mystery; but are, as it were, in the air." In other words, the cluster became a powerful mechanism for attracting and sharing knowledge about "a trade."

A rich pool of shared knowledge, combined with the pressure of intense competitive rivalry, made these clusters an exceptionally fertile ground for innovation. Not only was the cluster a powerful source of initial competitive advantage for a company to launch its global expansion, therefore, but it also provided a continuous flow of innovation. These innovations could be adopted and refined by the multinational's home base and subsequently projected around the globe through its existing network. As new innovations appeared in Silicon

Valley, for example, companies such as Cisco or Intel were able to turn these new ideas into improved products and services that they were then able to leverage around the globe.

THE TRADITIONAL MULTINATIONAL PROJECTOR

Exploiting the virtuous cycle of advantage and innovation in a home-base cluster, companies typically followed a sequential path from strength in the home market to global leadership. The early history of most multinationals shows a number of marked similarities—the "1-2-3" steps to internationalization described in figure 2-1.

Step 1. Build on the Core Strengths from Your Homeland to Gain International Advantage

Before today's leading companies became large, successful multinational organizations, nearly all were already large, successful domestic organizations in their respective home countries. Their business mod-

**Figure 2-1   The Development of the Traditional
Multinational Corporation**

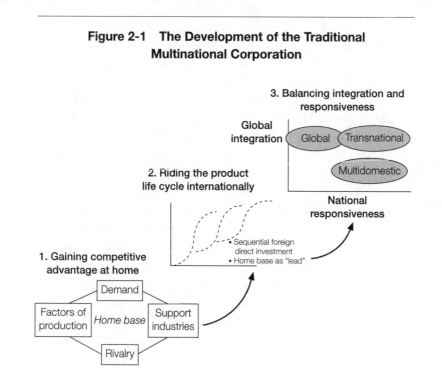

els were created in their original national location. Their strategic advantages evolved out of the critical capabilities and opportunities found there.

Brown Boveri (the BB in ABB), for instance, became a very early multinational on the strength of high-pressure hydroelectric turbine technology developed initially by Charles Brown to suit the energy needs of Switzerland, the Alpine relief of which offered numerous opportunities for hydroelectric power stations. Brown Boveri eventually developed into a full-range supplier of electricity generation and distribution equipment, but its initial home-oriented advantage in high-pressure turbines spearheaded its internationalization.

The mass-manufacturing processes that Ford developed—particularly the moving assembly line—were driven by the need to provide affordable vehicles to the masses of farmers in turn-of-the-century America. This led to the 1908 introduction of a mass-manufacturing process for the Model T that gave Ford a significant cost advantage over small-scale European manufacturers and allowed Ford's post–World War I penetration of European markets, starting with investments in the United Kingdom and Germany.

Step 2. Project These Strengths into the Global Arena along the International Product Life Cycle

Successful multinationals learned to leverage their homegrown advantages on an international scale.[7] To achieve sales growth, they began by selling in "nearby" countries (where cultural and economic closeness was more important than geographic distance). The focus was on innovative products for which demand was fairly homogeneous and therefore less dependent on local culture and context. Thus it was possible to enter new markets without significantly changing specifications. (For this reason, services and highly customized products were seldom the basis of multinational expansion.)

Many multinationals followed the product life cycle as their businesses fanned out across the globe. As production costs fell with economies of scale and learning, companies targeted new, lower-priced markets for growth. Poor global communications and limited mobility of key personnel extended the early advantage over foreign competitors, giving time for a gradual expansion abroad.

Multinationals monitored the level of disposable income in an emerging market. When disposable income reached the takeoff point, the multinational introduced the product into the market. The international product life cycle could be stretched out over many years, or even several decades.

As their product's life cycle reached maturity and price/costs moved higher on the strategic agenda, companies began to move production to countries with lower cost factors, starting with the less skilled/more labor-intensive operations.

The aim of Step 2 is to maximize revenue and minimize costs on a global scale. Efficiency is the driving force, and it serves to sustain the competitiveness of the domestic operation. The domestic economy remains the company's "strategic" market. Some researchers refer to traditional multinationals as "national firms with international operations."[8]

Step 3. Balance Local Responsiveness with Global Integration

As they expanded into more markets and built more sourcing plants, multinationals added new sophistication to the basic formula.[9] The multinational organization (by now a worldwide configuration of operations) faced a key strategic decision: Should it emphasize global coordination and integration of its activities, responsiveness to national characteristics, or both? Being "global" generates economies of scale and scope (and therefore lowers costs), while being "local" enhances differentiation and responsiveness to customer needs (and therefore raises revenues).

Figure 2-2 charts the new corporate forms that evolved as multinationals responded to this integration-responsiveness dilemma. We include all of these organizational types in the category of "traditional multinational companies." Each type, however, embodies a different corporate choice about how to operate in the multinational economy. The epitome of "global projection" (often referred to as the "export model"), in the top left quadrant, chose to emphasize global efficiency and coordination. These firms became such world-class projectors as McDonalds, Siemens, and CNN.

"Multidomestic" companies, in the bottom right quadrant, placed their emphasis on local responsiveness. They differentiated them-

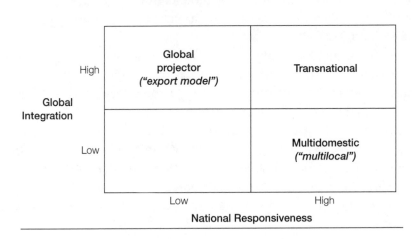

Figure 2-2   Multinational Strategy: Standardization versus Adaptation?

selves by adapting to local preferences. Unilever, Nestlé, and more recently Amazon.com (which has developed separate subsidiaries and supply chains for retailing its products in each of its major markets) are prime examples of this multidomestic strategy.

In the 1980s, a number of companies, such as Asea Brown Boveri and 3M, repositioned themselves toward the top right-hand quadrant. CNN.com is a more recent example. The goal of these companies is to be sensitive *both* to local needs *and* to global coordination. Companies using this approach were categorized as "transnational."

Transnational structures varied across individual companies, but their core intent was to create integrated networks of national subsidiaries, each with different roles. Some subsidiaries would act purely as implementers of the strategies and formulas developed by headquarters or dominant sister subsidiaries. The strongest subsidiaries would become "strategic leaders," building core advantages that the transnational would project around the world. Transnationals are still international projectors. They are more sophisticated ones in the sense that they project competitive advantage from lead subsidiaries as well as from headquarters.[10]

Having shifted key operations abroad—often to diverse locations—to take advantage of competencies and economies outside their home countries, some firms established specialist units or centers of excellence with a mandate to absorb and disseminate local skills and know-how.

But what about potentially valuable knowledge that is scattered around the small, peripheral subsidiaries of a traditional multinational? What about the rich seams of technology or new customer needs that emerge in places where the transnational has only a token presence or where it doesn't operate at all? In a world in which the profits from global projection in its various forms are declining annually, in which traditional multinationals desperately need to find new sources of differentiation, can these unorthodox sources of new technologies and market intelligence continue to be ignored?

THE NEXT OPPORTUNITY

Historically, peripheral pockets of knowledge and market intelligence weren't critical to global success. As long as their traditional home-based clusters led their industry, traditional multinationals continued to perform well. In the past, exploiting learning scattered around the world was for the multinational an "optional extra"—a windfall to boost growth and profitability from an unexpected source—but not the lifeblood of the firm's innovation. But the global game is changing:

- The capabilities of global efficiency and local adaptation are becoming a table stake, not a distinctive source of competitive advantage.

- With each new generation, the product/service life cycle grows shorter, and how it spreads across global markets is less predictable. The idea of riding the life cycle of a standardized product through waves of international expansion, as successive countries develop, becomes less and less tenable.[11]

- The technologies and customer knowledge that a global leader must absorb are becoming more diverse. Perfecting an innovation using one source of technology or designing a new product or service around the needs of a local customer base is no longer sufficient to ensure a world-beating product.

- The knowledge that a global company needs to win is becoming increasingly dispersed around the world. It is no longer to be found in a single cluster, or even a handful of industry hotbeds in major markets.

The rules of this new game threaten to undermine the profitability of the traditional globalization strategies we just described. But they also create enormous new opportunities for companies that are able to tap the potential of ever more diverse and specialized knowledge dispersed around the world.

Knowledge Is Increasingly Diverse and Dispersed

To understand these new opportunities, managers need to recognize that the knowledge that their companies need is becoming more diverse and more dispersed. There is no better example of this than the information industries. We tend to equate the dominant source of innovation in this sector with Silicon Valley. But a recent *Wired* magazine survey listed ten world hotspots, each offering unique technologies and market intelligence: Austin, Texas; Bangalore, India; Boston, Massachusetts; Cambridge, England; Helsinki, Finland; Salt Lake City, Utah; Seattle, Washington; Singapore; Sophia-Antipolis, France; and Tel Aviv, Israel.[12]

Yesterday it was possible to designate one country as the lead market, another as the fount of innovation, and yet another as the major source of global supply. Today there is no single lead market for most products and services. There is no single hotbed with a monopoly on technological innovation. Is the lead market for mobile telephone applications the United States, Finland, or Japan? It is impossible to say.

It is misleading even to talk about a lead country for technology or consumer trends. Today countries are poor proxies for where new technologies or novel market needs might be found. Are consumers in Idaho any more likely to point the way to new market needs than those in Milan or Hong Kong? Why, then, is the United States designated the lead market? Will the next breakthrough in semiconductor technology come from Cambridge (England) or from Austin, Pittsburgh, Grenoble, or Kyoto? If the answer is unclear, why limit chip research to a single laboratory in the United Kingdom?

The range of knowledge that companies need in the global innovation race is increasingly diverse. Companies in the agricultural
chemicals business used to prosper with a deep knowledge of chemistry. Today agri-chemicals companies need to master biotechnology,
genetic engineering, and seed production, among other disciplines.
Pharmaceutical companies such as Novartis and GlaxoSmithKline
now face a migration of their knowledge base from traditional chemistry toward biotechnology and genetics. Because the hotbeds of each
of these technologies are in different locations, the requirement for
more *diverse* knowledge often means coping with greater knowledge
dispersion as well.

Eight fundamental forces are driving this trend toward greater
global dispersion of the knowledge that companies need to win globally. We group them into two categories: those driving the dispersion
of technological knowledge and those driving dispersion of market
knowledge.

Forces Driving Dispersion of Technological Knowledge

- **Industry convergence.** As industries converge, different streams
  of technology converge, and companies will need to master a
  more diverse range of technologies. But these industries and
  technologies have tended to grow up in different locations
  around the world. To access the new technologies, companies
  must therefore draw from a wider range of locations. For example, because the pharmaceutical and biotechnology industries
  developed in different places, the convergence of these industries
  means pharmaceutical companies can no longer rely on their
  home base as the source of innovation. They need to draw technology from a broader set of locations. Or witness the way in
  which the convergence of publishing, broadcasting, and the
  Internet has increased the range of technologies (and hence the
  geographic sources) that companies such as AOL Time Warner or
  Bertelsmann need to reach consumers in the electronic age.

- **Technology transfer.** As multinationals transplant competencies
  to new locations through their subsidiaries, new pools of competencies will develop. As a result, the pools of specialist knowledge
  a company could usefully access for innovation becomes more
  dispersed. When Hewlett-Packard moved its process engineering

skills from the United States to Singapore to manufacture calculators, for example, it set off a chain of events in which the engineers there began to alter the calculator designs, gradually building a design competence that was then applied to keyboards and eventually to the complete design of inkjet printers, so that a new competency pool emerged on the other side of the world.

- **Offshore sourcing.** As companies use contract manufacturing located outside traditional clusters, the sources of new knowledge that flow from manufacturing process improvements will also become more dispersed. Today, for example, Taiwan has an almost 70 percent share of the world manufacturing of scanners and a more than 60 percent share of the world manufacturing of computer keyboards and mice.[13] Although the core technologies may have originated in California, it is inevitable that new knowledge about the manufacture and design of these components will be generated in Taiwan. Again, this drives increased dispersion of the knowledge that companies need.

- **Technological complexity.** As products become more complex, the relevant sources of knowledge needed to design, market, and deliver them to customers become more dispersed. Most of the knowledge required to produce a simple, standard product may be found in a single location. But consider what knowledge is required today to develop and build a new aircraft. Hundreds of specialized technologies from materials science to advanced avionics and artificial intelligence must be brought together, along with a detailed understanding of the different economics of individual airlines' route structures and service aspirations. As Boeing discovered when it set out to develop its 777 aircraft, the plethora of knowledge and capabilities required simply didn't exist in the United States, let alone Seattle, despite the city's long history of airframe design and manufacture.

- **"Random" breakthroughs.** New technological breakthroughs still have a large element of serendipity. Random events don't always occur in the strongest existing clusters or locations with the most resources devoted to a particular problem. For instance, the creation of the "www" (World Wide Web) and "http" occurred in Geneva, Switzerland, at the European High-Energy Particle Physics Lab, CERN (around 1990), as a tool to enable collaboration between physicists and other researchers. A couple of years later it was picked up by a few students at the University of Illinois at Urbana-Champagne, and Mosaic (the precursor of Netscape) was born. In early 1997, the world was amazed by Dolly, a lamb cloned from the DNA of an adult sheep mammary. Dolly was "created" by researchers in Edinburgh, Scotland—not the most obvious source of a breakthrough in genetic engineering.

Forces Driving Dispersion of Market Knowledge

- **New customer interactions.** As products and services are introduced into new, formerly peripheral markets, new knowledge about potential customer applications or tastes will emerge from fragmented locations. In adapting its product to the Buenos Aires market for ice cream, for example, Häagen-Dazs developed its "dulce de leche" flavor, named after the popular Argentine caramelized milk dessert. Within a year, the new Argentine flavor was introduced throughout the United States and Europe, where it sold more than all but vanilla in the stores carrying it.[14]

- **Globalization of customers.** As corporate customers, distributors, and retailers themselves become more global, the relevant knowledge they have accumulated will become more dispersed in small pockets across their own organizations. In seeking the knowledge of hard disk drives it needed from Seagate, for example, STMicroelectronics discovered that the information was dispersed throughout Seagate's operations in the United States and Asia.

- **Solution selling.** As more and more companies sell "solutions" rather than separate products or services, they will need to bring together dispersed knowledge, as the know-how that underpins all of the pieces of a complex solution is unlikely to be found in a single location. As IBM has moved away from selling hardware alone and toward selling solutions, for example, it has found an increasing need to bring together knowledge of the customer with hardware, software, and systems-integration expertise from sources both inside and outside IBM in different locations spread around the world.

These eight forces are combining to drive ever-greater dispersion in the knowledge sets that companies need to win in the new global economy. A survey we conducted among U.S. and European multinationals in 1998 underscores the trend. On average, respondents expected that over the next five years almost half of the breakthrough technologies in their industry would come from outside their home continent. Likewise, they anticipated that 42 percent of the most innovative products would emerge outside their home continent.

A TREND TOO IMPORTANT TO IGNORE

Companies ignore the increased dispersion of relevant knowledge at their peril. Witness the fate of computer companies based on the East Coast of the United States when the leading-edge technology moved west.[15] Likewise, bioMérieux, in Lyon, France, was a leader in the businesses of in vitro diagnostics of infectious diseases (its local capabilities tracing back to the work of Louis Pasteur and his colleague, Marcel Mérieux) until the emergence of automatic diagnostic machines based on specialist mechanics, robotics, and electronics. Almost all of the new, critical knowledge for the machines was in the United States, not in France. Recall the damage to Motorola when it ignored the pool of telephone technology emerging in Finland. Nokia was an upstart competitor drawing on unfamiliar digital technology in a location that was peripheral to Motorola. As Motorola discovered, this is not just about lost opportunities for fostering innovation and creating new types of advantage. Ostrichlike behavior in the face of global knowledge dispersion will eventually threaten a company's competitive position.

Some multinationals are already responding to increased knowledge dispersion. By 1990, an analysis of U.S. patent data found that among European-owned industrial firms, some 31 percent of patents were based on research conducted outside the home country. But does any one of these companies really believe that 69 percent of all new technical knowledge relevant to its business is being produced in its home country? Or does historical inertia cause these companies to stick to local sources?

American firms seem to be even farther behind in leveraging knowledge scattered around the globe. For U.S.-owned firms, just under 9 percent of patents came from research conducted abroad.[16] Is 91 percent of the research they need really located in the United States? With the luxury of a technologically advanced home market, American firms can easily fall into the delusion that they don't need to access foreign technology and ideas. Motorola now knows otherwise.

Other data confirm that many companies have failed to appreciate the potential of leveraging global knowledge. Surveying 144 of the world's largest industrial firms about the role of their different geographic units in building competitive advantage, John H. Dunning concluded that "the sample firms perceived that their domestic operations and/or indigenous resources and capabilities of their home countries continued to provide the main source of competitiveness— especially in terms of technological capacity and skilled professional manpower."[17] Despite the inherent risks of blind spots and the lost potential for new competitive advantage, it seems that most traditional multinationals have failed to break free of their geography. The questions that remain are Why? and What does it take for a company to reach beyond its geographic roots?

One possible explanation is the attitude that, for most industries, there is little worthwhile new technology, skills, or market information to be found outside a few well-known hot spots. This view might be summed up as "if you're in electronics, it's enough to be learning what Silicon Valley has to teach." But, as we saw earlier, the powerful forces driving increased knowledge dispersion are creating worthwhile knowledge about technologies and market behaviors outside the well-trodden handful of locations.

The alternative explanation is that, for all their complex organizational structures and processes, traditional multinationals understand the metanational imperative but simply don't know how to respond. Breaking free of geography might seem straightforward. In practice, however, shedding geographic shackles is fraught with management issues because it strikes at the heart of our ideas on the sources of competitive advantage. Tapping new sources of technological and market knowledge requires radical new ways of thinking and behaving. It means questioning the established mindsets and systems that made a company great.

Our 1998 survey data support this second view. Respondents were noticing the danger signals, but they wondered how to absorb breakthrough technologies emerging in regions where their own operations were weak or nonexistent. Would the answer lie in strengthening their presence in these key locations? But what if the local market there was small and the technological community was impenetrable?

Take a few moments to fill out table 2-1. Your entries will help show you where to begin looking for the knowledge you will need to win in the future. Use this information to start mapping the size and complexity of the metanational opportunity for your company in the global knowledge economy.

Table 2-1   Sketching the Impact of the Global Knowledge Economy in *Your* Industry

Source of Future Competitive Advantage	Locations (Countries, Regions, Cities)	
	NOW	FUTURE
Lead Markets and Customers Where are the most demanding customers? Where are the new ways of using your product or service emerging? Where do you find trendsetting changes in regulation or industry structure? Where are the maverick competitors being born?		
"Defining" Technologies and Competencies Where are the critical new technologies in your industry originating? Where are the most exciting new products in your industry being developed? Where will you find the most innovative suppliers or potential partners?		

Where will your company need a presence it does not yet possess? Where will it be important to gain a sensitive understanding of new types of customer demand? Where are the emerging hotbeds of new technologies and other types of capabilities? Where will it be important to creep into the minds of maverick competitors who may overturn the existing rules of the game?

How will your company access this new knowledge? How and where will it move it about and combine it with existing capabilities or new know-how gleaned from elsewhere? How can you go about using the new knowledge to create better products and services, improve the supply chain, and cut costs? How will you leverage these new advantages around the world? Does your company have the right mindset, incentives, structures, and systems to make all of this happen? If not, what barriers will you need to overcome?

THREE BARRIERS

Three barriers, deeply rooted in organization design, power structures, and corporate beliefs, make it difficult to break free of geography even when a company recognizes the opportunities and threats that global knowledge dispersion brings.

The Primacy of the Home Base

Blinded by the power of clusters and the projection strategy, most multinationals find it inconceivable that their birthplace, with its associated home market, is not the primary source of competitive strength. Their structures—which invariably locate the CEO, strategic decision-making, and the bulk of R&D close to headquarters—reflect a rock-solid belief in the primacy of home.* Subsidiaries do R&D, but

---

*Consider the following statistic: Among the multinationals in the motor vehicle industry (widely considered one of the most "global" industries), 23 percent of sales, 32 percent of assets, and 36 percent of employees are outside the parent's home country, but only 7.5 percent of R&D is conducted overseas. In a recent survey of companies with more than 500 employees, 43 percent ranked "near headquarters" as the most important criterion for locating R&D facilities.

with heavy emphasis on the "D" to adapt their products to local market conditions.

Within most multinationals, employees and other stakeholders have tremendous emotional attachment to their home city, region, or country. Even among global giants, very few companies ever move their headquarters far away from the place where they began in business. On the rare occasions when they do move, it is an emotionally traumatic step. This was true even when Philips NV relocated its headquarters to Amsterdam—still in the Netherlands, but away from Eindhoven, where the company was born.

The Idea That "Weight Equals Voice"

The second barrier is that in decisions about strategy and investments, "weight equals voice." Even where some power has been given to other parts of the network, national subsidiaries with the largest markets, asset bases, investments, and numbers of people tend to have the greatest influence on key decisions and investments. How often does a voice from the periphery truly influence the largest, most profitable subsidiaries with the idea that some unproven technology or emerging market need requires a fundamental change in the business? Motorola was hardly likely to give much weight to the views of its people in the Nordic countries when they claimed that the digital GSM standard would rapidly take over the world market. After all, the company had few assets and sales there. Its R&D was based in the United States and Japan. Finland, for example, was a peripheral market.

The Assumption That Local Adaptation Is Relevant Only Locally

The third barrier is the implicit assumption that local adaptation is relevant only locally. Even multinationals that excel in local adaptation of their products and services, developing locally tailored marketing campaigns—building local brands, launching local product formulations, and adjusting distribution strategies—often regard these as deviations from the global blueprint that undermine their worldwide efficiency. Therefore, they fail to recognize the potential for learning from adaptation by transferring local success stories to other markets. Even if that potential is understood, few firms have the mechanisms in place to link the new knowledge with existing international competencies to create new products, services, and systems that can be leveraged globally.

These three legacies turn companies into prisoners of their historic geography. Even with a global network of manufacturing, sales, marketing and service centers, and R&D laboratories, a multinational will never be able to take full advantage of the untapped potential being created by global knowledge dispersion while these three legacies remain.

THE BENEFITS OF BREAKING FREE OF GEOGRAPHY

There are significant prizes available for companies that accept the challenge of breaking free of their geography. Specifically, those who can escape the chains of their geographic heritage will be able to build the next layer of competitive advantage over their rivals by accomplishing the following:

- Accessing untapped technologies and lead consumers that are outside the traditional "capitals" of their industries and beyond the large, mature markets and production sites—new knowledge that will provide the raw material for discontinuous innovation and sustained advantage.

- Understanding and exploiting new technologies, processes, and systems drawn from other industries, even when these are concentrated in locations outside the places at which they currently operate.

- Combining technologies and knowledge about emerging user needs drawn from places that have not been previously connected.

Breaking free of geography to tap the world for knowledge that will differentiate you from competitors is an important first step toward building a new layer of competitive advantage. But it is only a first step. Ultimately, what matters is the way in which you use this knowledge: how effectively you apply it to fuel innovation that can be leveraged across world markets. This is the metanational challenge.

To understand how a company can rise to the metanational challenge and unlock competitive advantage by breaking free of its geography, we looked around the world for companies that had already embarked on this journey. Perhaps not surprisingly, we found few pioneers among the global giants that had succeeded by projecting their homegrown strengths into every corner of the globe. Instead, it was the unlikely global winners—companies that had succeeded on the world stage despite starting out in a peripheral or disadvantaged location—that were pointing the way. Chapter 3 explains what we can learn from these companies about prospering in the global knowledge economy.

Chapter 3

Metanational Pioneers: The Benefits of Being Born in the "Wrong" Place

WOULD YOU PICK Finland as your home base from which to storm the international market for mobile telephones? Would you select Switzerland as your launching pad to break into the international market for guided missile systems? Would you choose Japan as the location from which to compete with Steinway in the global market for pianos? Would you rather try to build a global leader in the personal computer business from a base in Silicon Valley or from Taiwan? Would you dream of China as the best place to start a global insurance company? If you wanted to dominate the global market for integrated business software, would you locate your headquarters in Germany?

Chances are you wouldn't do any of the above. Yet Nokia became the world leader in mobile telephony from a base in Finland. Oerlikon broke into the international market for missile systems from Switzerland. Acer of Taiwan grew to be the number three personal computer company in the world. Yamaha of Japan has become the world's largest supplier of pianos. AIG, one of the most successful international insurance companies, got its start in China. SAP of Germany became the world's largest supplier of integrated business software.

All of these companies were born in the "wrong" place, in the sense that they were outside the traditional capitals of their industries. A large part of the knowledge they needed to compete globally was not available in their home country. At first glance, they may seem an unlikely place to look for the keys to future competition in the global knowledge economy. But in fact, it is these global leaders born in the wrong place that are most advanced in the game of unlocking the potential of knowledge imprisoned in local pockets scattered around the world. Because the knowledge they needed was not available at home, they had to develop the skills of sensing, mobilizing, and operationalizing technologies and market knowledge drawn from abroad. They learned these metanational capabilities because they had to. Necessity was the mother of invention.

Apart from the incentive to search the world for new technologies and market knowledge, all of these companies shared another characteristic: top management with a deeply cosmopolitan mindset. Their CEOs and senior executives not only had international experience; they shared a deep interest in and appreciation of the strengths of local cultures in different parts of the world.

In this chapter we begin to learn from these unlikely global winners how to unlock the potential of globally dispersed knowledge. We identify six core capabilities that these companies have begun to develop. We then show how these capabilities can be shaped into a metanational corporation that builds competitive advantage from unexpected places.

THE METANATIONAL ALTERNATIVE

In the past, few companies achieved global leadership starting from a home base located on the periphery of their industry. Those that did were seen by most managers in established companies as little more than interesting curiosities. But in a world where the relevant knowledge is now globally dispersed, the special skills of companies born in the wrong place are of great relevance to mainstream corporations and to startups aspiring to become global. Their success is testimony to the fact that geography is no longer destiny; a company does not have to be headquartered in the "capital" of its industry to succeed. They demonstrate that the strategy of global projection—spreading advantages created at home around the world—is not the only path to success.

These global winners who were born in the "wrong" place point the way on a new metanational path to success. None of these companies could yet be described as a full-fledged metanational. But we believe they are the forerunners of tomorrow's winners in the global knowledge economy.

The key differences between the traditional projection strategy and the metanational alternative are well illustrated if we compare and contrast the stories of Intel and STMicroelectronics—two successful, global players in the semiconductor industry.

STMICROELECTRONICS VERSUS INTEL: DISTINCT PATHS TO SUCCESS

Intel and STMicroelectronics share a number of common characteristics. Among the top ten semiconductor manufacturers that have led the industry's growth over the past decade, only Intel and ST did not rely largely or solely on sales to captive customers within a corporate group. Both companies were founded at roughly the same time. Intel is widely admired for its domination of processor chips for personal computers. While ST is less well known, its growth in market share of value-added chips has been second only to Intel. It has become a world leader in the customized chips we find inside cars, televisions and TV set-top boxes, mobile phones, hard disk drives, and the heads for Hewlett-Packard inkjet printers, or on smart cards.

Intel and ST have several other things in common. Most of their top managers and technologists were trained as electronic engineers and were by and large from a very small number of American companies, tracing their lineage back to Fairchild Semiconductor. Very charismatic leaders drove both: Andy Grove, a Hungarian-American, at Intel, and Pasquale Pistorio, a cosmopolitan Sicilian, at ST.

There is, however, at least one dramatic difference between Intel and ST. Intel was born in Silicon Valley, the world capital of semiconductors. ST has its roots in Milan and Paris—locations that are more readily associated with high-fashion clothing than with high-tech semiconductors. If Intel was born with a silicon spoon in its mouth, ST's cradle was in the "wrong" place.

To build their businesses, both companies had to access, mobilize, and leverage a complex set of technologies and market knowledge. Intel, however, had practically all of the knowledge it needed to build a powerful position right on its doorstep in Silicon Valley. Intel accessed knowledge from Stanford University and such firms as Applied Materials, Cadence, Hewlett-Packard, Seagate, AMD, and MIPS, just to name a few, all within close proximity to Intel's Santa Clara headquarters.

Intel has also had joint development projects or marketing partnerships with customers. Examples include IBM, VLSI, DARPA (a U.S. government agency), AT&T, and Pacific Bell. But they are all American. Intel's long-term strategic partner has been Microsoft, another U.S.-based corporation. Intel was, therefore, largely able to sidestep the problems associated with the international dispersion of critical knowledge that we described in chapter 2.

Intel's Global Projection Strategy

Because the main technologies and market knowledge it needed to sense and mobilize were available locally, Intel was also able to minimize its exposure to challenges of managing sophisticated and sticky knowledge across vast distances and different contexts. With the bulk of the knowledge it needed located in Silicon Valley, Intel found that the process of using that knowledge was facilitated by proximity. Frequent and informal interactions between the various parties were relatively straightforward—a matter of half an hour's drive to a meeting. The necessary knowledge was mostly available in the heads of people who shared the same language and understood the local context of chip development—everything from implicit roles and responsibilities to accepted development cycles.

Despite its Silicon Valley base, Intel did have to access a certain amount of technology and knowledge from overseas. Some of the wafer lithography technology Intel used, for example, came from Japan. In sheer technical terms, this technology is obviously highly complicated. But it is relatively simple to move across distances with precisely articulated operating manuals and vendor training programs. And part of the knowledge about wafer lithography that Intel needed was actually embodied in the equipment that was shipped from Japan to Santa Clara and other Intel fabricating plants (or "fabs").

Intel has been careful to minimize its exposure to the problems of sensing, mobilizing, and exploiting complex knowledge at a distance. It does so by creating most of its intellectual property assets in its home-base facilities using the wealth of complex knowledge available locally. Where it has had to augment this knowledge base from remote sources, it has made sure that the knowledge it transfers is available in well-articulated forms such as data, equipment, or procedures—knowledge that can simply by "slotted in" to its operations.

This strategy has been supported by Intel's focus on developing and manufacturing standard digital products, memories first and then microprocessors, for personal computers and workstations—a focus that minimizes complexity and largely eliminates the need to customize the final product to subtle differences in user needs around the world.

Intel's strategy, then, is that of the classic global projector: It accesses and mobilizes a complex set of knowledge largely from its immediate backyard to create world-beating products, systems, and processes within facilities at its home base. It then projects this powerful formula around the globe, exporting its products and know-how and replicating its systems and processes across a global manufacturing and service network.*

ST's Metanational Strategy

The situation at ST could hardly be more different. Lacking the depth of local technologies and market understanding around its birthplaces in France and Italy, ST had to source a great deal of specialist, often tacit, knowledge from outside its "home" countries.

One obvious way to fill this knowledge deficit might have been simply to source all the technology and market understanding it needed from Silicon Valley. ST could have tried, for example, to acquire one of Intel's American competitors. At best, however, that

---

*Intel follows a replication strategy (its "Copy Exactly") when it moves its technology and processes from a lead "fab" or R&D center in the United States. Intel has design centers outside the United States, however. In particular, the design center in Haifa, Israel, has been more and more involved in the design of new products—it already played an important role in the development of the Pentium MMX, for example. Even Intel had to consider a move away from its strong projection strategy.

approach might have allowed it to match its U.S. competitors. Fishing in the same pool as local competitors who were born in the Valley would almost certainly have relegated ST to a game of catch-up, forever a second-rank player.

Imagine, on the other hand, if ST could unlock the potential of knowledge imprisoned in pockets of local expertise scattered around the world. Then it could exploit knowledge that its Silicon Valley competitors were either unaware of or had chosen to ignore because of the perceived difficulties in accessing it. If ST could successfully extend its knowledge net to scoop up promising technologies and new applications needs from anywhere in the world, it would be able to innovate in ways that Intel or other rivals had not even thought of. ST would be in position itself to build fundamentally new types of competitive advantage.

In practice ST's strategy wasn't quite this deterministic. Serendipity played a role. The lack of customers near its major facilities in France and Italy forced ST to search for customers in distant locations and with very different semiconductor applications. As ST combed the world for new customers, it was confronted with the limitations of standard semiconductors in satisfying these different user needs. From there came an awareness of the opportunity to go beyond producing standard semiconductors, sold as components, to create integrated, customized chips that could perform a set of functions for specific applications. This would allow, for example, the hard disk drive (HDD) controller boards of a customer like Seagate to be shrunk onto a couple of chips. Thus emerged the idea of putting a complete "system on a chip."

But if ST were to produce integrated system chips, it would need to overcome two further challenges. First, it would need to augment its current stock of technologies with knowledge that lay outside its organization and that was, in fact, scattered around the world. Second, it would need to achieve a massively complex integration between all of these pockets of knowledge about technologies, processes, and the customer's application needs in order to design and produce a system chip. To produce a motherboard the old way, components from diverse sources had to be brought together and integrated. To design and produce a system chip, ST would have to mobilize and integrate *knowledge* from diverse sources instead of components.

We often assume that knowledge is easily mobile. But as ST discovered, the difficulties of mobilizing and integrating the specialist and sticky knowledge it needed to create a system chip made moving and integrating *components* look like child's play.

First, ST had to understand the customer, the customer's product application, and the overall "system know-how." Most of this knowledge is deeply embedded within the customer and its people, in the form of engineering and design principles, intelligence about end-user needs, industry norms, and competitive practices. There is a quantum leap from the technical specifications for a chip—one that is designed separately to be a modular part of a larger system—to the functionality of ST's system-on-a-chip that is heavily dependent on the specific context of the application it has to serve. In the former case, the product specification is all quite explicit. It may designate, for example, a certain voltage in a particular pin of the chip when a certain voltage is applied to another pin. By contrast, the potential supplier of a system chip is informed, for example, that the platters of the HDD must accelerate in a particular way or that the battery of the mobile phone must last for at least a given number of hours.

The maker of a system-on-a-chip must learn how to interpret these specifications and designs with its customer. But ST has customers in several industries, and each industry has its own language, its own logic. And the challenges of accessing this diverse knowledge only increase when the customers are in countries physically and culturally distant from the home of ST.

Some of ST's "lead" customers were located relatively close by. Thomson Multimedia and Gemplus, for example, are both headquartered in France. Thomson Multimedia is a leader in video applications (televisions and TV set-top boxes), and Gemplus is the number one company in the world for smart cards. But more often than not, ST looked afar to find demanding, lead customers that forced it to become an "insider" in world-class clusters. In many of these customers (such as Seagate and HP in California, Pioneer in Japan, Bosch in Germany, Nokia in Finland, and Nortel in Canada), knowledge about a particular application was spread across specialized sites in different locations, regions, or countries.

ST also needed to come to grips with the fact that the leading semiconductor process technologies and product innovations do not come out of France and Italy. There are certain exceptions, such as the world-class digital engineering in the high-tech cluster of Grenoble, France, and the leading analog technologists in Castelletto, Italy. Both confer unique advantage to ST. But ST needed to anticipate the advances in its own industry in order to keep its silicon know-how at least on par with its rivals in the United States and Japan.

So how did ST sense, mobilize, and operationalize the kinds of knowledge that it required to become a winner in the global semiconductor game? To begin with, ST reversed the mindset of global projection and instead put worldwide learning at the center of its activities.

Sensing Dispersed Knowledge. ST extended its search area far beyond its original locations. A top priority was to begin gathering knowledge from Silicon Valley. There is nothing surprising about that: Multinational corporations often establish subsidiaries with full-functional capabilities in a promising market, projecting the corporation's advantages by replicating its home-base organization and business model abroad. In many multinationals, however, these successful, well-located subsidiaries become almost autonomous businesses—local fiefdoms inside the company.

The picture is quite different with ST's foothold in the Silicon Valley. While ST operates design centers, prototype labs, business units, and sales offices in the Valley, a key role of the staff there is to keep in close contact with nearby research institutions and universities. This structure ensures that ST has several functions and professions anchored in the hotbed of silicon know-how: scientists, technologists, application engineers, designers, customer engineers, operations managers, production workers, sales reps, and marketing staff.

These individuals are not part of any single product group, division, or business unit; nor do they constitute ST's American subsidiary. The nodes of ST's network in the Valley are linked more strongly with the local community and with other distant parts of ST in Europe or in Asia than they are among themselves. They are not in Silicon Valley to replicate what ST does in its home base. Their strategic role is to learn. As Francesco Carobolante, an "ST emigrant" in the United States who set up the San Jose design center in the early 1990s, explained it: "We are an ST design center. *But we are also the eyes and ears of ST.*"

ST also had co-development projects with competitors: Siemens (Germany) and Philips (Holland), and more recently with Hitachi (Japan). But one of ST's major guidelines for sensing necessary knowledge has long been that of learning with leading customers. For that purpose, ST established strategic alliances in the late 1980s and early 1990s with half a dozen lead global customers in key industries or for particular applications. Examples include Seagate (United States) for disk drives, Nortel (Canada) for telecommunications, Bosch (Germany) for automotive electronics, Thomson Multimedia (France) for video applications, and Pioneer (Japan) for consumer electronics. All these strategic accounts themselves have dispersed R&D activities, dispersed manufacturing operations, and a penchant for a global strategy. These alliances continue to be the principal learning tool about industries, applications, system know-how, and product development driven by the global market, not by the home market.

Over time, what ST had put in place was a world-beating "sensing network" that allowed it to prospect for and access a wide range of technological expertise and in-depth knowledge about customer needs and emerging applications.

Mobilizing Dispersed Knowledge. Once ST had accessed a rich portfolio of technology and knowledge about user needs, it faced the problem of how to mobilize this knowledge from dispersed sources and different contexts into innovative products and services. In the case of its HDD chip projects, for example, the silicon know-how had been drawn from across ST's international network, while the system knowledge that would need to be designed into the new product had come from a fragmented set of customer sites also dispersed around the world.

To mobilize these specialized pieces of knowledge, ST created a purpose-built structure of strategic global account units.[1] Each of these units was designed to create a link between the specialist knowledge within particular customer sites and the people in ST that could use this knowledge in the design or production processes used to create a system chip. Importantly, these special business units were not part of the normal matrix: They formed a separate organization with a direct link to the world headquarters in Geneva. This organization was not subject to the tyranny of P&L accounts, and it was effectively ring-fenced from the other measurement tools and mechanisms that ST used to manage the efficiency of its operations. The purpose of those global account teams was to share and mobilize complex knowledge between ST and the customer.

What ST had created, then, was a dedicated organization whose task was to sense specialist knowledge from around the world and integrate it with technology and know-how dispersed in pockets within ST, in order to fashion an innovative solution for a major customer.* Once ST was able to use this organization to integrate its silicon know-how from several sites around the world with the system know-how from Seagate, other HDD customers, and even competitors, it succeeded in replacing the traditional HDD motherboard with designs involving just a few system-level chips. Because these new system chips were customized to the needs of the HDD industry, they reduced manufacturing costs and improved HDD performance: They were more valuable than an assembly of standard chips.

Lacking this organization and its access to the unique bundle of knowledge that ST had drawn from around the globe, a competitor would find it very difficult to match this innovation. By sensing and then mobilizing underexploited pockets of knowledge, therefore, ST had created a potentially powerful source of competitive advantage that was difficult for its rivals to imitate.

Operationalizing Metanational Innovations. By sensing and mobilizing global knowledge, ST designed an innovative product that could be used to leverage its existing fabrication sites in France, Italy, the United States, Morocco, and Singapore for competitive advantage. To fully leverage this innovation, however, ST's operating network would need to market and produce system chips for other major customers with slightly different applications around the world.

Encouraged by the flow of orders won at Seagate and later with Western Digital, ST's operational network accepted the challenge of building on this experience. The next goal was to design and produce system chips as a set of application-specific standard products that could be adapted and used by any customers for a wide variety of data

---

*Of course, the managers at ST and other companies we studied did not use the terminology *sensing, melding, magnets,* and other concepts and metaphors that we use to describe and interpret their behavior.

storage device applications. These devices were sold to customers such as IBM, Quantum, Samsung, and other major HDD manufacturers, and also for related applications such as ZIP drives and CD-ROM drives. By 1996, ST's sales of chips to the HDD industry surpassed $500 million.

A global projector like Intel would have designed an improved chip to meet the needs of its domestic market. It would then "project" this chip design from its home base into different national markets across the world, adapting it where necessary. By contrast, ST developed a design based on knowledge from around the world for a leading global customer. It subsequently leveraged this design across an ever-expanding set of global customers and user applications, adapting the product to different customer and applications needs.

ST's experience suggests another key difference between the projection strategy and its metanational alternative: the *sequence* by which an innovation is exploited. In the case of projection, expansion proceeds across countries. In a metanational strategy, the innovation is global from Day 1. Expansion takes place across new customers, new global market segments, or new applications.

LESSONS FROM OTHER COMPANIES BORN IN THE WRONG PLACE

ST's experiences illustrate some of the capabilities and processes that underpin the metanational strategy. Our extensive research into the behavior of other winning companies born in the "wrong" place has surfaced some consistent patterns that show the kinds of capabilities companies are building to take advantage of the opportunities described in chapter 2.

Lessons for Sensing Globally Dispersed Knowledge

When Acer, the third largest personal computer company in the world by 2000, set out to expand from its humble beginnings in the early 1980s, among the problems it faced was its image as a Taiwanese company. Chairman Stan Shih summed it up this way: "Taiwan's reputation was for low end products. Even bankrupt computer companies in Silicon Valley had a better image than companies from Taiwan."[2]

This poor brand perception would have been of little consequence had Acer decided to become just another efficient manufacturer of IBM clones. But it had a more ambitious goal: It wanted to become a global PC brand and an innovator in its industry. At the time, some observers cautioned that such a goal was foolish: Apart from a poor brand image, Acer lacked access to the sources of new technology in the PC business—technology that was mainly being developed in the United States and Japan. "Didn't Acer realize," the skeptics said, "that while it was well located to be a manufacturer of PCs for others, it was born in the wrong place to be a global leader in branded PCs?"

Acer countered with an unorthodox strategy. Lacking the funds for a massive, international advertising campaign, Acer decided it needed to get free publicity from press and magazine editorials that would demonstrate to the world that Acer was capable of delivering sophisticated technology. It did so by repeatedly trying to beat its rivals to market with genuinely new technologies—innovations that would grab the media's attention.

But these new, attention-getting technologies weren't being developed locally in Taiwan. To get ahead of its rivals, Acer would have to become a successful prospector—a company that was able to anticipate where in the world the "hot" new technologies were coming from before these sources became well known.

In 1982 Acer (then called Multitech) discovered an 8-bit technology that had been developed by a small company in far-away California and cloned it to launch its own machines in Taiwan, the United Kingdom, Germany, and Hong Kong. That small California company was Apple Computer. In 1986, having seen the potential of Intel's new 386 chip, Acer launched a 32-bit PC based on the 386—and it did so ahead of IBM. The news of "David beating the IBM Goliath" led to great fanfare in the press. Acer subsequently continued on its path, beating its American rivals with the next generation of American technology in Germany and Japan.

Become a Global Knowledge Prospector. Making a virtue out of necessity, Acer became a compulsive global prospector, searching for new technologies throughout the world. Looking for all types of useful skills and knowledge that were not found in Taiwan, the company scoured the world for hidden pockets of knowledge. From a small design shop in the United States, it accessed skills in ergonomic design that led to the sleek, gray Aspire machine. Acer discovered unmet needs among small- and medium-sized businesses in Mexico and created a successful new range of computers that it subsequently sold to small businesses in emerging economies around the globe.

Acer implemented this strategy by viewing every unit in its global network as a knowledge prospector. Its sales units were not just there to sell, but also to learn from their distributors, their consumers, and their suppliers, looking for new knowledge that could point the way to the future. The company's management, R&D staff, and manufacturing people also constantly combed the world for emerging technologies and potential partners who were pushing out the frontiers. Through these initiatives, Acer was able to build a *capability for global knowledge prospecting* that surpassed any of its competitors.

Build the Capability to Access Pockets of New Knowledge. Once new sources of knowledge were identified through global prospecting, we observed that successful companies spent considerable effort to find efficient ways to access and internalize the new technology or market knowledge. When the required knowledge was well codified, the problem of accessing it proved quite straightforward. The company could, for example, buy blueprints or market data, license a technology or employ a local research firm to collect the relevant information and package it in an easily digestible form. In the case of more tacit knowledge, it was often possible to hire individuals who possessed the knowledge and could teach it to a new team.

But consider what happens when the newly located knowledge is subtle and very hard to codify. In this case, accessing it requires more than sourcing information or hiring a few individuals. Companies who wish to exploit this kind of knowledge face a significant problem of how best to access or "plug into" it efficiently—without either alienating its source (such as a customer or supplier) or transferring it in a misleading form. In overcoming the inadequacies of their birthplace, our unlikely global leaders put in place effective mechanisms for tackling this difficult problem.

Such was the challenge when Shiseido, based in Japan, sought to plug itself into local French knowledge about how to design and develop perfumes.[3] Fragrances accounted for only around 1 percent of the cosmetics market in Japan. But they are key to accessing distribution in the West, accounting for more than 40 percent of the cosmetics and perfumery market in France and from 30 percent to 40 percent in other Western countries. If you want to be a global cosmetics company, you need to understand perfume.

Plugging in to this type of complex knowledge requires living and experiencing it in order to learn. It cannot be accessed through market research reports or a search of the Internet. A company learns the perfume business by having some of its people experience what goes on in a successful perfume house, so that they can "creep into the minds" of people who have spent years honing their subtle skills.

Initially, Shiseido only partially recognized just how difficult it would be to access the knowledge it needed about perfume in France. It set up a 50/50 joint venture with a French cosmetics company in 1980, with the aim of accessing accumulated local knowledge about perfume development, the subtle interplay with customer behaviors, and the required logistics and information systems. It also established Shiseido Europe TechnoCentre to gather market information for the head office, with Japanese expatriates working as links to Japan. But neither of these initiatives proved sufficient to plug into complex knowledge about perfumes. Attempts at launching fragrance products under the Shiseido brand met only rather limited success.

In 1990, Shiseido management decided that it wasn't enough to access knowledge about the French market and then use this intelligence to develop and produce products in Japan. To plug into the fragrance knowledge base in France, Shiseido had to be in that business *in France*. Shiseido created BPI (Beauté Prestige International) in Paris, a 100 percent subsidiary specializing in the development and sales of fragrances.

BPI aimed at the top segment. Its success would be assessed by French, not Japanese, standards. Shiseido hired a French female CEO (another bold step for a Japanese company), very well reputed in the French fragrance trade, who had expertise in fragrances and in creative marketing, as well as the strong will that proved indispensable to keep the project on track. In 1992, Shiseido opened its own plant in Gien, a town on the Loire, south of Paris, in the French perfume industry "cluster." A Japanese expatriate with twenty years of training in fragrances in Europe was placed as operations manager there—with a view on technology transfer to Japan later on.

To learn about customers, and consistent with its practice of providing "beauty consulting" for cosmetics in stores in Japan and America, Shiseido acquired two prestigious beauty salons in France, Carita and Alexandre Zouari, in 1986. In 1992, it opened Les Salons du Palais Royal, a high-end beauty parlor in Paris, simultaneously with the launch of its perfume Feminite du Bois. Besides the obvious task of helping to sell cosmetics and fragrances, these salons were expected to serve as a source of information to be provided to the rest of the (Shiseido) world.

In 1992, BPI introduced two "designer brand" perfumes: Eau d'Issey (by Issey Miyake, a very cosmopolitan Japanese fashion designer) and Jean Paul Gaultier (named after its creator, the trendsetting French fashion designer)—representing two top names in the fashion business. The products were made at Shisheido's Gien plant.

Initially, Gien fell short of the quality and design expectations set by BPI, which favored subcontracting manufacturing as an alternative to in-house production at Gien. But Shiseido continued to insist that BPI products be made in-house, as a way to learn new capabilities. An experienced French manufacturing executive was hired to head operations in Gien. The BPI product lines became a resounding but unexpected success, and more have followed. Gien later started to produce "Shiseido lines" for Japan, where most of the concept development and final fragrance adjustment was done in Japan with Japanese consumers.

Shiseido had managed to successfully plug itself into the cluster of knowledge about perfume design and development that it needed from France. Despite many conflicts of a cultural nature, in areas such as research, planning, marketing, and sales, the Japanese decided to let the French people do things their own way. But the company learned by close observation and interaction, and Shiseido now applies some French managerial techniques in Japan for other products—an added bonus from plugging in to France.

The Shiseido experience illustrates a second critical sensing capability for companies born in the wrong place: *the ability to access complex knowledge* that is available only far away from their home base, by plugging in to an unfamiliar environment.

Lessons for Mobilizing Globally Dispersed Knowledge

The ability to prospect for and then access scattered pockets of specialist knowledge is of little use if a company is unable to mobilize its new knowledge to create innovative products, services, or processes. The first stage in mobilizing dispersed knowledge is to connect the fragmented pieces of knowledge about new technologies or market needs and use them for a particular problem or opportunity.

Our metanational winners created specific goals, projects, structures, and other mechanisms to help mobilize the new knowledge they acquired. We use the term *magnets* to describe the activities and systems they designed to attract critical knowledge and direct it toward specific challenges. In the case of ST, with HDD electronics, for example, Seagate (and the global account unit that served it) provided the necessary magnet.

Create a Magnet for Specialist Knowledge Accessed around the Globe. We observed the use of such magnets in U.K.-based Advanced RISC Machines (ARM), a 400-employee company whose market capitalization surpassed $12 billion in 2000, when Intel finally agreed to license ARM's semiconductor designs after a decade of head-to-head competition. Cambridge, England, may seem to be a reasonably auspicious birthplace for a chip developer like ARM. Nevertheless, much of the technology and user application knowledge ARM needed were to be found only in distant places like California, Texas, and Tokyo. Even today only 13 percent of ARM's sales are in Europe.

ARM describes itself as an independent silicon chip research, design, development, and licensing company. Its success comes from licensing its RISC (Reduced Instruction Set Computing) microchip designs to the world's largest semiconductor and consumer electronics companies. These chips are embedded in everything from mobile telephones to games, machines, and handheld PCs.

ARM draws knowledge about emerging technologies, wafer fabrication, and end-user needs from more than one hundred partner companies scattered from Korea and Japan to the United States and Finland. ARM's partners also include universities such as Cambridge, Manchester, and Southampton in the United Kingdom; Hanover in Germany; and Austin in Texas; these partnerships form a global collaborative research network. The company uses a mix of local subsidiaries, roundtables, and joint design teams with these far-flung partners to access critical knowledge. In more or less continuous rounds of meetings, ARM gets the best technical ideas from each partner and monitors the emergence of different customer needs.

At the core of ARM's success is a sophisticated network and a set of processes for locating, accessing, and mobilizing specialist pockets of knowledge around the world. This discipline is reflected in the three criteria ARM uses in looking for potential partners:

1. **Could this partner help create a global standard?** If the technology or application opportunity gleaned from a partner cannot contribute to the design of a better global standard, then ARM turns it down.

2. **Will the partnership develop into a "two-way" learning program?** ARM will license its technology only to partners that will contribute useful information on emerging technologies and market needs that ARM can use in the next round of development.

3. **Will the partnership help fill an emerging capability gap in ARM's portfolio?** In other words, ARM proactively looks for partners not only as potential buyers but also as future sources of capabilities.

Once it selects appropriate partners, ARM faces the challenge of using the pool of dispersed, specialized knowledge it gleans from them. It needs a powerful magnet to bring this dispersed knowledge together. ARM's magnets take the form of projects to create global-standard microchip designs—for example, a chip to power "Bluetooth" cores that will allow such devices as telephones, refrigerators, and TV sets to talk to one another. Each ARM project is run by a design project team in which employees, semiconductor partners, and user-industry partners can, as CEO Robin Saxby puts it, "interwork globally."

In ARM's case, then, the magnet is neither the R&D laboratory nor even a place. It is a *virtual* magnet—a project to create an emerging global platform that embodies the best combination of technologies to support the greatest feasible range of end-use applications. The manifestations of this magnet are the global team built to deliver it, the champion that leads it, and the budget allocated to it.

ARM's approach illustrates a third capability that we observe in companies that have begun to unlock the potential of the global knowledge economy: the *ability to identify and move globally dispersed knowledge by creating a magnet* that brings the knowledge to bear on a specific task.

Meld Dispersed Knowledge into Innovative Products and Services. Once knowledge is brought together by a magnet, it must be combined and melded into innovative products, services, or processes that can ultimately be leveraged by the company's global operations. We use the word *meld*, from the combination of *melt* and *weld*, to denote the alchemy of metanational innovation. Melding combines and transforms the component pieces of knowledge so that they become unrecognizable even after a thorough reverse engineering process.

As mentioned in chapter 1, PolyGram is deft at mobilizing the international potential of artists or groups from nonmainstream national markets. To achieve these minor miracles, it must meld a set of very complex pieces of knowledge to create a precise package of recording, public relations, marketing, and distribution expertise.

PolyGram's "raw material" for innovation consists of three types of knowledge:

- Its understanding of the style, appeal, and potential of local artists.

- Its understanding of the ever-changing consumer tastes for entertainment in particular markets around the world.

- Its knowledge about promotional, marketing, and sales techniques that will help propel a particular record to become a "hit" in its target markets.

These relevant pieces of knowledge are dispersed in different locations around the world. PolyGram brings this knowledge together by using one of its International Repertoire Centres (IRCs) as a magnet.

The first task of professionals working in an IRC is to glean knowledge from their sales and marketing colleagues about emerging fashions and tastes in local markets around the world. They also spend much of their time understanding the distinctive potential of artists who have been identified by the artists and repertoire (A&R) scouts in the area served by their IRC. Some of these artists may already be local stars. But keeping abreast of emerging local talent is not sufficient. Because their ultimate brief is to maximize international sales, the IRC professionals also need to keep abreast of innovative promotional and sales techniques being pioneered in different markets around the globe.

Having brought together the dispersed knowledge in the minds of IRC professionals, PolyGram's next task is to meld that knowledge to produce the record and associated promotional, marketing, and sales plans that will "click" with consumers in the target markets around the world. The necessary interactions are complex. The artist's repertoire and style may need to be adjusted to suit the tastes of international consumers, without losing the distinctive aspects of the performance. Promotional, marketing, and sales plans will have to amplify the distinctive appeal of the performer and the repertoire, rather than overshadowing it. An assessment must be made as to which innovative marketing technique will suit both the repertoire and the markets to which it is targeted. Staff at the IRC must accomplish this melding to come up with the right package. The process will generally involve countless iterations, as the IRC staff interact with the artist and his or her manager, A&R, sales and marketing people in numerous PolyGram local subsidiaries, international promoters, radio stations, music magazines, and so on.

What PolyGram has created in its ICRs and the processes they manage is *the ability to meld knowledge from dispersed sources around the world* into a new record, packaged with PR and marketing. This is the fourth capability that metanationals use to unlock the potential of the global knowledge economy.

Lessons for Operationalizing Innovations

Innovation alone, however, is clearly not enough. A final feature of globally successful companies born in the wrong place was their ability to leverage their innovations across a world market. This capability has two aspects. First, the necessary knowledge must be relayed to the people responsible for day-to-day operations. Then these people need to make sure the innovation is leveraged for increased sales or profits.

Consider what happens to one of PolyGram's potential international hit records once the IRC has shaped the right product and promotional package. PolyGram still needs to transfer the whole package smoothly into the hands of the operating subsidiaries that manufacture and distribute the product and implement the local marketing and sales campaigns.

Obviously, this is not just a matter of shipping a master tape and a mockup marketing package to a local subsidiary. Complex knowledge about the distinctive potential of the repertoire and the artist needs to be communicated to the operating subsidiaries, which may then need to adapt it to their local market without losing that distinctiveness. Likewise, the message behind the prototype marketing material must be communicated so that it is not lost in the process of local adaptation. Finally, the manufacturing and distribution chains need to be synchronized with the launch and promotion schedules around the world.

Transfer Critical Knowledge to Operations. IRC staff visit local subsidiaries, train local staff, and participate in the preparation of local launch plans to make sure that all the complex knowledge is effectively transferred. The process may also involve a concert tour by the artist that must, in turn, be choreographed to best position the record in each target market. PolyGram's local sales forces, meanwhile, need to be motivated to push the unfamiliar repertoire in their local markets.

These aspects of PolyGram's IRC system demonstrate another capability required to create metanational advantage: the *ability to effectively relay innovations* derived from globally dispersed knowledge *into the supply chain of day-to-day operations* where they can be exploited for profit.

Leverage the Innovation for Increased Global Sales or Profits. The final step in exploiting globally dispersed knowledge entails scaling up innovations by expanding them across new customers, customer segments, or applications. Recall that ST took its customized "system chips"—initially developed for Seagate—and turned them into a product range that was sold to most of the major manufacturers of HDD and other data-storage appliances. What started as a specific product for a single global customer was rolled out across new customers and similar applications. To leverage its innovation in this way, ST drew manufacturing and marketing capabilities from a wide range of sites within its global operating network; these include facilities in Italy, France, the United States, Morocco, and Singapore.

We observed that companies born in the wrong place scan the world for locations with the necessary capabilities in production, marketing, and distribution. Their concern is "How do I assemble the operating capabilities I need to leverage this innovation globally?" These capabilities may come from sites either within their own network or from partners outside it. The global projector, by contrast, asks, "How do I roll out this innovation across my national subsidiaries in the right sequence?" To the global projector, operations are a set of national subsidiaries. To the budding metanational, operations are a global supply chain assembled from capabilities drawn from different sites around the world—owned or not.

PixTech, the electronic display company we discussed in chapter 1, is a good example of this "How to leverage?" mentality. Seeking a way to operationalize its flat-panel designs, it accessed high-volume manufacturing skills from Unipac of Taiwan and distribution power through an agreement with Sumitomo of Japan. Likewise, when Acer wanted to expand global profits from the small-business PC it had developed by melding diverse technologies with its understanding of the needs of small enterprises in Mexico, it harnessed marketing, design, and manufacturing capabilities from throughout its operating network in Europe, Asia, and the United States.

Companies that are born in the wrong place, then, seem to have developed the *ability to leverage their innovations across global customer segments or applications and to assemble an efficient global supply chain.* They do so by flexibly combining operational capabilities from different sites—either within their existing network or from external partners. This is how they extract increased revenues or profits from their metanational innovations.*

SUMMARY: SIX KEY LESSONS

Let us review the six key lessons we extracted from our detailed study of companies that are beginning to unlock metanational potential from the global knowledge economy. These companies have, to varying degrees, taken initiatives in six different areas. These initiatives are summarized in table 3-1.

APPLYING THESE LESSONS TO BUILD ADVANTAGE: THE METANATIONAL IDEAL

Our winners from the periphery offer important lessons for unlocking the potential of the global knowledge economy. But many questions remain: How can these kinds of initiatives be shaped into a coherent strategy? What capabilities, structures, and processes do I need to create value from specialist knowledge scattered around the world? How can I make sure our innovations are fully leveraged by our operating network?

Today, no single company is a perfect example of a full-fledged metanational. Rather than focusing on one emerging winner or trying to impute the ideal from a handful of case studies, we now set out a blueprint to help managers create metanational companies in the future.

The metanational ideal is an organization finely tuned to sense, mobilize, and leverage pockets of specialist knowledge dispersed around the world. These capabilities will open the door to new and powerful sources of value creation and competitive advantage that traditional multinationals are not able to harness. The metanational

---

*In the process of operationalizing an innovation, the operating units of metanational organizations incrementally improve the initial innovation. This happens, for example, through R&D units that follow established technological roadmaps. As we discuss later, this process may produce new pockets of knowledge scattered within the company that can, in turn, be used to fuel a new innovation cycle when combined with specialist knowledge from elsewhere.

Table 3-1   Six Lessons from the Periphery

Initiative	Examples
Become a global knowledge prospector	Acer prospecting the world for new technologies and untapped market needs that could be used to create new PC products; PolyGram searching for new artists and repertoire who might have global potential in small markets.
Find ways to access or "plug in" to pockets of new knowledge	Shiseido set up an operation to design and manufacture perfumes in Gien, a center of the French perfume industry, and acquired two prestigious beauty salons in France to access complex knowledge required to develop, launch, and market new perfumes; ST created specific units designed to access information from lead customers like Seagate and from hotbeds of technology and know-how dispersed from Silicon Valley to Singapore.
Create a magnet to bring together specialist knowledge accessed around the globe	ARM used a magnet in the form of global platform projects, like its "Bluetooth Core," to bring together a wide variety of technologies from around the world, creating a global standard semiconductor design that would underpin the widest possible range of end-use applications; ST used its system-on-a-chip projects for the same purpose; PolyGram used its IRCs as a magnet for globally dispersed knowledge.
Meld knowledge from dispersed sources to create innovative products and services	PolyGram created global hits from local repertoire by melding its understanding of the style, appeal, and potential of local artists with its understanding of consumer tastes in particular markets and its knowledge about promotional, marketing, and sales techniques; ST brought together knowledge of customer applications like HDDs with digital and analog processing technologies and process know-how to create its innovative HDD controller system chips.
Transfer an understanding of the innovation and its potential to staff responsible for day-to-day operations	PolyGram's IRC staff visit local subsidiaries, train local staff, participate in the preparation of local sales and marketing plans, and create concert tours in order to transfer an understanding of what it will take to make unfamiliar repertoire a local and global hit.

(continued)

Table 3-1   Continued

Initiative	Examples
Leverage the innovation across a world market for increased sales or profits	Through its international network of sales, marketing, R&D, and manufacturing operations, ST took its customized system chips developed for Seagate and turned them into a product range that was sold to most of the major manufacturers of HDD and other data storage appliances. What started as specific products for a global customer were rolled out as a standard for new customers and similar applications. PixTech leveraged its new FED flat-panel display technology by in-sourcing manufacturing and distribution from partners in Asia.

will be able to innovate in unique ways, to leverage this innovation for higher sales revenues and greater profits, and thus to create more shareholder value than its rivals.

So what kinds of organization structures and processes must be put in place to build metanational advantage? What would a coherent metanational look like?

THE THREE ORGANIZATIONAL PLANES IN THE METANATIONAL

In chapter 1, we identified three levels of competition in the global knowledge economy:

- The race to identify and access new competencies, innovative technologies, and market knowledge that are scattered around the world.

- The race to innovate by mobilizing and integrating this globally dispersed knowledge.

- The race to leverage this innovation through an efficient and flexible network of operations.

Tomorrow's metanationals will need to build organizations that can win in all three of these competitive arenas. Each arena requires different units, locations, roles and responsibilities, processes, performance measures and incentive systems, and skill sets. Therefore the metanational organization must be designed around three distinct planes (or suborganizations), each focused on one of these competitive arenas. We term these the *sensing plane*, the *mobilizing plane*, and the *operating plane*. This set of "planes" provides a way of visualizing the basic framework around which a metanational can be built.

An Organization Charged with Sensing New Knowledge from around the World

The *sensing plane* is composed of a set of probes into the pockets of specialist knowledge that the metanational corporation needs for innovation. These probes allow the metanational to plug in to hotbeds of emerging technology or bellwether customers that foreshadow future trends. These probes could take many forms, including customer, supplier, or distributor partnerships; links with local universities; targeted acquisitions; and so on. The driving forces of the sensing plane are exploration and discovery. Its key role is to access new and uncommon knowledge that the metanational can use for discontinuous innovation.

An Organization Charged with Leveraging Innovation

The *operating plane* is composed of the set of operational units that produce, distribute, market, sell, and service the metanational's global offering. This plane also includes R&D centers involved in local adaptation of the global product, service or process, and units responsible for continuous improvement in operational processes. It also encompasses supplier and distributor relationships and other partnerships that have been set up in the name of operational efficiency (part of "make versus buy" decisions) rather than primarily for the purpose of innovation and learning. The driving force of the leveraging plane is the maximization of revenues and operating efficiencies. Its role is to extract maximum value from the knowledge the organization has gathered.

The Missing Link: An Organization Charged with Innovating by Mobilizing Knowledge Scattered around the World

The sensing plane amasses a rich stock of knowledge that the day-to-day operations can use to create competitive advantage. For example, an alliance with a university in China may reveal a technology with the potential to create a new production process. At the same time, the organization may notice an emerging need among customers in California that could be served using the Chinese technology—if we could create an appropriate offering. To achieve this, we would have to draw on product design expertise in Milan. But all of this knowledge is virtually impossible for operations people to use due to any of the following impediments:

- It is scattered around different locations.

- It will create value only if it can be brought together and melded into an innovative solution, product, or service offering.

- It is in a form that would be misinterpreted or misused if it were to be communicated directly to the operational people—either because it is highly dependent on its original context or because it is seen as an unwanted disruption to existing operations.

Before the metanational corporation can create competitive advantage from the knowledge it has accessed around the globe, therefore, it must find a way to bridge the gap between the world of the sensing plane and the world of operations. It must find a bridge between the world of the "explorers" (whose role is to access) and the world of the "farmers" (whose role is to harvest) within its own organization.

This challenge is depicted in figure 3-1. The gulf between these different planes is not just an information gap. The gulf reflects fundamentally different mindsets, roles and responsibilities, and measures of success between the planes. It cannot be bridged simply by setting up a common internal database, by distributing a global telephone directory, or by connecting everybody into some Intranet. The gap can only be bridged by putting in place a set of structures and processes that are capable of turning new knowledge into innovative products or services that the operating people can appreciate and use. In other words, it requires a set of processes for moving, melding, and relaying complex knowledge from different places around the world.

Figure 3-1   Bringing Two Worlds Together

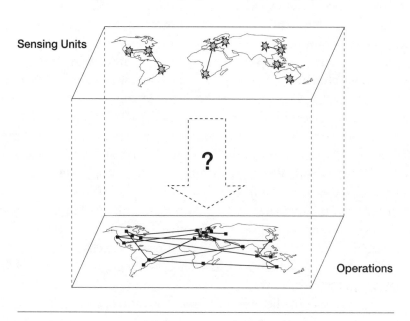

Bridging the Gap between Sensing and Leveraging

As we have seen, the first stage of bridging the gap between the sensing and leveraging planes in figure 3-1 is to create a *magnet* that can draw together the dispersed technologies, skills, and market understanding that are captured through the sensing network. A magnet usually takes the form of an innovation project with a focused objective and clear deliverables. It could be a project designed to create an innovative solution for a lead customer (as in the case of ST). Or it might be a project designed to create an innovative, global product platform (as used by ARM). Or it might be an activity, such as the one PolyGram uses to turn promising local acts into global hit records.

Just like any physical magnet, it needs a source of energy to pull together dispersed knowledge relevant to its cause. The energy source in a lead customer magnet will be some mix of customer pressure, the desire to maintain reputation, and the promise of economic reward. If the magnet is a product platform, its energy will be drawn from excitement about the opportunity to do something bigger and better, from peer pressure, or from senior management commitment. When the magnet is a global activity, the energy may come from the desire to prove the global excellence of the function to internal or external constituents, the enthusiasm for future potential, the commitment from senior management, or the discipline of performance.

Magnets may be set up by senior management for a particular purpose. Alternatively, they may emerge given certain preconditions that motivate a set of individuals within the company to create the magnet. Magnets are sometimes permanent structures that support a continuous flow of innovation. Others are temporary structures that are disbanded when an innovation is successfully handed off to the operating network. Sometimes the magnet has a physical locus—its own site or a customer's site. In other cases, it is a virtual structure, and sometimes it includes elements of both. Sometimes magnets are designated as separate profit centers. In other cases, their performance is judged by the quality of innovations that result. (In chapter 7, we discuss how magnets should get established in a metanational and how they should work.)

The missing link between the sensing and operational planes, then, is the set of structures that act as magnets to collect and meld dispersed pieces of knowledge into innovative business models, product and service designs, or processes and systems. We term this the *mobilizing plane*. Projects and "virtual" teams reside in the mobilizing plane and are built around selected lead customers, global platforms, or global activities. The driving forces of the mobilizing plane are entrepreneurship and innovation. Its role is to promote the identification, moving, and melding of technological and market knowledge drawn from around the world to create innovative solutions that the metanational can leverage globally.

Knowledge Flows in a Metanational

Each of the three planes in the metanational organization has a specific role in creating advantage. But to be effective, knowledge clearly needs to flow between the planes.

The sensing plane must be fueled by information about emerging hotbeds of new technologies and market trends. This requires a process by which the metanational can *prospect* for new sources of knowledge, as we saw in Acer.

Specialist knowledge from each of these locales needs to flow into the mobilizing plane. This requires a process by which that metanational can *identify and move* the requisite technologies and market knowledge so that they can be focused on an innovation problem, as we saw in ARM.

The resulting innovations need to be handed over into the operating plane, where they can be turned into sales, profits, and shareholder value. This requires a process by which the metanational can *relay* the innovation and the bundle of knowledge about what makes it unique and how it might be exploited to those responsible for leveraging it.

In light of these three distinct planes of activity, therefore, the successful metanational will need three specific processes to manage these flows of knowledge within the organization. This complete structure for unlocking the potential of globally dispersed knowledge is depicted in figure 3-2.

Figure 3-2   The Metanational Process

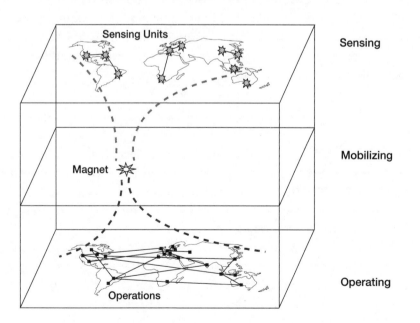

SIX CAPABILITIES THE METANATIONAL WILL NEED TO BUILD

We began this chapter by exploring the lessons to be learned from unlikely global winners who were born in the wrong place. We extended those lessons and started to draw the implications together into a coherent strategy for exploiting the untapped potential of specialist knowledge scattered around the world. We then asked what kinds of structures and knowledge flows might be required to implement that strategy in a systematic way. A picture of tomorrow's metanational corporation began to emerge: an organization with three distinct planes of activity and three key processes for managing the flow of knowledge among these activities.

To put it all together, metanationals will need to develop six capabilities that correspond to these core activities and knowledge flows. Table 3-2 details the six capabilities required.

Together, these capabilities will allow the metanational to sense, mobilize, and operationalize underexploited pockets of knowledge scattered around the world. The resulting organization will consistently outpace competitors in the race to take advantage of the opportunities emerging from the increased dispersion of relevant knowledge, as discussed in chapter 2. The challenge, for budding global competitors and existing multinationals alike, is to develop these capabilities and the organizational structures, processes, and incentive systems to harness them.

TWO HIDDEN TRAPS

Developing the six capabilities may seem a deceptively simple task, especially for existing multinationals that already see themselves as "transnational" entities. As we mentioned in chapter 1, however, two hidden traps threaten the path for traditional multinationals attempting to become metanationals.

First is the mistaken belief that the six metanational capabilities can simply be "shoehorned" or squeezed into the existing structure of a multinational organization. Chapter 4 explains how to recognize this trap and why such shoehorning won't work.

Table 3-2   Six Capabilities the Metanational Will Need to Build

Goal	Capabilities
Sensing new knowledge faster and more effectively than competitors	*Prospecting Capabilities:* The predisposition to prospecting for emerging pockets of innovative technology and new market needs. This prospecting capability allows companies to anticipate emerging hotbeds of relevant knowledge ahead of competitors.
	Accessing Capabilities: The ability to "plug in" to innovative technology and new market needs through an established network of relationships with foreign customers, suppliers, distributors, universities, and technical institutes. This provides access to emerging pockets of relevant knowledge.
Mobilizing dispersed knowledge to innovate more creatively than competitors	*Moving Capabilities:* An effective process for setting up "magnets" (such as projects undertaken to serve global customers or to build global product or service platforms) that can identify and move globally dispersed knowledge so that it can be marshaled for innovative problem-solving.
	Melding Capabilities: A capability to meld knowledge about new technologies and novel customer needs from diverse sources into coherent innovation, overcoming the problems associated with melding complex knowledge and integrating it into solutions.
Operationalizing innovations more efficiently than competitors	*Relaying Capabilities:* An ability to transfer newly created solutions, in usable form, into the day-to-day operations that underpin the supply chain.
	Leveraging Capabilities: The capability to leverage innovations across global customer segments or applications and to assemble an efficient global supply chain by flexibly combining operational strength from different sites. These may either be established sites in an existing network of operations or sites operated by a partner.

The second trap lies in the common belief that, given ever more powerful information and communication technologies (ICT), mobilizing dispersed knowledge will simply mean finding the appropriate set of wires and screens to connect sites and people. Some may believe that advances in ICT herald the "death of distance" for intangibles such as knowledge. But this is tantamount to equating knowledge with information. It fails to recognize that the most valuable knowledge to mobilize is tacit and context-specific. Such pieces of complex, sticky knowledge are very hard to move and to meld. Chapter 5 explores this trap and examines the real challenges of mobilizing complex knowledge.

Chapter 4

Shoehorning Won't Work

PERUSING THE LIST of six capabilities that underpin metanational advantage as identified in chapter 3, many multinational managers might retort: "So what, we have most of that. Our transnational network of subsidiaries already reaches into all the important parts of the globe. We are well plugged in to local environments. We already have a highly interdependent organization that is capable of leveraging our strengths for global success."

Among those that do recognize the need for new capabilities, most will probably respond optimistically: "We can do that!" They envision tweaking the existing multinational organization or their transnational network, and perhaps making a few more dramatic structural changes. In general, they believe their integrated operating networks provide what is necessary to match the emerging metanationals.

Companies that are planning to become more global, meanwhile, might rightly ask the question: "Don't we have to build a traditional multinational network first before we try to unlock metanational advantage? Isn't it necessary to walk before you try to run?"

In this chapter we demonstrate why the "shoehorn" approach—trying to squeeze metanational goals into an existing multinational structure—does not work. Our message is not that the measures, incentives, and other systems used to drive a multinational's operating network are wrong. Rather, we argue that the multinational operating network needs to be seen as separate from the metanational processes that are concerned with prospecting for, accessing, and melding knowledge for innovation.

Specifically, we argue that managers of even the most highly developed of today's multinationals need to recognize that in the era of the global knowledge economy:

- Their existing international network doesn't include all the locations they need in order to create metanational advantage by accessing, mobilizing, and exploiting relevant pockets of knowledge dispersed around the world.

- Their operating roles, responsibilities, and allocation processes don't include the full range necessary to build metanational advantage.

- Their performance measurement and incentive structures are too narrow to motivate individuals to build and sustain metanational processes.

- They lack some of the important skills necessary to create and exploit metanational advantages.

The good news is that "old dogs *can* learn new tricks" when they decide to augment their existing organizations with fundamentally new capabilities, processes, and organizational structures to master the new, metanational game.

For entrepreneurs and managers trying to transform their national champion or startup into a global player, the message of this chapter is this: Don't build yesterday's global company. Instead, try to leapfrog existing competitors. Evaluate the strengths and weaknesses of traditional multinational strategies and structures in the emerging global economy. Cherry-pick the best features. But put your emphasis on developing the metanational capabilities you'll need to win in the economy of the future. In that global economy, the key to victory will be your ability to sense, mobilize, and leverage knowledge scattered in disconnected pockets around the world.

STRENGTHS AND LIMITATIONS OF EXISTING
OPERATING NETWORKS

At the core of most of today's multinationals is a network of sales, marketing, R&D, distribution, and production or service operations. We call this the operating network. It serves two objectives: to maximize sales and to minimize the costs of supply to a given quality standard, thus creating profits and shareholder value. These goals remain intact as a company moves from global to metanational. They are the end result of the corporation's multinational endeavors.

Most of today's multinationals concentrate their effort and resources almost exclusively on making their operations network hum. They focus on maximizing the revenues and operating efficiencies to be gained by exploiting and adapting their global formula. They are highly tuned machines for these activities, which we call *leveraging* or *operationalizing*.

To succeed in the global knowledge economy, however, it is imperative to recognize, and compete in, the two other arenas we identified in chapter 1: preempting sources of new knowledge (sensing) and attracting and melding that knowledge from dispersed sources for innovation (mobilizing). The key questions for traditional multinationals, then, are these: "How effective is our existing operations network as an instrument to win on all three levels of competition?" and "What would it take to improve our effectiveness across this broader set of arenas?" To answer these questions we must understand both the strengths and limitations of existing operating networks in a world where companies are increasingly striving for metanational, not just multinational, sources of competitive advantage.

We have chosen Asea Brown Boveri (ABB) as a core illustration, along with 3M and other examples, to explore this issue. ABB has been frequently held up as a paragon of leading-edge practice in multinational management. With its broad global network of subsidiaries whose roots extend deep into their local environments, ABB embraced the challenge of building a "transnational" organization. Yet we will discover that even ABB does not possess all of the capabilities, structures, incentive systems, and skills necessary to meet the emerging metanational challenge. The same is true for other examples we examine in this chapter, including powerful global innovators such as 3M and icons of corporate best practice such as General Electric.

ABB has one of the world's most extensive operating networks. At its peak it counted 210,000 employees in more than 1,300 companies, spanning more than 140 countries.[1] The mission of this operating network reflected the company's belief that "worldwide economic growth requires dependable and efficient electric power," emphasizing that "ABB is committed to help meet this need by promoting energy efficiency, higher productivity and quality in all its activities." But four aspects of ABB's organization constrain its effectiveness as a launching pad for success in an era of metanational competition:

- The company's choice of operating locations.

- The roles and responsibilities given to different groups of managers within its global matrix, as well as the information and decision making processes they use.

- The performance measures by which those managers and their operations are evaluated and rewarded.

- The skill set that shapes that performance.

In the sections that follow, we discuss each of these aspects in turn.

OPERATING NETWORKS DON'T INCLUDE ALL THE LOCATIONS NECESSARY TO EXPLOIT METANATIONAL ADVANTAGE

In choosing the locations that make up its operating network, a company like ABB seeks to "optimize its business globally." Two sets of considerations dominate:

- *Cost efficiency.* Specializing production of components to drive scale economies and take advantage of local cost advantages (in labor, raw materials, concessionary finance, tax regime, and so on).

- *Revenue maximization.* Putting down local roots in major markets, recruiting local marketing and sales talent, adapting the product to improve local sales, and working with governments to increase exports.

These two core considerations determine the location of a traditional multinational's national subsidiaries, including manufacturing plants, operations and service centers, sales offices, and distribution facilities.

In most traditional multinationals, even the locations of R&D laboratories reflect tradeoffs between cost efficiency and potential value creation (hence, ultimately, revenue maximization). 3M, for example, maintains its core R&D activities at its home base in St. Paul, Minnesota. It has sited additional R&D laboratories around the world to deliver roughly "50 percent local technical service, 25 percent assistance to local manufacturing, and 25 percent local adaptation of products." Quite sensibly for a traditional multinational, the R&D labs are located where 3M has significant local markets and manufacturing capacity. When designing for efficiency, why set up R&D facilities that aren't near major markets or production centers—even if you want an organizationally independent "skunk works"?

When traditional multinationals designed their operations networks, it simply didn't make sense to locate activities on the periphery, in the proverbial Timbuktu—unless the site gave access to lower costs or underserved local customers. When these companies did establish a presence in a peripheral location, the subsidiary's purpose was either sales and service or low-cost manufacturing. Learning was an incremental activity delegated to locations where the multinational was already well established. As the authors of General Electric's annual report put it: The goal is "to search out and attract the unlimited pool of talent *available in the countries in which we do business*" (italics added).[2]

Yet, as we saw in chapter 2, new hotbeds of technology are emerging in locations that are neither low-cost production centers nor even major markets: biotechnology in Israel, for example, or speech recognition and automated translation in Belgium. Likewise, the "lead" markets, where novel applications and consumer behaviors are emerging, are no longer necessarily the established, major markets for a multinational. These markets are often large but mature. They no longer embody the future direction of the industry.

The Finnish market's early leadership in the use of mobile communications is a classic case in point. For Motorola, the world leader until recently, Finland was outside the operating network. The low priority status appeared justifiable: Finland was neither a large market nor a globally cost-competitive production base. But in the global competitive battle with Nokia and Ericsson, the fact that Motorola's operating network did not allow it to "get inside" Finnish market developments proved a critical gap that the company continues to pay for in lost market share.

In its industrial automation business, ABB also discovered the limits of relying on an existing operating network as the sole foundation for building competitive advantage. ABB operated strong subsidiaries in the United States and Europe, providing local automakers with robotics for the painting stations on automobile production lines. But when it identified opportunities to sell its equipment in the burgeoning car industry in Southeast Asia, it found the key customers were Japanese. ABB's existing operating network was unable to provide the detailed insights into Japanese automakers' needs and operating policies—an understanding that could only come from close interaction with the auto manufacturers' engineering and production departments back in Japan.

ABB had significant Japanese presence in some other businesses. But in industrial automation systems—where the market potential for ABB was deemed limited because of major competitors' strengths—its Japanese operations were small. Considering the cost/revenue dynamic of the operating network, it did not make sense to operate an industrial automation systems business in Japan.

Without Japan as part of its operating network, ABB Industrial Systems faced an important handicap in the battle to preempt new knowledge—in this case the needs and behaviors of Japanese car makers that were expanding capacity in Southeast Asia. The lesson became clear to ABB and other multinationals: Competing for the emerging global knowledge relevant to a particular business may require a company to learn from locations and markets beyond the reach of its operating network.

The solution is not to extend the operating network into these new territories. It might not make economic sense, for example, for ABB to try to sell or produce industrial automation systems in Japan. Instead, as we will discuss in chapter 6, companies faced with this problem need to find new ways to sense and access critical knowledge that lies beyond the reach of their operating network. Extending the operating network to perform the sensing role would be like trying to use a power generation turbine to do the job of a thermostat.

OPERATING ROLES AND RESPONSIBILITIES DON'T SPAN THE FULL RANGE OF METANATIONAL NEEDS

Just as a multinational's choice of locations reflects the cost/revenue equation, its allocation of roles and responsibilities is designed to achieve the same ends. The tradeoff between global coordination (minimizing costs) and local responsiveness (maximizing revenues) is a paramount concern in designing roles and allocating responsibilities. Frequently, traditional multinationals establish a global product/market matrix to manage the tension between global integration and local responsiveness. For most of the 1990s, ABB operated under just such a matrix structure, with a business dimension and a country/regional management dimension.

The Country/Regional Dimension

The regional dimension of ABB's matrix involved more than 1,300 separate operating companies that were incorporated and domiciled in over 140 countries. Each operating company was led by a president (or a company manager) and a management board. The company manager focused on the operation of that business in that country, with the specific responsibilities including adapting the global strategy to the needs of the national market, local human resource development, and ultimately the sales and profitability of the local business. Company managers, in turn, reported to a regional manager who was typically responsible for all the operating companies in a particular country. The head of ABB for the United States, for example, was responsible for more than 110 ABB companies operating there.

These regional roles and responsibilities were designed to provide ABB with the necessary "local responsiveness" to customers, suppliers, governments, local employees, and the local community, while ensuring local coordination of all the ABB global business activities present in the country or region.

The Product/Business Dimension

The product dimension of ABB's matrix, meanwhile, consisted of more than sixty "business areas" (or BAs), each representing a different worldwide product market, such as high-voltage switching gear, cables, and electric metering. A typical BA manager's responsibilities included the global strategy for the group of products under the BA, the allocation of production across individual ABB companies, and ultimately worldwide sales and profitability for that BA. "Global optimization" was the primary goal, achieved by allocating resources between different product and sales sites. BA managers also guided internal transfers of operating know-how in design, production, and quality improvements for their product areas. Functions such as purchasing, R&D, and risk management were all coordinated globally.

ABB's matrix was designed for the dual objectives of being global (creating economies of scale, leveraging technology inside the organization, and maximizing purchasing benefits) and being multidomestic (establishing a high degree of local responsiveness and deep local roots in each country where ABB operated).

A product-geography matrix like ABB's might appear to cover every conceivable role and responsibility a multinational requires—and then some. But multinationals have increasingly discovered that it is easy for such a matrix to lose track of customers' needs. Nowhere are individual customers, or key accounts, directly represented within the structure. This has proved particularly problematic when the demands of individual customers cut across product and geographic boundaries within the matrix. As a result, some multinationals, like IBM, have expanded the ABB-style product/geography matrix by adding a customer dimension.

The Customer Dimension

This third dimension of the matrix is often referred to as the global (or key) account management, or customer relationship management organization. While the precise terminology varies, all of these roles seek to coordinate the multinational's interactions with a particular customer, regardless of the product line and of where those interactions take place in the world.

The global "customer responsiveness" role has generally been introduced to overcome the traditional product/geography matrix's limitations in addressing the needs of demanding global customers with purchases spanning multiple product groups. Specifically, while the traditional matrix coordinated the global approach to a particular product group, it didn't necessarily coordinate policies across different product groups. While it responded to the differences between countries, it didn't necessarily produce a coordinated, global response to *customers* operating across many different countries.

The customer dimension of the matrix typically encompasses roles such as coordinated customer interface (the "one-point of contact"), global contracting (standard or umbrella contracting with country-specific conditions), global pricing, and worldwide service infrastructure. The major goal of Global Account Management initiatives is revenue maximization through higher sales growth, using several mechanisms:

- Enhancing global customer satisfaction to obtain a higher share of the customers' global purchasing (or share of wallet), where the customer already buys a certain product or service.

- Extending existing product purchases in a few countries by offering similar lines to the customer's subsidiaries in many other countries (a geographic synergy).

- Cross-selling products from other business areas that the customer was unaware of and that had not been able to get into the customer by themselves (a divisional synergy).

Thus the global account management organization aims at leveraging existing knowledge, resources, and relationships with global customers to increase existing business with existing products—while doing so in a globally coordinated, customer-responsive, and cost-effective mode. Global account management is a relevant and valuable job in the traditional multinational, but it remains essentially a sales job.

Limits of the Multinational Matrix

The roles and responsibilities specified by the traditional product/ geography matrix, sometimes augmented by a customer responsiveness organization, are designed to manage the tensions between global efficiency, local adaptation, and the needs of individual customers within a multinational. They promote revenue maximization and cost efficiency, while trading off global coordination with the need for local and individual customer responsiveness.

Consider, however, whether these traditional multinational organizations are suitable for building the six metanational capabilities we identified in chapter 3. Are these structures, and the associated roles and responsibilities they create, well attuned to identifying and exploiting metanational advantage? Do they help a multinational become a successful global prospector for new knowledge? Do they encourage efficient melding of knowledge that is scattered in local pockets around the world? Do they really encourage the process of leveraging knowledge that is dispersed across the globe, rather than simply projecting a well-honed formula from home base or from a dominant local subsidiary?

The answer to these questions is a resounding "No." For all their strengths as a tool for managing international operations, the roles and responsibilities, resource allocation rules, performance measures, incentive systems, and skill sets within a traditional multinational structure are not designed to build metanational advantage. Even a highly developed transnational matrix network such as that of ABB leaves important gaps when compared with the roles and responsibilities necessary to build metanational advantage in the global knowledge economy. Let us take each of the key metanational capabilities identified in chapter 3 and ask whether the traditional matrix could deliver.

Prospecting the World for New Pockets of Knowledge?

Consider the following question: "What specific activity in the traditional multinational matrix, like the one at ABB, focuses it on prospecting the world for new pockets of knowledge?" Certainly a regional or BA manager inside ABB may become aware of new knowledge, but is either one focused on prospecting the world outside the places where they have existing operations? We would argue that the country and BA jobs we just listed place the focus on leveraging know-how already inside ABB. A BA manager's brief emphasizes reaping global synergies across the organization to use existing technology and reap economies of scale. The regional or company manager, meanwhile, concentrates on his or her national market.

You might argue that traditional multinationals have armies of people whose job it is to search the world for new sources of low-cost inputs and for innovative suppliers. Isn't that exactly what Nike and Adidas do when subcontracting the manufacturing of sports shoes, what Sony and Philips do when purchasing components, or what Saks Fifth Avenue and Carrefour do when ordering apparel? Of course, purchasing people may learn valuable information as a by-product of searching out new sources of supply.

But the primary emphasis of the worldwide procurement role is to maximize cost efficiency by finding suppliers or new inputs that can enhance a well-defined existing specification. This is not the same as anticipating new sources of knowledge that, if combined with far-flung market needs and pockets of technology, might lead to a break-through innovation. In short, if global sourcing structures create some metanational advantage, it will be by coincidence and good fortune. The global prospecting in which metanationals excel is a much more focused, disciplined, and relentless process that requires clear intent and dedicated resources and responsibilities.

Accessing New Sources of Knowledge?

Many multinationals are good at plugging in to the needs of their local customers and understanding the peculiarities of local labor markets, government regulations, and operating environments in which they have a significant existing presence. Each local company within the ABB matrix, for example, is well plugged in to local customers, suppliers, governments, and, in some cases, local research centers. Indeed, one of the critical roles of a company manager is to establish deep roots in the local economy.

But the company manager's mandate is to serve the local market, to articulate strategies for local customers, and to implement global strategies in the local market. True, the final item in an ABB company manager's job description is "leveraging ABB's local presence to enhance the group's global position." But does a company manager in a local market really have the necessary perspective on the group's global operations to make this happen? In most cases, under the pressure of time and the discipline of P&L, her priority will be to ensure success in the local market (the ultimate goal for six out of seven company manager responsibilities) before attempting to interest others in the uncertain global potential of locally discovered knowledge.

In sum, even where a traditional multinational has subsidiaries, the roles and responsibilities within a traditional matrix structure do not generally focus individuals on acting as a conduit between the local environment and the corporation's global knowledge needs. The organizational emphasis is on plugging in to what matters for local success, not on building metanational advantage.

Mobilizing Knowledge from Dispersed Sources?

Where in the traditional matrix organization are the magnets for new knowledge? Whose job is it to meld knowledge gathered from diverse global sources to create innovative solutions? There is a critical gulf between the roles and responsibilities in a traditional multinational matrix and the aspiration to build metanational advantage.

ABB's many profit centers and companies reflected its desire for "far-reaching decentralization of responsibility into 'self-contained and manageable' units." Managers were charged with integrating global policies with their knowledge of the BAs to provide solutions for local customers. Innovation took place at two levels: (1) within the R&D and product development functions controlled from the BA headquarters, and (2) at the local level, where innovation meant adapting proven technologies, products, and services to the unique needs of local customers.

The BA's global R&D function is one potential candidate to act as a global knowledge magnet. In most multinationals, however, global R&D is a "giver" of new technology and products rather than a "receiver" from the regional sales, marketing, and product subsidiaries. Global (or central) R&D labs are generally located in environments deemed most fertile for leadership in a particular technology. Their role is more often to project technological advances to sub-sidiaries around the operating network rather than to act as a magnet for untried ideas or unfamiliar customer needs from operating sub-sidiaries around the world.

The Result: In a Transnational Matrix, Unlocking the Potential of Dispersed Knowledge Is the Exception Rather than the Rule

As we have seen, even a transnational matrix like the one at ABB is poorly suited to unlocking the potential of knowledge scattered around the world. Sometimes it does happen, but that is generally despite the transnational matrix structure rather than because of it.

Take the case of 3M, a company famous for innovation. 3M's Ger-man R&D labs were trying to adapt a new adhesive technology for cars that researchers in the United States had discovered to make the adhesive stronger—a requirement considered vital for the German automotive industry. By chance, the adaptation effort yielded a fun-damentally new adhesive technology that achieved great success in the German market. In a further piece of serendipity, 3M Japan became aware of the new technology and used it to enter the market for adhesives among Japanese carmakers. Eventually, the potential of the "German" technology was recognized back in the United States, and it was launched into the American market.

This quasi-random series of events is a story often told in sophisti-cated transnationals: The strong and resource-rich home base devel-ops a new product interacting with nearby customers; later, a national subsidiary R&D lab goes out of its normal role, or some new customer need is unveiled in a smaller national market, and the benefits of such feats are exploited locally, then in other subsidiaries. Later on, in some cases, the innovation is even brought back to home base (revers-ing the usual knowledge flow). Such events are hailed as the miracle of a transnational structure, with global reach at work: Specialist knowledge that is dispersed around the world is successively lever-aged and melded to create a world-beating innovation.

This sort of story is, indeed, a miracle when it happens inside a tra-ditional matrix, because there is little or nothing inside that structure to encourage the melding of dispersed knowledge to create break-through innovation. There are no magnets for dispersed knowledge to migrate to. It is no one's role or responsibility to make this kind of thing happen. Therefore it can only happen by happy coincidence—the smile of fate. But because metanational advantage requires just such a confluence of knowledge, we need a set of roles and responsibilities to make the process of melding knowledge from dispersed sources more systematic than pure chance.

Consider the following facts. To uphold its reputation for quality and technological innovation in the auto industry, Daimler of Germany is a most demanding customer for its suppliers. Furthermore, German autoworkers are the best paid in the world—so productivity improvements are critical for survival. It is therefore not surprising that German customers like Daimler were pushing even harder than their U.S. counterparts for an adhesive that would improve both quality and labor productivity. So why was the basic 3M adhesive technology for auto applications developed in the United States *without* taking into account the corporation's knowledge about the German and Japanese car industries and *without* the specialized skills of 3M local scientists and technicians in those countries? Why, in the first place, was knowledge not brought together from across geographies and melded as part of an integrated innovation process?

Despite its powerful capability to innovate using the knowledge within its home base, or inside a powerful subsidiary elsewhere in the world, 3M—like other traditional multinationals—faces a gaping hole when confronted with the challenge of melding globally dispersed knowledge to create a metanational advantage.

PERFORMANCE AND INCENTIVES: YOU GET WHAT YOU MEASURE

Given the twin goals of maximizing revenue at minimum cost, managerial life in the traditional multinational's operating network tends to be dominated by budgets. At ABB, budgets and plans were monitored by a global, computerized reporting system named ABACUS. Each month, ABACUS collected performance data on all 4,500 profit centers. Using these reports, senior management was able to monitor new orders, invoicing, margins, and cash flows in each business area and subsegment around the world.

Control and information systems, while necessary for efficient operations management, create a bias toward optimization, replication, and predictability. They tend to drive out disruptive learning. Responding to new and unfamiliar knowledge may have long-run benefits, but it typically involves short-run adjustment costs and possible losses associated with experimentation.

FARMERS' REWARDS VERSUS EXPLORERS' REWARDS

The performance measures and incentive systems that guide managers in the operating network tend to encourage stability: "more of the same" and "incrementally better." Senior managers tend to operate in "review" mode, looking for exceptions to the norm as danger signals that may need to be corrected. To use a slightly different analogy, the control of the operating network, often rightly, is dominated by "farmer's rewards and punishments": Strive for continuous improvement in cultivating the fields you know. Do not waste time and resources by straying from your field.

To build metanational advantage, by contrast, some managers need rewards and punishments designed for "explorers": rewards that motivate them to prospect the world for new technologies and emerging customer applications, to assemble this dispersed knowledge, and to use it for innovation. It is equally important that other groups of managers cultivate that innovation and optimize its efficiency within the operating network. The two contributions are complementary. Neither one alone is sufficient to deliver metanational advantage. The key point is that each type of activity requires its own performance measurement and incentive system.

Barriers to Global Teamwork

Incentive systems often create barriers to cooperation that falls outside what is specifically prescribed. ABB avoids duplication and customer confusion by allocating specific markets to particular operating companies. This may make sense for the operating network, but it creates a problem for metanational interaction. For example, ABB allocated the U.S. market for power transmission and distribution to its U.S. company. However, ABB also decided that for specialized gas-insulated switching gear, technical development and production should be consolidated in Switzerland, its strongest company in this specialist technology, in order to achieve maximum scale economies across a relatively small worldwide market.

In the course of developing a specialist, gas-insulated substation project in the United States, one of the Swiss sales managers built a close relationship with a U.S. customer—a construction company that was actively involved in building power plants in the United States. When this U.S. construction company won a contract to build a plant in the United Kingdom using gas-insulated technology, the bid had to be submitted through ABB's U.S. subsidiary because the contract would be with a "U.S. customer" even though the majority of the work would be done by ABB's Swiss subsidiary. But because the project was to be undertaken in the United Kingdom, a market that had been allocated to ABB in Sweden, the Swedish subsidiary would be required to run the project.

Moreover, ABB's internal transfer-pricing rules meant that the manager in charge of the Swiss company would lose between 2 percent and 4 percent of his total revenue recognition by virtue of having the sister subsidiaries involved. This would adversely affect his ability to achieve his profit budget in the Swiss company, a target on which 50 percent of the manager's bonus depended. The system created a clear disincentive for the Swiss unit to seek this business over an alternative project that could be sold and managed directly from Switzerland.

The process of marshalling and melding dispersed knowledge—Swiss technical know-how, U.S. knowledge of the construction company's systems and practices, and Swedish knowledge of project management in the United Kingdom—was hampered by performance measurement, incentive, and market allocation systems that were designed for the perfectly valid objective of maximizing operational efficiency.

Along the path to becoming a metanational, most multinationals will face similar issues. STMicroelectronics, for example, had to address the fact that its system for income recognition was a barrier to global cooperation. Most of the sales development for HDD was in the United States (where global customers such as Seagate had their central functions and R&D), but the billings were in the Asia Pacific (where the customers' plants were located). This separation distorted performance indicators such as expense-to-sales ratios. The different divisions, routinely optimizing their P&L accounts, were not motivated to "lend" scarce R&D or design resources to another division that would do the invoicing and get most of the margin. The individuals in the San Jose design center had mixed feelings about being accountable as a design center while also being charged with the more nebulous task of acting as "the ears and eyes of ST around here." While the benefits of this role for the corporation were not explicitly recorded in revenues, the San Jose unit had to carry the full costs of its broader role.

Local Performance, Local Rewards

The major professional service firms, such as Ernst & Young, and information business companies such as Reuters and Dun & Bradstreet offer superb examples of earlier knowledge-intensive organizations that continue to prosper on a global scale. Nevertheless, like ABB, they are discovering that their performance measurement and incentive systems are best attuned to projecting home-base knowledge and ignoring local knowledge or keeping it in its place. Each manager or partner is evaluated on the basis of his or her national or regional subsidiary or office. Although the head office may encourage a global attitude, what really counts is that "Europe is losing money" or that "the São Paulo office is doing great." And managers feel it in the pocket: Bonuses are geared toward local performance.

Some multinationals have started to introduce a global component to incentive packages for local managers, partners, or account executives. But the global component is usually small, as it would be hard to deprive a local subsidiary of a hefty bonus when its own performance was stellar, even if the rest of the world had a mediocre year.

One barrier that PolyGram faced in its metanational development was that its national operating subsidiaries were measured and rewarded on local sales and profits. Equally problematic was the fact that the national sales and marketing people lacked the subtle understanding of overseas markets required to judge which local acts really had international potential. This lack of global capabilities and incentives meant that much of the repertoire with scope for international exploitation was "imprisoned" locally. Its regional or global potential was lost, depriving the company of shareholder value. As we saw in chapter 3, the "solution" was not to adjust the incentives of the national subsidiaries but to add the dedicated IRCs, whose rewards were based on global performance measures.

The Curse of the "Internal Market"

The increasing popularity of "market mechanisms" as the way of managing interactions inside a multinational also hinders the development of metanational advantage. Under an internal market structure, Sales is a customer of Manufacturing, Corporate R&D licenses technology to a Division, business units handle internal transactions at arm's length. Subsidiaries are free to buy wherever they please (to encourage competition), and "market prices" are used as internal transfer prices (to encourage transparency). Profit centers are ubiquitous.

There are obvious efficiencies to be gained by organizing a complex multinational network on the basis of internal "customers" and "suppliers." Markets and market prices are the best-known mechanism for optimizing resource allocation in a (static) economy. But building metanational advantage is about learning and innovation, not allocation and efficiency. "Transactional" performance measures are unlikely to solicit the behaviors necessary for effective global sharing, melding, and leveraging of dispersed knowledge.

Taking these conflicts as a whole—the tension between farmers' rewards and explorers' rewards, barriers to global teamwork, the tight link between local performance and local rewards, and the popularity of "internal markets"—the implication is clear: The performance measures and incentive systems inside today's multinational are frequently at odds with the process of building metanational advantage.

The Operating Network Often Lacks the Skill Base to Achieve "Discontinuous Learning"

Metanationals will have within them the skills to grasp unfamiliar knowledge of a complex nature that is embedded in distant clusters, prepare it for sharing, and make that new and disruptive knowledge usable by the rest of the organization. They will be able to share and synchronize innovation across distance and across cultures by orchestrating and combining the relevant pieces of knowledge. And they will know how to exploit "stateless" innovations effectively and efficiently in the global arena, even when they come from outside the mainstream operations. The special capabilities and mindsets are not yet familiar to most traditional multinationals. Specifically, unlocking the potential of globally dispersed knowledge requires that people possess the following skills:

- Knowing where and how to prospect for new knowledge. This includes being sensitive to the indicators of where new knowledge "gold" may be found.

- "Listening and seeing"—and understanding in diverse contexts.

- Becoming an insider in distant lands.

- Recognizing "gold" when you see it.

- Learning to be "in tune" with others from different backgrounds—a key factor in the process of melding new knowledge.

- Melding knowledge from diverse and dispersed sources.

- Translating innovations into language that the operating units can understand.

- Scaling up and leveraging innovations.

The last point on our list—the leveraging skills that support worldwide economies of scale—exists to varying degrees in all multinationals. But throughout our research, we found that the first six requirements—the skills that allow a company to access and meld knowledge from around the world—are often lacking in traditional multinationals.

Even General Electric exhibits the difficulties of unlocking potential "learning from the world" to create metanational advantage. When questioned about the impact of information technology on the company's ability to access knowledge from around the world, CEO Jack Welch observed, "These days information is available to *everyone* about *every place*, so there are *no hidden markets* waiting to be discovered." In other words, sitting in Fairfield, Connecticut, with data from far-flung subsidiaries should be enough to develop a fully informed global business judgment. When commenting on the underperformance of GE's consumer goods business in not-very-distant Latin America, however, Welch said, "We have not found *all the clues* to the flow of goods *there*" (italics added).[3] GE has an immense amount of information about Latin America, but the company was unable to "unpack" that information to find "all the clues" in those markets. Some of the "listening and seeing skills" necessary to sense and access distant knowledge were clearly missing, even in GE.

THE TROUBLE WITH SHOEHORNING

Traditional multinationals may be tempted to address the deficiencies in their structures, incentives, and skill bases by "shoehorning" extra locations, roles, incentives, and skills into their existing operations networks. But as we will see, this approach is doomed to failure. At worst, it may simply increase overhead, add to the frustration of managers who will be pulled in too many directions at once, and paralyze the organization with complexity.

Adding New Locations

Adding locations to cover the few parts of the map where a multinational lacks access to new knowledge may seem simple and straightforward. Imagine the business case, however, for Motorola to establish a significant presence in Finland. In such a small market with entrenched competitors, any investment would be hard put to clear the traditional profitability hurdles. To justify the investment on the basis that it needed "eyes and ears" in the home territory of its major rivals, Motorola would have to bend its normal capital budgeting rules beyond their breaking point.

Even if a new subsidiary were approved by the capital expenditure committee, as a standard sales or production operation it would not serve the knowledge-gathering purpose. Witness the difficulties and false starts that Shiseido experienced in expanding its network to capture perfume know-how in France. Shiseido not only had to establish a new set of subsidiaries in France, but it also had to change the fundamental nature of those subsidiaries—hence the unorthodox move of buying and operating beauty parlors in Paris.

Adding New Duties in Existing Units

Another manifestation of failed shoehorning is the spectacle of centralized multinationals attempting to draw dispersed technologies and market information into their home base "headquarters" organizations. When a traditional industry capital no longer has a monopoly on relevant technology and information, and other locations and industries contribute important innovations, these companies argue that all they need is to increase the power of their home-based "knowledge machine."

This is a seductive argument because it avoids the need for any fundamental change in the primacy of the headquarters. It does not upset the organization's power structure, in which voice is equated with the weight of assets and people in a particular location. Nor does it require fundamentally new structures or processes.

Unfortunately, responses that rely solely on a more powerful headquarters organization will generally not create the necessary skills. In essence, this is because understanding, capturing, moving, and deploying knowledge is a formidable task that generally can't be accomplished from the comfort of headquarters' "mission control."

Using the headquarters or a corporate function as the global magnet has the obvious advantage of administrative simplicity. Well-established channels are already in place to communicate (or perhaps prescribe) innovations back to the global operating network. Yet this approach suffers severe limitations:

- Of all the nodes in the network, the head office is perhaps most wedded to existing ways of doing things. Headquarters may reject innovations, especially where they challenge deep-seated implicit assumptions about customers' behavior, the drivers of cost efficiency, and the "right" way to run the business. Headquarters departments are seldom known for their skills as listeners, especially when the message is coming from a peripheral location that is insignificant as an existing market or production site. This is hardly surprising, given that most headquarters organizations have historically played key roles in projecting their own know-how and controlling the "wayward" or "centrifugal" tendencies of far-flung subsidiaries. When you are at headquarters, standing on the "sun," everywhere else looks dark.

- The traditional headquarters power structure casts the sensing network in a passive role, simply supplying what headquarters requests, not becoming actively involved in the deployment of new knowledge for problem-solving or innovation. This increases the risk that new knowledge will be misinterpreted or misapplied. At worst, the sensing network may be relegated to "telling the headquarters what it wants to hear."

Other operating units may seem more likely candidates for shoe-horning than headquarters. The designated magnet could be a leading national subsidiary known to have contributed several innovations to the whole corporation, or a dynamic global business unit, or even an R&D lab. All of those units, however, will probably have narrow windows of experience that will tend to constrain them even more than corporate headquarters. With a skill base narrower than necessary for understanding and orchestrating diverse types of knowledge, they may assign lower priority to their metanational duties as compared with their primary operating roles. Simply taking those units "out" or partially out of the operations network is not feasible. Doing so may actually lower the entire multinational's operational performance.

Promoting Global Learning

Many global firms have tried to become "learning companies" by setting up local or international suggestion schemes, offering incentives to reward initiatives from their employees, and paying out bonuses to far-flung operational staff who contribute to knowledge databases. But these motivation drivers are usually ignored, or even contradicted, by the global corporation's operational goals. Employees may be asked to learn and capture new knowledge, but if they continue to be evaluated on results, their ideas will stay in the background.

Attempts to shoehorn metanational objectives into traditional structures may not only fail to produce results; they may actually be dysfunctional as well. Take the case of a leading U.S. consultancy that initiated a number of "learning projects" to help expand its business scope by reaching into new issues and competencies. It was a highly visible endeavor, and the project leaders were given generous budgets along with the latitude to explore new territories.

As is typical in a product/geography matrix, the projects were led by principals and senior consultants who were otherwise engaged in normal operations. Over time, the learning projects slowly became "bins" for expenses outside the normal operating budgets or for extra hires required by client engagements that turned more demanding than anticipated. As a result, potentially interesting new ideas were buried under an artificially high "learning expense" and further obscured by the generalized discomfort with the whole exercise. The learning program was cancelled only two years after its inception—and the organization is probably not ready for another "learning" program in the near future. Again, shoehorning had failed.

Encouraging Internal Entrepreneurs

In recent years, multinationals have relied on various forms of corporate venture capitalism to foster learning and adapt to fast-paced markets. This strategy, however, has not reduced their dependence on the home base. Nor has it broadened their knowledge search area or allowed them to meld dispersed knowledge. The magic formula—add a dimension to the matrix, create global product lines, cultivate "decentralized entrepreneurship" and networking, reward bottom-up initiatives—has rarely worked the expected wonders for shareholders.

Encouraging individual enterprise, responsibility, and "ownership" among employees around the world is another well-trodden path. But such efforts to diffuse entrepreneurship and stimulate multiple initiatives can fragment the company into literally thousands of small, isolated, self-contained units. Each micro-unit may have learned something, but this learning was in isolation and not necessarily in areas of relevance to the total corporation.

We remember vividly the bemusement of one CEO whose global company had encouraged decentralized entrepreneurship: "For 90 percent of the employees, it seems nothing has changed. They take as little initiative as previously and, if anything, because the rules are now less precise, they spend more time checking before doing anything. For the other 10 percent, I am sometimes afraid they will turn into juvenile delinquents." In many respects, then, encouraging internal entrepreneurs actually works against the goal of connecting dispersed pockets of knowledge. It results in greater fragmentation, not less.

Centers of Excellence and Global Mandates

Many companies have recognized the fundamental conflict that we have highlighted in this chapter: The operating network's drive for maximum efficiency naturally chafes against structures, performance measures, and incentives designed for prospecting and melding new knowledge that is dispersed around the globe. Savvy multinational managers also appreciate the limitations of simply ordaining headquarters as the natural knowledge magnet and the crucible of innovation. To avoid these difficulties, many companies have set up "centers of excellence": locations that serve as repositories for specific corporate competencies and related innovation.[4]

Early centers of excellence tended to be sited at the corporate headquarters. More recently, it has become fashionable to establish the center of excellence in a national subsidiary, with a global mandate to lead development and disseminate innovation for a particular product, technology, system, or other capability.

Simplicity and efficiency of communication are the two main arguments in favor of centers of excellence or global mandates. The traditional multinational chooses the new hotbed of technology—for example, European pharmaceutical companies seeking biotechnology expertise would choose California—and locates a center of excellence there. The center captures the technology or market information, develops new products and processes, and provides these new sources of advantage to the existing global operating network. By placing responsibility for making the product or activity "world class" in one location, proponents of this approach argue that communication will be efficient and local "economies of agglomeration" will be achieved. Moreover, the existing operating network can remain more or less intact. It will suffice to link the single center of excellence back into the existing network of operations with a one-way flow of knowledge, products, or processes.

Centers of excellence offer real advantages, yet they have important limitations in a world of increasingly dispersed technology and market information:

- For more and more industries, there is *no single* hotbed of new technology; nor is there a single lead market: *Multiple* sources of new knowledge need to be accessed. Therefore, establishing a center of excellence in a single location will not provide access to the range of new technologies and market developments that are needed to be a global leader.

- Increasingly, as knowledge crosses traditional industry boundaries and as peripheral markets suggest new consumer applications, it will be necessary to access knowledge from outside the multinational's current network of subsidiaries. Therefore the solution does not lie in designating an existing subsidiary as the center of excellence, but in extending the reach of the existing operating network.

- At best, establishing a center of excellence in a single, existing location will allow a multinational to achieve competitive parity with those who are already located (or headquartered) there. To lead the competitive race, a company needs to access and leverage a mixture of new sources of technologies and market information that no other competitor possesses either in its home base or at one of its centers of excellence.

Centers of excellence may transform the multinational from a network with a strong projecting center into one with several projecting centers. However, the fundamental principles and mindset of projecting from "capital" locations still remains. Worse, having failed to develop the ability to manage complex knowledge at a distance, the corporation with several centers of excellence or several divisional head offices will surely lose the natural advantages it enjoyed when its key people shared one location and a common culture.

AUGMENTING THE OPERATIONS NETWORK

Shoehorning approaches fail because they try to force *accessing and mobilizing* activities onto the *operating* network. In a worst-case scenario, they can actually undermine operational excellence and imperil the company's very survival, leading to increased complexity, managerial confusion, and a high-cost "global debating society."

Managers seeking to win in the global knowledge economy must face up to an unpalatable fact: The rules of the game for an efficient operating network are fundamentally different from those required to access, mobilize, and innovate using new knowledge that is dispersed around the globe.

The strategic task of the operations network is *exploiting knowledge* by achieving international scale for advantages created in the home base node. Strategists at the head office optimize resource allocation, distributing scarce capital among internally competitive units. To compete in price-conscious global markets, the operating network becomes a very efficient structure, with all nodes in the "right" locations: sourcing and manufacturing units for cost minimization, marketing and sales units for sales maximization.

The operating network manages continuous flows of minutiae—detailed information that must be in the right place at the right time, powerful organizational knowledge in the form of formal rules and unwritten routines. It is a world of patience and dedication. It is also a world of proven and sometimes boring technologies, of mathematical models, of necessary bureaucrats. Even the most creative of companies needs a well-honed operations network to survive globally for any length of time. Even the most innovative of companies in Internet-based e-businesses must still make sure that customer orders are met, that cash is collected, that books are kept, that pension funds meet regulatory requirements, and that all the other tedious details of the operations network are handled.

A company seeking metanational advantage must understand that the processes of prospecting, sensing, attracting, melding, relaying, and leveraging new knowledge from dispersed and diverse locations are very distinct from the routine operations. They are the activities of explorers and prospectors, not farmers. Theirs is a realm of increasing returns, of peer-to-peer relationships, of creating strong links with those outside the corporation, of working in parallel across space and time. Their contribution targets not the efficiency of the metanational today, but its global performance tomorrow. This is a world of strategic advantage drawn from the "wrong" locations, of strange conversations across the wires, of ad hoc get-togethers, of working "inside" leading customers-to-be, of expeditionary marketing. It is a world of discovery.

Table 4-1 illustrates the fundamental differences in worldview that separate the operating network from the sensing and mobilization networks. The underlying principles are so profoundly different that we

Table 4-1 Two Different Worlds

The Canons of the Operating Network	The Canons of Knowledge Sensing and Mobilizing
Knowledge exploitation	Knowledge discovery
Allocation of resources	Integration of knowledge
Budgets are internally competitive	Knowledge interaction has increasing returns
Internal interdependence	External connectivity
Geographic configuration for static efficiency	Geographic configuration for dynamic efficiency
Vertical hierarchy	Network of local units and "virtual" teams
Power vested in resource controllers	Influence flows to knowledge entrepreneurs
Information flows designed for coordination	Information flows designed for knowledge creation
Maximizing predictability	Maximizing learning
Self-interested interactions	Joint innovation
Farmers' rewards and punishments	Explorers' rewards and punishments

see them as separate organizational canons. Is it any wonder that even the most highly skilled multinationals have trouble bridging the gap?

BEYOND "TRANSNATIONAL" TO "METANATIONAL"

Transnational corporations attempt to combine local learning with global coordination, arguably the pinnacle to which a multinational organization can aspire. The transnational solution relies on projection and knowledge flows between subsidiaries in the existing operating network. "Worldwide learning," if it exists at all in the transnational, is the icing on the cake. Even ABB, perhaps the consummate transnational, found it difficult to transcend the operations plane and develop new organizational canons for sensing and mobilizing complex knowledge dispersed around the world.

The critical task is to lift at least part of the organization's sight from its focus on current costs and volumes. The metanational path calls for a shift of mindset about what the company's organization, processes, and people set out to accomplish: It calls for a dual focus on knowledge discovery and exploitation where the critical knowledge is geographically dispersed and deeply embedded in its local context.

We can see the beginnings of a metanational mindset by observing how a company views itself, how it displays itself on the Web, how it talks about itself. A traditional multinational (even a transnational such as ABB) sees itself as it sees the world—as a set of "countries." The country is the key building block of traditional multinationals: Roles and resources are allocated to national subsidiaries, performance is broken down by country, and the local component of the incentive system is based on country performance. The metanational sees itself differently. Countries or nation-states are not a foundation for its strategy or for its organization—for the very simple reason that nation-states make poor proxies for pockets of knowledge. Localities are key: High-tech "is" Grenoble, not France; Silicon Valley, not the United States; Bangalore, not India; and so on.

To break out of the shoehorning trap, the country or national subsidiary must be abandoned as the basic building block on which the international corporation is built. It is worth noting that the word *country* no longer appears in STMicroelectronics's vocabulary. Although for some purposes sales and profits are aggregated by country,* it is the statistics on global segments and global customers that dominate the decision-making circles of management. ST's units carry the names of towns or cities in which they are located: ST Agrate and ST Catania rather than ST Italy; ST Grenoble and not ST France; ST Ang Mo Kio and not ST Singapore. Each unit is viewed not as part of a national fiefdom, but in terms of the specialist knowledge and capabilities it contributes to the global system. ST's worldview features a global canvas dotted with specialist capabilities and knowledge. The company's legal home is Amsterdam, and its headquarters' functions were split between Geneva, nearby St. Genis in France, Agrate near Milan, and Paris. When we asked CEO Pasquale Pistorio where his company's home base was, he seemed puzzled at the question and replied, half-jokingly, "Perhaps the world?"

We devote much of the remainder of this book to exploring how traditional multinational structures, processes, and incentive systems can be augmented to cover the six metanational capabilities we identified in chapter 3. Our task is to help companies move beyond being global to become metanational. For managers of existing multinationals, our prescriptions entail reshaping organizations to succeed in the global knowledge economy. For companies intent on building new global organizations, we show how to leapfrog existing multinationals into a metanational world.

Before we embark on such a journey, however, we need to tackle another dangerous assumption, another hidden trap: the idea that technology solves the problems of connecting distant, disparate knowledge. Many believe that information and communication technologies can be used to create an elaborate knowledge management system that spans the world to access and collect all the knowledge a company needs for global innovation. But does surfing the World

---

*Of course, national subsidiaries exist as legal entities, and statistics are compiled for these legal entities in order to meet local taxation and accounting disclosure rules. Several ST managers also have formal roles in the various national companies. For example, one corporate vice president doubled as CEO of ST in his country of residence. Interestingly, when we asked him for a visiting card showing the latter role, he indicated that he had no use for one.

Wide Web in the comfort of one's home really make a person cosmopolitan? This would be tantamount to assuming that the Web *is* the world. The fallacy lies in assuming that information and knowledge are the same thing. Such illusions have proven both dangerous and expensive, as we illustrate in chapter 5.

Chapter 5

The Tyranny of Distance

CONSIDER A SIMPLE SMILE. At Disney World in Orlando, Florida, a guest (customer) always gets a smile from a Disney cast member (employee)—even in response to a complaint. It couldn't be any other way.

Now put yourself in the shoes of a manager charged with setting up EuroDisney just outside Paris.[1] You know that your ability to tap into the vast experience Disneyland has accumulated over the years in America will be critical to the project's success. So do you demand that your staff adopt the simple, yet powerful, rule—"always smile at the guests"—that has proven so effective in enhancing the Disney experience for customers at your sister theme parks in the United States? Will this initiative successfully transfer Disney's knowledge about how to make the customer feel valued and at ease?

Think about what happens when you take that seemingly simple shorthand for good customer service—"always smile at the guest"—and put it into a European context. First, the European cast will probably feel uncomfortable when asked to smile at someone who is not an acquaintance, and even more so if that someone is shouting about standing in a long queue, in a language that the cast member does not really understand. The employee's required smile will be uneasy and rather artificial. The European customer, coming from a culture where smiling is viewed as appropriate only in certain circumstances, may interpret the smile as mocking. The result could hardly be good for customer relations or employee satisfaction.

How can a straightforward piece of knowledge like "always smile at the guest" be the source of confusion and resentment when moved between distant locations? The answer is that this seemingly innocuous idea is actually only the tip of an elaborate knowledge iceberg. It contains a whole set of implicit assumptions about what generates customer satisfaction, how smiling at customers might ultimately be related to long-run profitability, and even the roles and relative status of employees in relation to customers. Much of this knowledge is tacit: It rests on assumptions that can't be articulated.[2] The rule about when to smile is also "context-dependent": In other words, if we transfer the rule to people who think and act in a different context, we will create misunderstanding. When you take the idea of always smiling at the customers out of a particular context and put in into a different context, it might not make any sense.

As we try to access and meld increased amounts of knowledge from locations scattered around the world, we will keep encountering these kinds of traps. Ideas or procedures that seem simple will be misunderstood and wrongly applied, because they actually conceal a whole bundle of knowledge that is tacit and context-dependent.

"Of course!" you may say, "but the solution is pretty straightforward: Don't try to move knowledge as a rulebook. Move people instead." It is true that moving people can help transfer parts of the knowledge bundle that are tacit and context-dependent. By working with colleagues in another part of the world, individuals will do a better job of explaining knowledge that isn't well articulated in the procedures manual. They may be able to explain to the EuroDisney staff, for example, the role of the smile in customer service and why it works in the American context. Together the team may be able to come up with a new customer service formula—including the appropriate use of the smile—that will be effective in Europe.

But we should not be lulled into a false sense of security by the idea of overcoming distance simply by moving people around the world. The dangers inherent in this approach are illustrated by the appliance maker Whirlpool in its quest to design a refrigerator to lead its push into Asian markets.

Whirlpool relocated ten engineers from its Singapore design center to work with its large engineering team based at its U.S. headquarters. The Singaporean engineers were well versed in the needs of Asian markets. They had worked with local marketing staff to assess functionality and designs that would appeal to Asian consumers. Over an extended period they worked closely with the U.S. design team to come up with a new, "Asianized" model. But the sales of this new refrigerator were disappointing. This was in sharp contrast to the success of a washing machine, for which Whirlpool had designed the features and machine styling *in Singapore,* based on an existing U.S. "core."

Much of the problem with Whirlpool's new Asian refrigerator design can be traced back to the difficulties in moving and sharing complex knowledge internationally. The Singaporean engineers had a deep understanding of their local context, values, and norms. But when removed from their context to work with designers at Benton Harbor, Michigan, they were overwhelmed by the sheer size of the Whirlpool American design organization. Their voices were lost in such a huge and unfamiliar setting; the Singaporeans were unable to share their knowledge effectively with individuals who lacked direct experience of the Asian context and had different values, norms, and backgrounds. As a result, the final refrigerator design did not meld knowledge from both sides of the Pacific in an effective way. In the case of the washing machine, by contrast, moving a blueprint from the United States, backed by some transfer of people from Benton Harbor, but with the design process being undertaken in the context of Singapore, was much more effective in producing a successful product for the Asian market.

The experiences of Disney and Whirlpool illustrate the tyranny of distance when we try to move knowledge around the world. Distance creates obstacles, despite the dramatic advances in IT systems and telecommunications technologies that, for some purposes, are "shrinking the world."

Perhaps paradoxically, as technology allows us to move information over greater distances ever more quickly and cheaply, the problems associated with global knowledge-sharing are likely to become even worse. Unless we recognize that much of the knowledge we are trying to move is tacit and context-dependent, we may simply spread confusion and misunderstanding at an ever-faster rate.

The development of information and communication technologies (ICT) has countered some aspects of distance: Information can be stored, retrieved, and moved between distant locations in a matter of seconds and cents. But information is only a very partial representation of knowledge. It is actually the least strategically valuable portion of knowledge—precisely because it is now so easy to access and copy. To build metanational advantage, it won't be enough to excel in moving information around the globe. As we saw in the examples of Acer, ARM, Nokia, PolyGram, SAP, Shiseido, and STMicroelectronics, metanational advantage accrues to companies that can access and mobilize subtle bundles of knowledge scattered around the world. This means overcoming the tyranny of distance that still reigns when we attempt to move tacit and context-dependent knowledge.

In this chapter, we dissect the reasons why the tyranny of distance remains a potent obstacle in today's high-tech, information-rich global economy. We explain the pitfalls that companies face as they try to mobilize distant, subtle knowledge and unlock its potential to create innovative products, services, and business models. By systematically attacking this knowledge-management problem, we help managers avoid the traps that lie in the way of building metanational advantage.

LEVELS OF KNOWLEDGE COMPLEXITY

The first step toward successful global knowledge management is understanding when and why a complex bundle of knowledge might be difficult to access, mobilize, and meld with other pieces of knowledge. Fortunately, some knowledge can be taken at face value and hence is easy to mobilize even if it is drawn from a distant locale. We term this "simple knowledge."

Simple Knowledge

The simplest form of knowledge is that which can be made fully explicit, by articulating or codifying it to be universally understood with little risk of misinterpretation, even by people who come from a different context. Most "scientific" knowledge is quite *simple* when measured in terms of the ease of accessing, mobilizing, sharing, and combining it with other knowledge. So is the technical knowledge that can be captured in a patent or a blueprint. It is knowledge that can be grasped by seeing and studying—rather like taking a picture. This does not mean that moving explicit knowledge across the world is always trivial or unproblematic. Wal-Mart learned this lesson when it opened one of its first supercenters in Argentina: a perfect replica of a U.S. store, right down to the 110-volt appliances—in a market where 220 volts was the standard.[3]

Nevertheless, advances in measurement, information, and communication technology are increasingly challenging the tyranny of distance for simple knowledge. They are allowing us to create and transfer explicit "pictures" of reality in greater depth and resolution. Despite the risk of information overload, the potential benefits justify devoting increasing resources to managing explicit knowledge. But managing simple, explicit knowledge is only one part of the metanational puzzle.

Multinational companies have long understood that some knowledge cannot be fully articulated or codified but instead requires learning through experience and practice. Most individual skills, organizational routines (such as the operation of an assembly line), and operating procedures, as well as some unwritten industry norms (like how to help a distributor manage excess inventory), are examples of *experiential* knowledge. This experiential knowledge represents the next rung on the ladder of knowledge complexity illustrated in figure 5-1.

Experiential knowledge can be transferred and understood by re-creating the experience. You need to practice using a new software tool to really understand it, but whether you are sitting in the United States or Singapore when you do so is largely immaterial. Experiential knowledge may be moved by moving people, by using simulators, or by demonstration over very rich media.

Complex Knowledge

It is when companies try to move knowledge that is further up the ladder of complexity that the difficulties and the potential traps become more severe. The first trap, as we saw in our Disney story, is to assume that merely articulating or codifying a piece of complex knowledge makes it easily understood. The kinds of knowledge we

Figure 5-1   Knowledge Complexity

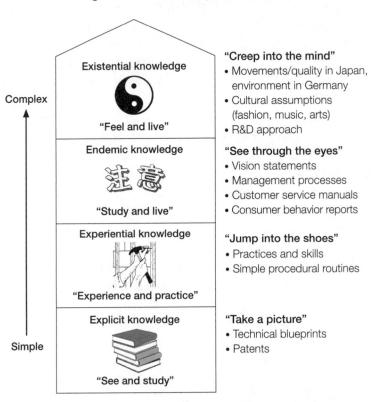

call *endemic*—like the Disney smile—are actually much more complex than they initially seem because, in order to understand them, you need to be cognizant of the context in which they are embedded.

We might think, for example, that because we have read a market research report on consumer buying patterns in India, we now understand consumer choice in India; or because we have access to a detailed policy statement about innovation in 3M, we can understand the ingredients for successful innovation inside 3M. But in fact, consumer choice in India and innovation at 3M are rather complex pieces of knowledge that require a lot of context in order to avoid misleading conclusions. This is true for most knowledge about markets (for instance, consumer behavior), about business practices (for instance, firm-government relations), about management (for instance, incentive schemes), or about operations (for instance, customer service systems).

Highest in complexity is the kind of knowledge manifest in cultural domains, such as art, music, and fashion: *existential* knowledge that is both tacit and embedded in particular contexts. To understand knowledge of this type, it is not enough to "jump into the shoes" of the source. One has to "creep into their mind"—or maybe even into their soul.

This kind of very complex, existential knowledge is relevant to business because it encompasses the values and emotions that drive successful "movements," such as the quality movement in Japan and the environmental protection movement in Germany or Scandinavia. Likewise, some capabilities like "Silicon Valley entrepreneurship" involve a great deal of very complex knowledge that could never be conveyed in writing or on a Web site. Sophisticated organizational routines also fall into this category—namely, those with few standards and many implicit, noncodified procedures.

We grasp existential knowledge by feeling and living it, through experience and practice, in the context where it resides. Transferring existential knowledge requires a long period of shared experience. It should not be surprising that General Motors took some twenty years to understand the Japanese "quality system" as Toyota understood it. The barrier to understanding was neither in General Motors nor in Toyota, but in the very complexity of the knowledge that was to be shared. Complex knowledge is very "sticky" to its origin.[4]

As we saw in some of the examples of transferring knowledge that we just described, a failure to recognize and manage knowledge complexity can lead to costly mistakes. Distance, both physical and cultural, often aggravates the problems associated with managing complex knowledge. When a company wants to mobilize and then share complex knowledge drawn from different places around the world, it is therefore critical for managers to understand where each piece of technology or market understanding they want to mobilize lies on the spectrum of knowledge complexity. It is a simple piece of knowledge that is explicit and well-codified, so that it can be transferred as data? Is it knowledge that the recipient will have to experience in order to understand it, in which case it will have to be transferred by moving people or by finding a way to re-create the experience for others? What should we do if the knowledge we need to transfer is endemic, so that it will be easily misinterpreted if taken out of context? What if it is existential, so that the recipients will have to "creep into the mind" of people from a different culture halfway around the world in order to understand it?

These problems are not new. Multinationals have had to deal with them since they began to spread across the world. But in managing complex knowledge, traditional multinationals have addressed the tyranny of distance in very specific, and limited, ways. These time-honored solutions served well in the past. But as we will see in the next sections, the traditional approaches are falling down badly in the new global knowledge economy.

KNOWLEDGE MANAGEMENT IN TRADITIONAL MULTINATIONALS

Multinational companies arose because they provided efficient conduits for the international transfer of good ideas: manufacturing processes and systems, sales and marketing know-how, service delivery systems, management capabilities. McDonald's and Coca-Cola didn't grow to be huge multinationals by moving beef patties or soft drinks around the globe; markets can do that just as efficiently. They prospered by finding ways to transport franchising and distribution know-how—expertise that the world trade system had no other way to move.[5]

Since their inception, in fact, multinationals have been movers of knowledge on the international stage. As we saw in chapter 2, however, that movement occurred almost exclusively outward from a home base. Multinationals typically sourced their special knowledge from a vibrant local cluster of expertise in their home base and "projected" it into new markets around the world. The home-based knowledge was projected in different modes: as products, components, machines, organizational rules and procedures, and even inside the "heads" of trusted expatriate employees. But how did companies generate that knowledge in their home bases?

In chapter 2 we saw that a virtuous cycle can take hold when a local cluster develops special expertise relevant to a particular industry. Researchers have discovered that local clusters enjoy unique advantages as engines to create new knowledge. In particular, proximity and shared values promote the right interactions among the players (producers, customers, suppliers of inputs and services, and researchers) who are located there. Multinationals use these same principles to create and manage knowledge, both internally within their home-base organization and externally between their headquarters and its local cluster.

When a company innovates (for example, when McDonald's created its business model), a number of processes unfold: identifying an opportunity, accessing existing knowledge, and creating new knowledge by melding relevant pieces of knowledge. Often, parts of the requisite knowledge exist outside the company—in customers, in suppliers, in universities, in other companies. But when the creative process occurs largely in one location and when all interested parties share some common context (language, national culture, technical or professional expertise), the process unfolds under the favorable conditions of co-location.

Co-location is the first of the time-honored principles that traditional multinational projectors follow in managing knowledge to create new products, services, systems, and business models. The second principle is to rely on the one-way transfer of knowledge from the center to the periphery (projection), rather than the more complicated processes of drawing on knowledge from multiple, scattered locations.

Tradition 1: Promote Co-location

Co-location reinforces a company's ability to recognize opportunities, to find the requisite pieces of knowledge (some inside the firm, some in the nearby environment), to access that intelligence, and to combine or meld it into a creative business concept or an innovative product or service.

Under co-location, these processes occur naturally, without an explicit awareness that managers are, indeed, managing knowledge. There are always some barriers to shared understanding, even inside the company, let alone in interactions with the outside. People from sales and production, for example, may have trouble sharing communication about customer complaints and turning that knowledge into an advantage. The problem may be further compounded for a multi-functional team. But such barriers are minimal when compared with the problems of sharing knowledge among people who are distant from one another, both physically and contextually.[6]

Co-location of the people who drive innovation is the key knowledge management strategy adopted by most of today's successful multinationals—even those, like Microsoft, that have risen to become global giants relatively recently. Microsoft's corporate campus outside Seattle, for example, houses all of the company's major developmental activities to ensure that team members communicate and solve problems quickly in face-to-face meetings: "Bill Gates insists on this. . . . [Microsoft employees] work in parallel teams, but 'synch-up' and debug daily. . . . [They] speak a common language on a single development site."[7] Whenever Microsoft accessed knowledge by buying a company in the United States, people were brought in from the acquired company to the Microsoft campus.

Similarly, on the other side of the world, Toshiba uses co-location as its primary tool for handling complex knowledge. In its site known as Yanagicho Works, in Kawasaki City, Toshiba has brought together its manufacturing experience with other functional practices (R&D, design, engineering, marketing, and so on), creating a multiproduct, multifunction site where it produces more than ten different product categories, from smart cards to machine tools.[8]

Toshiba has purposely co-located all of the relevant knowledge, skills, technologies, and processes. Furthermore, the company took great care to reinforce connectedness among its staff located together at Yanagicho. The workforce there is essentially Japanese—carefully selected, well-educated, and motivated to strengthen collective norms, values, and assumptions. Most managers have considerable shop floor experience, and the workforce is encouraged to be multiskilled and to develop experience across multiple functions.

Tradition 2: Transfer Knowledge by Projection

The second knowledge management principle used by traditional multinationals is the projection of knowledge from the home base outward. Projection emphasizes market penetration (understanding where and how to exploit what the company knows best at home) and transfer of knowledge (technology transfer, training employees abroad).

As we saw in chapter 2, most multinationals began by projecting into markets that were relatively near and similar to the home market: Sharing a natural language is often the key criterion for international expansion. Some companies have maintained an almost pure projection strategy. These companies act like radio broadcasters: In projecting home-base knowledge, companies essentially ignore the recipient's context. This strategy can work if you are projecting knowledge that is context-free or when the new context is similar to the old. Intel deliberately creates such a situation for its semiconductor manufacturing facilities. In its "exact copy" policy, Intel replicates its semiconductor plants to the last detail. This ensures that the original physical context of its process knowledge is passed along.

Other companies have found the need to adapt their home-base formula significantly to meet the needs of local markets. But even as they expanded to markets quite dissimilar to their home bases, the fount of knowledge creation in traditional multinationals still came from headquarters or from a handful of major subsidiaries. Their global innovation initiatives remained co-located, and the new products, service platforms, or processes they created were then projected around the world. What these companies added was the capacity to adapt their global innovations locally. On receiving an innovation, local subsidiaries adapted it to respond to local conditions.

This "projection and adaptation strategy" meant that most of the *creation* of new knowledge—the process of innovating by melding knowledge about different technologies and market needs—could remain co-located. Major innovation projects were co-located either at headquarters or at one of a few centers of excellence in major subsidiaries elsewhere in the world. Local adaptation, which involved melding knowledge projected from headquarters with an understanding of local conditions, could also be co-located—in this case within a national subsidiary.

In this way, traditional multinationals largely sidestepped the problems of sensing, mobilizing, and melding complex knowledge from around the world. They co-located the processes of global innovation, on the one hand, and local adaptation, on the other. The link between the two was provided by projection.

At stake in projection is the efficient *use* of knowledge, not learning and creation of new knowledge. Product components, machines, or complete manufacturing units can be sent as "carriers" of knowledge. People in the distant receiving location will then use the projected knowledge and meld it with local knowledge to adapt either to the local market or to local operating conditions.

Make no mistake: This combination of co-location and projection was a powerful solution to the problem of international knowledge management. But in the new global knowledge economy, the intelligence a company needs to innovate is simply not available in any single location. Rather, innovation must draw on knowledge that the company accesses and mobilizes from pockets of specialist knowledge scattered around the world. Tomorrow's winners won't be able to combat the tyranny of distance by using co-location and projection.

To win in a world of knowledge dispersion, companies will need to ask how they can achieve the kind of melding of complex knowledge that occurs naturally when people and knowledge are co-located. There are basically two solutions to this problem:

- Find ways of compensating for the absence of co-location.

- Re-create the co-location of dispersed knowledge by moving it around.

The first solution requires a thorough understanding of how knowledge actually gets melded when the relevant people and knowledge are co-located. The second solution, re-creating co-location, demands that we understand how to move complex knowledge that can't be reduced to bits and bytes and is often embedded in a local context.

THE HIDDEN ADVANTAGES OF "CO-LOCATION" FOR MELDING COMPLEX KNOWLEDGE

In the past, most innovation took place under conditions of co-location. We have grown so accustomed to these favorable circumstances that we often take them for granted. We hardly notice the subtle knowledge exchange and melding that occurs quite naturally when people share the same physical context. Thus we seldom explicitly manage the exchanges that take place when people access and use the same hardware and software, the same tools and templates— when they share the same experience and see what the other sees.

When we look below the surface at what is really happening when people and knowledge are co-located, we see four hidden advantages constantly at work:

- The ultimate in "high-bandwidth" communication.

- High frequency of interaction.

- Chance encounters and serendipity.

- Being "in tune" and "in synch."

If we are to replicate these advantages to combat the tyranny of distance, we need first to understand how they work.

High-Bandwidth Communication

Close physical, cognitive, and emotional proximity makes the management of knowledge much more straightforward. When people are together, they experience the ultimate in two-way, high-bandwidth communication. This goes far beyond simply hearing the facts—the explicit articulation of knowledge. We also see gestures, feel the emotions and the energy the communicator uses to make a salient point. We impart meaning to the silences.

The recipient does the same, by "sensing" the understanding that we convey with our own gestures, our displays of comfort and discomfort, and so on. We also have the ability to "show" the other person using physical aids to provide concrete points of reference.

When we are co-located we enjoy a quality of reciprocal feedback that cannot be matched when it is mediated through a piece of artificial technology. Every email user knows the difference between a typed message and face-to-face contact: the huge difference between the e-smile :-) and the real smile. Every videoconference user knows the difference between the cold screen and the greater emotional contact when the other person is in the same room.

High Frequency of Interaction

Co-location facilitates frequent interaction, which makes it vastly easier to share implicit knowledge. To fully grasp a set of poorly articulated ideas requires repeated consultations: "Now, I understand this bit, but now I can't see why. . . ." Co-location also permits easy "down-the-corridor" searches for help when you haven't clearly defined the problem and don't know exactly who or what you need—when you don't even know what you don't know.

Chance Encounters and Serendipity

Co-location dramatically increases the probability of chance encounters. Random encounters with colleagues—in the cafeteria, in the elevator—often provide that critical missing piece of knowledge for the birth of a new idea. Being part of the broader local community—say, in the San Francisco Bay area—makes it much more likely that a biochemist or a computer scientist will "run into" someone who works for a customer, a supplier, or a nearby university research lab, all sharing the same kind of problems, the same references, the same curiosity, the same language. Chance encounters, like molecules colliding in a solution, significantly contribute to innovation.[9]

Face-to-face interaction triggers joint exploration in serendipitous conversations—something rare when dialogue between people is mediated by technology. Some minor occurrence in the (shared) background—the noise of the air-conditioning system, someone entering the room, a new piece of equipment brought into the lab—brings about a conversation that could never be planned.

Being "in Tune" and "in Synch"

After years of working together in close proximity, people become "in tune" with one another. Co-location helps develop a shared language, a shared fund of knowledge, a shared way of learning, and a shared set of values and beliefs. All of these things support the exchange of tacit knowledge that can only be interpreted by understanding the context in which it resides. Being strongly connected with other people, both cognitively and emotionally, is the outcome of a relatively long period of co-evolution, of living together—facing, address-ing, and learning a particular pattern of problems and solutions. That is how we create culture, how institutions rise.

Being in tune allows us to use our oral or written language to understand each other effectively. It dramatically reduces the likeli-hood that contributors will be misinterpreted when communicating new knowledge to their colleagues. It also helps a team of people to stay "in synch." Our context, our "world," has a certain rhythm or set of rhythms. The pace and timeframes of those activities vary consid-erably, even within an organization. Accounting and sales depart-ments usually live on monthly cycles, within quarterly cycles, within yearly cycles. Production departments may live on daily or weekly cycles—or on a JIT clock. Near the end of the cycles, the activity often becomes frantic: Goals must be achieved; the period numbers must be made. The very meaning of time is not the same, and this is particu-larly true at the cultural level: Some peoples value punctuality, whereas some peoples are rarely on time (at least as seen from the point of view of those who are on time).

Communication can be very difficult between people who operate under different rhythms. It may simply be the wrong moment for dia-logue (remember the end-of-period syndrome), and no attention will be paid to the intended message. When people are co-located and in tune, these issues do not arise.

FROM CO-LOCATION TO DISPERSION

Co-location is a scarce luxury when we seek to meld knowledge that we have accessed in specialized pockets, scattered around the world. Unfortunately, losing the advantages of co-location often brings a raft of difficulties to be overcome. These are aptly demonstrated by the experience of Ciba-Geigy (CG), a major Swiss pharmaceutical com-pany (now Novartis), when it sought to meld its knowledge of drug development and therapeutics with specialist knowledge about new drug delivery systems that it found in California.

In the late 1970s, CG accessed new drug delivery knowledge by acquiring majority control of Alza, a small, entrepreneurial California company that specialized in this emerging technology. The venture created a classic problem of knowledge dispersion. To use this new knowledge to create an innovative range of products, CG would have to meld Alza's know-how with its own expertise, which was scattered across the CG organization in Switzerland, the United States, and other locations. Much of the knowledge involved on all sides was complex—tacit, hard to articulate (although CG's knowledge was more likely to be codified), and easily misinterpreted if taken out of context.

The melding process ultimately proved successful: It was at the origin of a profitable new business in "patches" sold for the relief of motion sickness, angina pectoris, cessation of smoking, and other applications. The collaboration between CG and Alza, however, got off to a rocky start.

Some early problems lay in the "distance" caused by unresolved differences between the two organizations concerning Alza's future strategy. But an even more important barrier was the failure to recognize the *different types of knowledge* the two companies were accustomed to handling.

At CG, knowledge was generally made very explicit, in accordance with usual practices and regulatory requirements in the pharmaceutical industry. At Alza, knowledge was emergent and experiential, bringing together multiple disciplines and technologies—many new to pharmaceutical applications—that were required for the development of delivery systems. As a result, Alza's methods and activities appeared disconcerting to CG.

CG's long experience with explicit knowledge created an assumption that melding its knowledge with Alza's would be a nonissue. CG felt that a simple sequence of decisions, based on a straightforward exchange of data and procedures, would suffice. Following joint decisions on product development priorities, Alza would "fit" substances into its delivery systems. Based on its own highly structured development process, CG expected that Alza would hand back the resulting formulations as soon as Phase 2 clinical trials were complete. CG would then shepherd them toward registration and market introduction, using a standard process that it followed for all of its products.

CG had conceived a highly structured process that minimized the interfaces between Alza and itself, assuming that the two sets of knowledge would be effectively melded by an exchange of codified information and specifications. A series of damaging assumptions and decisions arose from this failure to recognize the complexity of the knowledge to be melded:

- CG "sponsors" (scientists and managers from CG appointed to take care of Alza-originated products) were not allocated time to work intensively on the Alza products. The interfaces with Alza were simply added to the sponsor's preexisting work agenda.

- Alza's knowledge was assumed to be embodied in the product prototypes it would give CG, limiting the need for other ways to share knowledge. Joint teams were not deemed necessary.

- CG felt it did not need to allocate significant budgets for the projects with Alza (as little extra work and just a few extra interactions were anticipated).

- CG management assumed that the company's existing knowledge, beliefs, and prejudices would not limit its capacity to absorb new ideas for product development using Alza's technology.

Early on, both sides discovered that their systems had to be modified for specific product applications. The joint projects required true knowledge *melding*, in the dictionary sense of *melt* + *weld*. The new knowledge could not be achieved simply by stitching together existing bits of know-how, because one piece (say, the "Swiss" understanding about the interaction between the drug and living cells) affected another (say, the "California" knowledge about the flow of compounds from the delivery system). Finding the right delivery system called for small changes in the shape of drug molecules, which in turn had an impact on dosage, therapeutics, and so on. As these issues arose, projects were delayed. Suspicions started to creep into the relationship.

Other problems surfaced, linked to the different contexts within which the two organizations' knowledge was created and represented. Alza's R&D unit was organized by system type (transdermal, intestinal tract, infusion and mini-pumps), whereas CG's was organized by therapeutic area (either human "subsystems," such as cardiovascular or nervous systems, or disease categories, such as anti-infective). There were no obvious pairings between the two corporate structures, so CG set up a proliferation of matrix interfaces, which added to the confusion and exacerbated the lack of ownership.

An attempt to align CG's sponsors with the system logic at Alza did not gain much support at GC, given that the organization was still structured by therapeutic areas. The few successful sponsors were secure mavericks that set out to prove that delivery systems had a future, mainly around transdermal patches. In other areas, such as slow-release pills, where CG sponsors operated more by the book, but where knowledge melding needed to be reciprocal and iterative, little progress was made.

The two organizations' different knowledge creation processes only added to the difficulty. Alza's informal, trial-and-error approach relied on close and frequent interactions, which had been possible historically, when all of the researchers were located in the same building. By contrast, CG's practices reflected the need to document the development process in minute technical and clinical detail for regulatory authorities, often in distant countries.

These discrepancies did little to elicit mutual respect and understanding. To CG, Alza's knowledge management practices looked disorganized, disorderly, amateurish, and irresponsible. To Alza, CG's practices looked staid, ponderous, and bureaucratic. The differences were aggravated by the cultural contrast between an established and formal Swiss pharmaceutical company and an innovative, entrepreneurial California outfit. Furthermore, CG started to doubt the validity of Alza's technologies rather than to acknowledge that the knowledge melding process had been poorly designed.

The CG-Alza example illustrates many key challenges for companies trying to build metanational advantage without the advantages of co-location. The situation calls for significant managerial initiatives to address the critical requirements:

- The need to recognize and find a way of handling tacit knowledge, instead of relying on the exchange of explicit, codified knowledge, blueprints, or specifications.

- The need for the parties involved to share an understanding of their different contexts before complex knowledge can be transferred.

- The need to establish an effective structure to promote knowledge melding, rather than assuming it will happen either spontaneously or through a simple, linear process of handing over knowledge between separate organizations.

- The need for teams and champions with incentives, budgets, and overall responsibility for delivering metanational innovations.

- The need to structure a smooth process for transferring meta-national innovations to the operating network, taking account of the knowledge flows that must accompany the innovation and the prejudices that may stand in the way.

CG's experience with Alza also underscores our point from chapter 4. CG tried to "shoehorn" the problem of melding dispersed knowledge into its existing organizational structures. When that approach (inevitably) failed, CG learned that it needed to augment its existing structures and processes in fundamental ways. For companies seeking to mobilize and meld complex knowledge, the tyranny of distance demands a robust and well-planned managerial response.

RECREATING CO-LOCATION: MOVING KNOWLEDGE

Fortunately, it is possible to set up structures and processes that compensate for the lack of co-location in melding complex knowledge scattered around the world. One alternative, as we mentioned earlier, might be to re-create co-location by moving the necessary knowledge around the world.

When we talk about "moving" knowledge, it is important to recognize that knowledge *as such* cannot flow between two places. What actually moves is a "package" or "carrier" of knowledge: a blueprint, a person, a tool, a machine, and so on. This is more than a semantic distinction for two reasons. First, because the package or carrier incompletely and imperfectly embodies the knowledge, so that knowledge degrades to some extent when it is moved. Second, because when the carrier reaches its destination the knowledge is going to be recontextualized—in other words it will, by necessity, be reinterpreted by the recipient in the new context.[10]

No matter how good the carrier, therefore, moving knowledge from one place to another will change the nature of the knowledge. We need to recognize and anticipate these changes if we are to avoid misinterpretation and misunderstanding when we try to meld knowledge from different locations.

How the knowledge gets changed when it is moved will depend, in part, on the type of carrier we choose. Three types of carriers are commonly deployed to move knowledge across the world: information; tools, templates, models, and machines; and people. Each has its own strengths and limitations.

Information: A Partial Carrier of Knowledge

One of the major carriers of knowledge is information, as in files or spreadsheets full of structured data, formulas, text, and blueprints. Moving information is not problematic. The beauty of information is that it reduces the cost of transporting knowledge to distant locations or to the future. The problem is that one may believe that moving information is the same as moving knowledge. This is only true if the knowledge is simple and explicit, and if the language or code used to make the knowledge explicit is shared.

The process that Boeing used to design the 777 airplane shows how knowledge can be codified into information and moved around the world. Boeing devoted tremendous resources to design and engineer the 777 using computer-aided design (CAD) systems. A complete "virtual 777" was designed in three dimensions—using 2,000 computer terminals operated by as many designers and engineers. This extensive codification of knowledge avoided the costly and lengthy exercise of building full mockup planes. (By contrast, for the 747, there were five full-size "planes" by the time the design was finished.) The CAD files conveyed consistent information internally and to all suppliers, both domestically and internationally.

The process was similar for the Stealth bomber, a challenging project in which four different companies worked together across great distance in the United States to design and build the aircraft.[11] The use of CAD and an extensive set of common coding rules allowed designers and engineers in dispersed locations to share information on an almost real-time basis. But even with a common language, common technology, and a shared technical background in aerospace, the cabling for the Stealth cockpit had to be redesigned three times as the different "pieces" of the aircraft design were pulled together. Information does simplify knowledge sharing, and that is why we use it. But there are clear limitations: Information cannot convey the tacit elements of knowledge; nor is it exempt from the risks of recontextualization.

Tools, Templates, Models, and Machines

Other major carriers of knowledge are tools, templates, models, machines, and even complete plants or operational units. The advantage of these carriers is that the knowledge they transport can be put to use without being learned. They can convey knowledge far more complex than pure information.

Multinational companies have extensively used these kinds of knowledge carriers when they locate operations abroad. When we visit a Hewlett-Packard plant in Singapore or a McDonald's restaurant in Moscow, for example, we actually see vast amounts of knowledge that was created in the United States and replicated for use in a distant location.

People as Knowledge Carriers

Finally, we have one of the most important knowledge carriers: people. Multinationals have always relied on expatriated technicians and managers to project knowledge to their foreign subsidiaries. People can carry rather complex knowledge. When people move to a distant location, however, the quality of their knowledge decays, because the more complex knowledge is so sticky and embedded in the original context. An Italian designer will be less effective after a couple of years away from Milan. A financial market wizard will lose some of her performance when placed far away from Wall Street. They lose the benefit of being immersed in their original knowledge clusters. They cannot keep up with the new tacit knowledge circulating there. And they will be working in new contexts that they cannot fully comprehend—a different national culture, for example—contexts in which part of their knowledge is simply ineffective or even misleading.

ICT: AN AID, NOT A SOLUTION

Recognizing the limitations of their existing knowledge management strategies, many multinationals invest in tools to manage information flows within their organizations. Recent developments, such as multimedia productions, allow better "packaging" of knowledge to be shared. Videoconferencing permits richer, more frequent communication than was possible or affordable only a few years ago. It is now common to find Intranet solutions that go far beyond email and information posting to include discussion forums, bulletin boards, online documentation libraries, and virtual conference rooms. The internal Yellow Pages (a directory of the firm's experts worldwide) has become a ubiquitous tool.

Information technology and information networks can help integrate knowledge—for example, by communicating best practices inside multinational corporations. The companies for which knowledge is a critical capability, such as consulting firms like Andersen Consulting (AC; now called Accenture), are naturally among the more advanced. AC has more than 150 offices in some 50 countries that are expected to feed a thoroughly formal "knowledge" system, using standards and forms to guide the process. Some forms are even submitted by the clients.

Knowledge Xchange is the name AC gave to its system of articulating, storing, and sharing/transferring knowledge. It is a Lotus Notes–based worldwide network, with tens of thousands of users, started in 1992. Knowledge Xchange provides the infrastructure, the standards, and the tools for the codification of knowledge and the exchange of information. It contains the usual Yellow Pages and other tools, as well as a Solution Planning area (integrating best industry practices, business process models, methods, and leading-edge information technology documentation). There are also Community Pages, knowledge databases, and online discussion groups for various specialty areas.

Even the most sophisticated computer-based networks, however, suffer three major limitations for melding knowledge drawn from dispersed sources:

- They can only deal with knowledge that has been well articulated—a severe limitation when the greatest competitive advantage is to be derived from melding complex knowledge that is poorly codified, tacit, and context-dependent.

- They are generally constrained to integrating knowledge that already exists in-house—as external knowledge is generally in the wrong form for computer-based systems that require a high degree of standardization.

- The problems they are designed to solve must be formulated beforehand—hence they can seldom act as a direct source of innovation.

It is clear that ICT can play an important role.[12] But, as we have seen, its contribution is largely restricted to promoting the distribution of the simpler forms of knowledge. ICT solutions do not address the problem of managing complex knowledge globally. Think back to the cases of CG and Alza or to Whirlpool's experience with designing refrigerators for the Asian market. Could the problems of those projects have been solved by even the best computerized knowledge management system?

At best, these companies' problems could have been partially solved with appropriate IT-enabled communications systems and groupware tools. But the tasks of mobilizing and melding more complex knowledge would still remain.

TAMING THE TYRANNY

In the last two chapters we explored two dangerous traps for companies seeking to unlock metanational advantage:

- The trap of attempting to "shoehorn" metanational capabilities into an existing multinational organization.

- The trap of underestimating and misinterpreting the knowledge management challenge—failing to draw appropriate distinctions between simple, well-codified knowledge and the tacit, context-specific knowledge that is the hardest to mobilize; and wrongly assuming that moving people or investing in ICT will provide the panacea.

The remainder of this book is devoted to helping managers address these challenges. In chapter 6, we take up the issue of how companies should go about learning from the world—how they can sense new knowledge that will provide the raw material for innovation. This involves understanding how and where to prospect for untapped pockets of specialist knowledge, and how to go about accessing that knowledge, especially when it is poorly codified and embedded in a local context.

Chapter 6

Learning from the World

AT THE CORE of a metanational's advantage is the capacity to innovate by tapping and connecting pockets of knowledge scattered around the world. This innovation process draws its lifeblood from the ability to sense new pockets of knowledge before competitors recognize them, and then to access this new knowledge more effectively than the competition. Building this sensing capability— the ability to learn from the world—is therefore a critical prerequisite for winning in the global knowledge economy.

Sensing involves the following:

- The capacity to identify a *sensing need*. A goal, even if broadly defined, is essential to move from aimless exploration to purposeful reconnaissance work.

- The capability to *prospect* the world for sources of relevant knowledge, unearthing new pockets of knowledge ahead of competitors.

- The capacity to *access* new knowledge once its location is identified—not a trivial task when the required knowledge is complex (tacit, experiential, or embedded in a local context, as described in chapter 5) or when it needs to be pried loose from a tight-knit local club.

Even well-established multinationals will need to augment and bolster their sensing capabilities to compete in the global knowledge economy. Global projectors lack a "prospecting" mentality. Rather than actively looking for new hotbeds of disruptive technology, skills, and market needs, most global companies are trying to find the most fertile ground to project their standard, existing competitive advantages. Global projectors are attracted by similarities to their home base that will provide maximum returns with minimum adaptation. Metanational prospectors, by contrast, seek out environments and knowledge that are most differentiated from their home base, because diversity provides the best raw material for innovation.

Global projectors also lack structures that would allow them to access unique local knowledge. Their subsidiaries are well plugged in to the global corporate network—but not to the local, external environment. The subsidiary of a global company is designed to deliver rather than to question and learn the idiosyncrasies of the local environment.

Multidomestic companies generally have better developed local sensing skills. But companies with a multidomestic heritage also need to be careful not to bask in false security about their sensing capabilities. Their problem is that, while they may use the knowledge they access to build their businesses locally, they have difficulty sharing that knowledge globally. (We address this problem of how to mobilize scattered and locally imprisoned knowledge in chapter 7.) Furthermore, not all multidomestic companies are well-connected externally. Their local sensing capabilities are not necessarily high, particularly if corporate headquarters emphasizes reliable profitability more than growth and innovation. And because the location of existing subsidiaries is usually determined by local market potential or low operating costs, multidomestic companies may have only a token local presence in interesting, peripheral locations where new hotbeds of technology or bellwether customer behaviors are emerging.

In this chapter, we explore how multinationals can augment their sensing capacity: deciding what to sense, prospecting for new knowledge, and accessing (or "plugging in to") pockets of knowledge they identify both within and outside their existing organization. We lay out alternative channels for accessing new knowledge and discuss the pros and cons of each. Finally, we examine who needs to be involved in a sensing network (including the key role of senior management as knowledge surveyors), how the sensing process needs to be managed, how its success should be measured, and how its people should be rewarded.

IDENTIFYING A SENSING NEED

The concept of sensing new, globally dispersed pockets of knowledge can easily conjure up an image of executives aimlessly running up expensive travel bills in the hope of making a grand discovery. It is true that the sensing process needs to be given some space: We cannot precisely predetermine what nuggets of new knowledge we will find and when and where we will find them. Sensing is, in part, a process of learning. It thrives on surprise and serendipity. But sensing also needs to be purposeful. It needs to start out with a definition of the sensing need: an opportunity to be created or a problem to be solved. Merely being on the ground in distant markets is not enough.

Recall from chapter 3 that Shiseido had a clear purpose: to gain access to the complex know-how that had been amassed by the French fragrance industry and to use this knowledge to bolster its competitiveness against large global companies like L'Oréal and Estée Lauder. When it set out to achieve this goal, Shiseido couldn't have specified exactly the pieces of knowledge it was looking for—it simply didn't know enough about the perfume business to develop such a specification. But its purpose was clear. Likewise, when ST began its quest to create system chips, it didn't know exactly what knowledge it would need, or precisely where to look. Its purpose, however—to replace circuit boards with dedicated chips designed to meet the needs of a customer application—was well-defined.

Identifying key sensing needs will be an important role for the CEO and other senior management in tomorrow's metanational. This will be a critical aspect of setting the direction in a company that can win by learning from the world. The role will be difficult to perform from the proverbial ivory tower of an executive suite. It will require senior management to lead by walking about—in this case walking about the world—because identifying a sensing need is a subtle combination of defining where a company will seek future competitive advantage and what areas of emerging technology or market behavior might contribute to this advantage. STMicroelectronics' system-on-a-chip strategy didn't emerge simply from a corporate planning white-board. It emerged because senior management was able to listen and make the connection between customers' needs for improved perfor-mance and the newly available, but disconnected, technologies that could be deployed to satisfy them. That strategy, in turn, led manage-ment to begin to define a set of sensing needs.

Once a sensing need takes shape, it has to be refined. Sensing requires substantial investment, so companies must choose the loca-tions that seem likely to provide the best returns. A metanational can-not afford to sense randomly; nor can it search over an unlimited area for new knowledge. Sensing can be either too broad or excessively focused.

Finding the right balance requires tradeoffs. The choices revolve around three aspects of the sensing problem: *what* to sense, *where* to look for it, and *who* might provide a fertile source. Figure 6-1 depicts the process of homing in on a new pocket of knowledge.

Figure 6-1   Addressing Sensing Needs

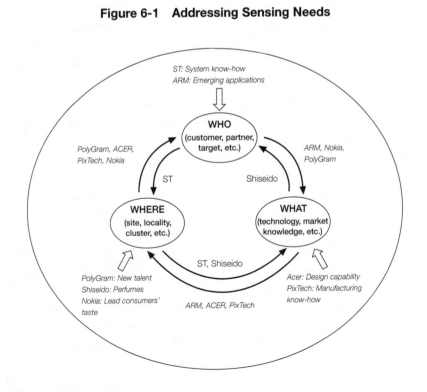

It is possible to enter the cycle illustrated in figure 6-1 at any point. ST began with an appreciation of *who* might have the systems knowledge it needed to build its system-on-a-chip: potential lead customers like Seagate. Early discussions with these customers helped ST define more precisely what it needed to sense. Armed with this understanding, it was able to identify *where* the knowledge might be found—inside Seagate's global network, within ST's own multinational organization, and from locations outside either of these networks. Similarly, ARM identified the partners that could help it set a global standard for embedded Reduced Instruction Set Computing (RISC) chips. They helped ARM define *what* new knowledge it required and *where* it could be accessed.

PolyGram, by contrast, entered the cycle with a guess as to *where* it might find the new talent from which it could fashion a global hit record. At the time, for example, there seemed to be an active group of young artists producing innovative music in Venezuela and Italy. PolyGram didn't start with a profile of the type of artist it was looking for, but by choosing a set of likely hotspots for musical innovation. It eventually homed in on the *who* (choosing an artist with global potential) and the *what* (finding suitable repertoire). Likewise, Shiseido started from a location, France, and developed from there its understanding of *who* could provide the knowledge it needed (small design companies and hair salons) and ultimately *what* it needed to learn.

Acer, on the other hand, knew *what* it needed to inject—new design skills—into its innovation process to come up with the kind of PC that users would be proud to have as an addition to their office furniture. This definition led it to California and, in turn, to discover the Frog design company. PixTech understood it needed display manufacturing know-how. This led it to Taiwan and ultimately to its partner, Unipac.

The winners in the global knowledge economy will generally be proactive about sensing, given the critical role it plays in creating metanational advantage. But this doesn't mean that a company gains all of its new knowledge by going out and searching for it. As we discuss in more detail later, it is sometimes possible to engineer a situation in which the relevant knowledge comes to you. One method may be to set up a venture capital fund that acts as a honey pot, attracting people with new technologies and other novel ideas.

Whatever method of sensing a company ultimately chooses, however, the key objective is to create competitive advantage. Those starting from behind may need to begin by sensing additional knowledge in places that its competitors have already mined in order to catch up. But to innovate and open up a competitive lead, the future metanational will need to be able to unearth emerging sources of technology and market behavior that its competitors haven't yet identified, possibly in places where competitors haven't even looked.

Catching Up and Keeping Up

Followers and aspiring challengers typically sense in locations where the industry leaders are already established—in the well-trodden capitals of their industry. For example, when Korea's Samsung entered the microelectronics industry in the 1980s, it was not difficult to decide where to establish its sensing activities. Silicon Valley was the uncontested world capital of that industry, and for Samsung, as a latecomer to that industry, sensing in Silicon Valley was a clear priority.

Samsung began by acquiring failing semiconductor firms in the Valley. The company used these firms to experiment with and sense manufacturing processes. Eventually it moved some of their production equipment to Korea to experiment with technology transfer. When Samsung decided to aim for mass production of a 64K DRAM with a high-yield ratio, in 1983, it set up two R&D teams. One was home-based, while the other was hired and settled in Silicon Valley. The latter consisted of five Korean-American Ph.D. students and three hundred American engineers who were recruited from the competition. This arrangement quickly enabled Samsung to catch up with the technology it needed.[1]

Sometimes, then, the choice of sensing location is obvious: You need to sense in the capital of the industry, and the issue boils down to choosing the "who" to use and the "what" to sense. It may be easier to sense from a weaker, smaller source than from a larger, stronger one, but the former may have less to contribute. But deciding to sense from locations your competitors have already discovered is a deceptively easy choice. For latecomers, sensing from the same knowledge sources as everyone else is unlikely to be enough to win.

By turning over the tailings in a gold field that your competitors have already mined, you may find the odd nugget that has escaped their attention—especially if you have better sensing tools. More likely, sensing in locations where your global competitors preceded you (the wait-and-see approach) will, at best, bring knowledge parity. The most rewarding, but also the most difficult, challenge for sensing is to discover new locations that your competitors are not yet aware of—perhaps by anticipating where new hotbeds of knowledge are starting to emerge before others do.

The same is true for identifying potential lead customers, partners, or suppliers—the *who* in the sensing cycle depicted in figure 6-1. Going to the large or dominant partners may only give you knowledge that competitors have already identified. By contrast, smaller customers or partners who are experimenting with new applications may offer the richest sensing grounds.

Likewise, looking for technological advances—the *what*—in your own restricted field may provide less scope for competitive advantage than anticipating the potential application of technologies developed in another industry that is about to converge with yours.

Getting Ahead: Moving beyond the Obvious

The winners in the new knowledge economy will go far beyond being customer-led. Witness the fate of several U.S. computer companies on the East Coast. They repeatedly missed out on personal and network computing, largely because of their intimate relationships with the data processing departments of large companies that were insensitive to individual users. Being too close to existing corporate customers blinded the industry to the shift from hobbyist computer nerds to individual users in large companies and then to network computing.

Anticipating the emerging hotbeds of knowledge ahead of competitors requires an insight into some tough questions. *What* disruptive technologies may affect my industry? *Where* are critical technology and market discontinuities likely to originate? *Who* will be the lead customers of the future?

In some cases, the answers are fairly predictable. The biochemistry-on-a-chip technology, fast becoming so essential to new drug discovery and development, could hardly have arisen anywhere but in a handful of places—the San Francisco Bay–Silicon Valley region in the United States or the Lyon–Grenoble region in France. There, and only there, were all the various underlying technologies, scientific insights, and venture capital acumen present in a single location. But was it obvious in the early 1990s that the critical new knowledge about mobile telephone technology and customer behavior would emerge in Finland? Surely the clusters around Bell Laboratories (which invented much of the underlying technology) or around the then industry leader, Motorola, would have been more likely bets. Would we expect one of the world's leading markets for Internet and mobile phone-enabled banking to be Brazil? Yet Brazil's largest bank, Bradesco, is a leader in the application of these technologies. It introduced Internet banking in May 1996 and had attracted 1.5 million online banking customers out of 14 million Brazilian Internet users by 2000.

Clearly there is no surefire way to anticipate who, what, and where to sense for the next technological and market advances. But failure is assured for those who don't even try. While forecasting is fraught with uncertainty, it pays to have a solid strategy for prospecting the world in search of new hotbeds of knowledge.

PROSPECTING FOR KNOWLEDGE

The most successful prospectors look for certain indicators of emerging knowledge hotbeds. Their experience suggests four rules of thumb for an effective prospecting strategy:

1. **Look for leapfroggers** among consumers least hampered by previous product experiences. These can be found by studying users' learning experiences with new technologies. Attention to leapfroggers often points toward the most innovative, leading-edge lifestyles and customers, but relevant knowledge can also come from other segments that leapfrog in less spectacular ways. Unilever's subsidiary in Brazil, Gessy Lever, sensed the emergence of a new, low-end detergent segment that had grown up in India following the entry of a local competitor there. This knowledge led Gessy Lever to open up a customer segment that Unilever had studiously ignored: the poor in the Nordeste and

the Amazon. The Brazilian unit developed and introduced quality detergents for lower-income consumers who were ready for "new" laundry products.

Leapfrogging also happens when corporate customers and partners are least hampered by an installed base. New knowledge is more likely to be generated in markets unencumbered by legacy technologies. Consider the emergence of smart cards, which have an embedded microchip rather than a simple, magnetic strip. The market leaders are from Europe: Bull and Gemplus in France, Siemens in Germany, Mondex in Great Britain, Danmont in Denmark. The fact that the card's inventor, Roland Moreno, was a European is not sufficient to explain this success in Europe. More important was the fact that smart cards leapfrogged traditional credit cards, in an environment where the legacy of magnetic-strip technology was less forceful. With a new, pan-European set of transaction standards, the smart cards also helped overcome the old country-by-country fragmentation of the financial industry.

Across the Atlantic, the smart card faced more resistance. The United States held on to the magnetic strip. Banks in the United States and Canada tested the smart card only sporadically in pilot projects, as the cost of change for the existing credit card transaction infrastructure was considered very high, notably for point-of-sale terminals. Furthermore, smart card manufacturers and U.S. banks competed to develop products with different technical standards, although compatibility is key to the smart card's acceptance.

2. **Think through metaphors from other industries.** Adversity forced Acer's founder and CEO, Stan Shih, to seek a drastic change in his company's business system. To stimulate his thinking, he took the metaphor of the fast-food industry that creates a standard approach to local needs but offers a large choice of fresh (read: nonobsolete) products. Computers would be assembled locally, in close contact with customers, using only the latest high-performance components. Shih divided Acer into forty independent local companies, partly owned by local entrepreneurs (like fast-food franchisees), which act not

just as assembly and sales outfits but also as local market sensors. He named the subsystems "perishable" or "nonperishable," based on the pace of new product introductions, and managed accordingly—for instance, minimizing inventories of perishable products. Acer adjusted as much as possible to local tastes: Production, distribution, sales, and service were adapted to the local market. With this unique structure, Acer reduced its inventory by 50 percent, thus avoiding the risk of inventory obsolescence, decreasing working capital, and lowering costs to create a strong advantage over its less-nimble competitors. Explicitly adopting the fast-food industry as a model gave Acer a consistent and profitable new approach to the computer business. A traditional PC maker would probably not have selected McDonald's as a place to sense new knowledge, yet understanding the McDonald's business system proved important to Acer.

Likewise, from its start in 1985, Dell kept costs down by using a direct-marketing business model inspired by catalog retailers such as Lands' End. By 1992, Dell was selling no more than 15 percent of its computers through resellers such as Staples. The rest was mainly sold directly via phone or mail orders, and increasingly on the Web. In the mid-1990s, Michael Dell understood that his low-price direct-sales positioning would no longer differentiate the company in the long run, so he focused on rapid, reliable customer service, enlisting underused local service forces from Honeywell and Xerox to provide next-day, onsite support for service, installation, and parts.[2]

3. **Identify locations where technologies are converging.** Here, mutually reinforcing innovative trends are likely to create a new knowledge base. The invention of biochips, for example, had its roots in the convergence of microelectronics and biotechnology in the San Francisco Bay area. Jim Neidel, the head of research for Glaxo Wellcome, which acquired the combinational chemistry pioneer Affymax in 1995, commented: "Affymax is in the right place, Silicon Valley, where innovation springs forth between computer industries, robotics, miniaturization, pharmaceutical industries, biotechnologies. The environment is right, the context is right."

The specifics of biochip development could hardly have been anticipated. But an astute observer in Silicon Valley could be certain she was looking in the right place, as the key enabling technologies and scientists were available there, waiting for someone like Affymax founder Alex Zaffaroni to unleash their combined potential.

Or consider the innovative use of global positioning system (GPS) chips in motor vehicles in Japan. GPS was developed in the United States. America arguably led the world in GPS electronics. But it was the convergence of this technology and a natural market need, in a hotbed of auto design where existing maps were a poor representation of a dense and complex street network in Japan, that engendered the new application.

4. **Look for lifestyle leaders.** Changing lifestyles can indicate the emergence of new technologies and market trends. IKEA's success in modern, affordable furniture, for example, could have been anticipated by looking for leadership in lifestyle trends. Is Hong Kong today a pilot of how consumers in a future, richer China would behave? Are there lifestyle indicators that will distinguish the technology and market trendsetters of the twenty-first century?

Other Signs of Emerging Hotbeds

Beyond leapfrogging customers, cross-industry metaphors, converging technologies, and emerging lifestyles, other indicators can be useful in anticipating new knowledge hotbeds. Savvy metanationals will further augment their prospecting strategies by doing the following:

- Staking out government/university science centers with resources, skills, and aspiring entrepreneurs. Stanford University was the original driving force behind the development of Silicon Valley. Bangalore's IT cluster was built on the site of the military software research labs that were located there after the British left. Hsinchu, in Taiwan, strives to "engineer" the birth of a Chinese Silicon Valley. Orsay and Grenoble, in France, thrive on spin-offs and subcontractors from the Commissariat a l'Energie

Atomique, which has major research centers in both cities. Cambridge University is at the origin of many new technologies, as are Los Alamos and Santa Fe, with their spillovers from the U.S. nuclear research programs.

- Watching for growth in long-distance and international phone traffic, and Internet nodes, denoting a concentration of educated, curious, and cosmopolitan communities.

- Monitoring the presence of complementary skills and precursor industries (such as for plastic molds in Portugal), suppliers, and customers.

- Identifying regulatory differences that promote innovation: for example, a fax has the value of an authentic document in Japan; advanced Internet encryption (based on regulatory requirements) facilitates e-commerce in the United States.

- Looking for locations with early regulatory approvals and sophisticated user communities: for example, microsurgery developed faster in Europe, where registration of new products and approval of new surgical procedures takes two years less than it does in the United States.

- Tracking the personal mobility of people and the incentives to innovate: Sense where the interesting people are migrating to live.

- Monitoring rapid changes in disposable income. Time-starved wealthy people invent new lifestyles that require new services and generate new expectations. Rapid declines in income (as in Asian countries that suffered massive devaluation in the financial crisis of the late 1990s) can also spawn innovation: The crisis in Thailand, for example, spurred the development of e-auctions to liquidate inventories and personal possessions.

- Seeking out the cradles of disruptive technologies, where maverick competitors are willing to break traditional industry rules.

At the end of the day, of course, prospecting is an art, not a science: It requires the proverbial helicopter view, informed by a good understanding of the world, as well as by creativity and a sense of the future. As we argue, it also requires a certain type of person, with the right role and possibly an unorthodox incentive system. And when the prospectors find important new knowledge, the organization has to know how to access it.

ACCESSING LOCAL KNOWLEDGE: PLUGGING IN

Accessing a pocket of local knowledge may involve very different degrees of effort. Sometimes knowledge can be accessed quickly and cheaply, requiring little more than casual observation. In other cases, gaining access is costly and protracted, requiring substantial, long-term investments (recall Shiseido's experience accessing knowledge about fragrances in France).

The difficulty of accessing knowledge from a distant location depends importantly on the nature of that knowledge. Recognizing the distinction between "simple" and "complex" knowledge, as discussed in chapter 5, is critical when choosing the right way to access it.

For simple, well-articulated knowledge that is publicly available, the problem of access is almost trivial. Desk research or short information gathering visits will usually suffice. A trip to the U.S. Patent Office, for example, will provide a wealth of knowledge about the technical specifications of, for example, mobile telephony. The rise of the Internet has dramatically reduced the difficulty of accessing distant yet simple knowledge.

In the case of complex, context-dependent knowledge, however (such as the learning Shiseido sought in France), accessing is a more involved process that occurs gradually and within the local environment. A hit-and-run approach will access only part of the complex knowledge bundle and so is bound to lead to misinterpretation. Accessing complex knowledge requires mechanisms for experimentation and immersion. One cannot imagine PolyGram's local talent scouts, for example, identifying new talent with global potential purely on the basis of what they can hear on a tape. Instead, they must endure the arduous task of attending an endless round of nightclub gigs and parties.

Accessing complex knowledge may be difficult because the holders may not be able to articulate it: They may not be conscious of what they know; hence they can't explain it. Their knowledge may be tacit. Another barrier, for both simple and complex knowledge, may arise if the knowledge holders do not wish to divulge what they know or lack the time to communicate it. In all of these cases, access will generally require some sort of collaboration. To learn what it needed from its lead customers, for example, STMicroelectronics had to set up alliances. These enabled it to locate an office for ST engineers at Western Digital headquarters in Lake Forest (not far from Los Angeles) and to establish a joint design team with Seagate in Scotts Valley (close to San Jose).

These kinds of interactions and alliances can be costly and time-consuming. How, then, can managers maximize the return on their investments in accessing new knowledge? The answer lies in choosing the right vehicle to access each type of knowledge that they need.

Choosing the Right Approach

The effectiveness of a vehicle for accessing knowledge is determined by the *quality* of the access it opens up rather than its size and resources. The fallacy of equating size and resources (or what we term "weight") with quality of access is illustrated by several Western companies that located large research centers in Japan. These multinationals recognized Japan as an important hotbed of technology and new processes, but their results were disappointing. Despite lavish resources, the new centers failed because they remained disconnected from the local scientific and technical establishment.

The myth that resources equate to quality of access may be fed by those with a vested interest in getting control of additional resources locally. They may argue that "you need to show the commitment of a large presence to be credible in the local community." But large, local investments may actually be self-defeating if, as often happens, the large research center or marketing office turns its attention inward instead of outward, toward accessing local knowledge.

The successful experience of the Japanese pharmaceutical company Eisai illustrates the advantages of emphasizing strong local connections over weight. In both Boston and Cambridge (in the United Kingdom), Eisai set up relatively small R&D labs, but they were headed by highly regarded local scientists, surrounded by doctoral students, and connected with top-notch local university biology laboratories.[3] A strong flow of new knowledge was quickly established.

Contrast this with Sony's multibillion-dollar acquisition of Columbia Pictures. Columbia had little interest in facilitating Sony's understanding of the movie business in Hollywood. As a large studio in its own right, Columbia had an independent agenda (which probably included maintaining its Hollywood-style spending levels) and little desire to help Sony access complex knowledge about content and entertainment. But it was just this kind of Hollywood-based knowledge that Sony wanted to integrate with its own hardware capabilities that came primarily from Japan.[4]

A second important rule for accessing complex knowledge from distant locations is that the job is best done by local insiders, who share an understanding of the local context, culture, and values. A local can sense subtleties that are unintelligible to corporate expatriates less attuned to the meanings that depend on context. Their outsider's bias for the explicit and the familiar will tend to get in the way. The U.S. Army understood this as far back as the eighteenth century, when it began using Indian scouts for reconnaissance in the Indian wars.

But how do you recruit top-notch locals when you are a newcomer from outside the system? For those seeking to access biotech knowledge in a new location, for example, it might seem a safe bet to go for Nobel Prize winners and pay them well. But this may lead you into hiring the voices of the past, not the future. And in less well-defined skill areas, such as movie-making, how do you spot new talents from outside and avoid hiring the wrong people?

It helps to get advice from local experts—for instance, venture capitalists who are increasingly specialized, who live and breathe the local environment and who are intimately familiar with the technology. Such advisers can also help you decide whether to establish a more permanent sensing node—a probe into a local pocket of knowledge. Sensing nodes can take many different forms, from external alliances to dedicated internal units or new task assignments in existing operating facilities.

External Alliances

Metanational winners find many ways of working with outsiders to access the intelligence they need. Each has advantages and drawbacks.

Customers. Alliances with customers can play an important role in helping to access market knowledge ("outside" the customer) or application knowledge ("inside" the customer). There are many potential benefits of learning with and from customers. Lead customers are the locus of industry knowledge about existing and coming needs.[5] Lead customers provide a proxy for being in the local environment and can help interpret and translate complex, local knowledge to be mobilized and leveraged elsewhere.

But not just any customer can serve as the basis of a local accessing node. We need to identify customers that possess relevant knowledge and have an incentive to share it with us.

Using its knowledge prospecting skills, ST identified Seagate and Western Digital as "strategic partners" from whom it could access the knowledge about HDD systems that it needed to create dedicated chips. Through these alliances with such customers, it located knowledge it needed in various customer sites in the United States and the Far East. To access this knowledge, it created a sales and support network that mirrored the customers' R&D and purchasing networks. This involved such steps as establishing a design center in San Jose, just a few miles from Seagate headquarters, and relocating dedicated staff inside Seagate's quality labs in Singapore. The customers' incentive to cooperate was the prospect of a global vendor that would provide new, more efficient system chips, customized to their needs and available ahead of competitors—advances that would differentiate their own products in the market.

In another case, ST and its customer Thomson Multimedia (TMM), the leading French consumer electronics multinational, jointly created a design center (named TCEC) in Grenoble, France's hotspot for high technologies. TCEC was set up in the early 1990s to develop new semiconductor products for home appliances, such as televisions and TV set-top boxes. TCEC's costs were split 50/50 between ST and TMM. Its 120 engineers and designers worked in teams that included one coordinator from ST and one from TMM to ensure good connection back with each corporation. TCEC's steering and product committees supported interaction between senior executives of ST and TMM. The link with TMM was instrumental in conveying to ST the needs of TMM's own distant American customers, like DirecTV, providing ST with the knowledge it needed to design chips customized to TV set-top boxes.

Using customers as the vehicle for sensing distant knowledge can involve substantial costs, including the costs of coordination and the need for at least partial co-location with customer development centers and operations. There are also potential strategic costs, which may be less obvious at the outset. Lead customers have an incentive to encourage excessive commitment of your resources to their local needs. Once their needs are served, they are unlikely to be sensitive to your further accessing needs, particularly if these involve other customers. You may become hostage to powerful customers who are not necessarily forthcoming about their intentions—they may let you know only what they want you to know.

Distributors. Distributors may also provide valuable access to complex knowledge about unfamiliar environments. In their drive to penetrate the U.S. market, for example, Japanese and Korean consumer electronics firms often relied on U.S. mass merchandisers, such as Sears and Wal-Mart, to specify products for them. This allowed them to access knowledge about the peculiarities of the U.S. market—knowledge that paved the way for later investments in building their own brands and distribution channels. Likewise, Acer used its distributors in Mexico to access knowledge about the needs of small and medium-sized businesses in a developing country. This knowledge played a critical role in helping Acer design a successful product for this market, which it subsequently leveraged across other markets throughout the developing world.

Dealers can offer access on an ongoing basis. Caterpillar, for example, works with dealers around the world so that "information about the customer constantly feeds back into the system and drives new product development and enhancements in service."[6] Like one's own sales force, however, distributors may be too focused on short-term responsiveness and problem-solving to be good sensors of really new important knowledge that does not have an immediate impact on day-to-day operations.

Suppliers. Suppliers can provide access to new knowledge. But it is important to remember that accessing knowledge from suppliers means going well beyond the kind of sensing that takes place in the traditional purchasing process. Purchasing offices may be useful sensing bases but only if they offer access and legitimacy in the local business and governmental communities. For the Taiwanese electronics giant Tatung, purchased components and other inputs amount to 70 percent to 80 percent of the final products' costs. Tatung used purchasing as a tremendous sensing engine to access technology and capabilities from the United States, Europe, Japan, and Korea. To do so, however, the traditional reporting structures, goals, and incentives of its purchasing organization first had to be augmented. Tatung's purchasing heads have explicit responsibility for seeking new product information, exploring materials and suppliers, and obtaining new technology for the Taiwanese headquarters. They report jointly to the heads of global purchasing and new product development.

At Nestlé, in Singapore, sensing tasks were differentiated from the operational short-term priorities of efficient purchasing. Nestlé's local R&D center had the secondary but nonetheless important task of monitoring quality assurance for suppliers in the Far East. It ensured that all the input products met Nestlé's standards. This close attention to the suppliers' activities allowed it to keep in touch with new market needs and emerging technologies within local suppliers.

Other Partners. Other partners can offer access to both technical and market knowledge. PixTech, as we saw in chapter 1, built a web of alliances for its flat-panel screens with that goal. Of course, partners also have limitations as sensing nodes: Like customers, they have their own agendas and may want to influence the scope of the alliance or limit it to dimensions they can manage. Obviously, some reciprocity is likely to be required, and it may be difficult to find a worthwhile exchange that goes both ways.

Targeted Acquisitions. When the pharmaceutical giant Glaxo Wellcome (GW) bought Affymax, a pioneer in solid-state combinatorial chemistry, it got more than a technology for speeding up its development pipeline. As a senior executive at GW put it, "There was a more strategic aim [than obtaining access to existing combinatorial chemistry techniques] when GW bought Affymax. It was to have a group of technologists and scientists in the San Francisco area, in the middle of the hive of innovation." So, through Affymax, GW firmly established a sensor in California, near and in tune with other companies innovating in computers and biotechnology.

Sony Music sensed local markets in Europe through minority ownership in a number of small independent music labels. This equity participation kept it aware of—and in tune with—the local music trends and talents. Likewise, recall the role of Shiseido's acquisitions of beauty parlors and specialist perfumeries in accessing French knowledge about fragrance design and marketing.

Sometimes it is difficult to use small technology acquisitions effectively as a vehicle for accessing complex knowledge. There is a temptation to believe that "We own them, thus we have their knowledge at our disposal." In fact, as we discuss later, it takes tremendous effort for a global corporation to internalize the knowledge embedded in a small acquisition.

Venture Capital Funds. Venture capital funds can provide a way of accessing emerging technologies and ideas for new business models by attracting entrepreneurs in search of funding. Rather than going out in search of new knowledge scattered around the world (which can be like looking for the proverbial needle in a haystack), companies can launch a venture fund to attract some of the knowledge they need. The Finnish telecommunications company Sonera, for example, has successfully partnered with an experienced Californian venture capital company to access new knowledge that complements its own strengths in emerging mobile telephony technologies.

Local Universities and Research Centers. Local universities and research centers can offer powerful ways of accessing new technical and scientific knowledge. Sponsoring local research helps to engage local scientists who can blend academic and corporate research programs and link them to other projects. Mere sponsorship, however, may be ineffective unless there is a parallel investment in local presence or staff. When Eisai first began to move outside Japan in the 1980s, instead of opening sales offices, its first move was to set up a biology laboratory in the United Kingdom. It signed a fifty-year contract with the University of Cambridge, which stipulated that Eisai would operate on campus doing research, enroll its scientists in doctoral study programs, benefit from teaching positions, and collaborate with local scientists to keep up with the latest basic or applied research. On its side, the university enjoyed the benefits of Eisai's funds and scholarships, scientific information, and visiting world-class scientists on campus.

Knowledge Brokers. Another vehicle for accessing distant knowledge is to seek out companies that generate knowledge as a by-product from their operations. What is operational data for one may be a source of new and valuable knowledge for another. Dun & Bradstreet, for example, sells what it calls "the largest company information database in the world," which is built from its clients' exhaustive databases and can therefore become an extremely useful sensing tool for others.

Emigrant Populations. Emigrant populations that have penetrated distant hotbeds of new knowledge can provide very valuable links. Some individuals may even be lured back to the old country as it grows, liberalizes, and creates opportunities, reversing brain drain. Acer, for example, has accessed knowledge about where new technologies were emerging by recruiting Taiwanese engineers and scientists working in the United States. Likewise, Israeli companies have tapped into Jewish scientists living abroad and programmers moving from Russia to Israel. These people may have the added advantage of being cross-cultural integrators able to translate knowledge from one local context to another. But beware of emigrants who have turned their backs on their original country and have done their best to disappear into their country of adoption: They can be out of touch. Examples might include Indians or Chinese who moved to America long ago, central Europeans who fled communism, and others who have outdated perceptions and feelings about their home countries.

Competitors. Although the idea of accessing knowledge from competitors may seem counterintuitive, it can work if there is potential learning for both sides. Consider the case of NUMMI, a 50/50 joint venture between Toyota and General Motors. NUMMI was established in 1984 at an existing GM car manufacturing plant in Fremont, California. The two partners took joint responsibility for managing the plant. GM's goal was to access the complex bundle of existential knowledge that comprised the widely respected Toyota production system. Meanwhile, Toyota wanted to access an equally complex bundle of knowledge about managing a U.S. workforce in an American legal environment, as well as to gain insights about the supply chain, marketing, and distribution of vehicles in the United States.

When the NUMMI project was launched, the first of about 450 American team leaders traveled to Toyota's Takaoka plant in Japan for three weeks of classroom and on-the-job training. These initiatives were followed by further on-the-job training in which team members worked side-by-side with Toyota trainers.

In 1998, NUMMI—by now producing more than 300,000 cars per annum, including the Toyota Corolla sedan, the Toyota Tacoma truck, and the Chevrolet Prizm—won the United States' National Association of Manufacturers Award for Workforce Excellence. Both companies accessed a great deal of complex knowledge by working together in the NUMMI joint venture (although GM found it difficult to integrate this new knowledge into its mainstream automaking operations back in Detroit).

The Dangers of Overreliance on Third Parties

Each of the approaches just outlined offers practical mechanisms to help a company access new knowledge in distant pockets outside its organization. All require a degree of commitment and investment in order to obtain that knowledge. All involve partial reliance on the competence of third parties and their willingness to cooperate. As such, they require proactive management of the relationship. And they require that the third party learns with you, too. A passive approach (effectively relying on the third party to take the initiative and "tell you what you need to know") both increases your dependence and reduces the likelihood of successfully accessing the knowledge you need. Overreliance on third parties is dangerous for a number of reasons:

- The third parties may have limited resources or little interest in revealing everything that would be useful for you to learn, or they may themselves have an incomplete understanding of the local technology or market knowledge that you wish to access.

- The third party may control your pace of learning, even without you fully recognizing that this is happening.

- The third party can be of only limited help in addressing the problem of translation: Complex, context-dependent knowledge obtained locally still needs to be made meaningful to the potential users elsewhere in your organization.

- Overreliance on a third party may give you a false sense of security that keeps you from recognizing the need for firsthand learning, so instead you rely too much on vicarious learning.

The risks of overreliance on third parties for sensing can be mitigated by setting up internal sensing units.

INTERNAL SENSORS

Your sensing units (or probes) may take the form of a laboratory, a plant, a design center, or a marketing center. On the surface, they may look like the familiar day-to-day operations that supply, market, or distribute products and services, but they have a very important additional duty. Management must recognize the dual role of these units as both sensors and operational sites and actively promote double-tasking to capture the valuable knowledge that arises as a by-product of selected operations.

Some internal units may be solely dedicated to the sensing function. Dedicated sensing units can more easily include people, structures, and incentive systems that are appropriate to the task of sensing but that sit uneasily within the mainstream network of operations.

Dedicated Sensors

The stand-alone status of a dedicated sensing unit has both advantages and disadvantages. On the positive side, a dedicated sensing unit can be used to establish a presence where the company has no other operations at all. This means the company can access pockets of new knowledge where it doesn't make sense to have a sales, a supply, or even an R&D operation.[7] By contrast, a company that limits the location of its sensing units to places where the company has established operations may find that important pockets of new knowledge remain outside of its reach. Dedicated sensing units also have the advantage of pursuing their mission free from the constraints of the operating plane.

Recall the successful strategy followed by Shiseido when it established sensing probes to access hotbeds of knowledge about the fragrance business in France. The units it established and acquired had a clear mission: to learn, uncompromised by potentially conflicting objectives that would have between introduced if Shiseido had asked these units to be responsible for large-scale production, sales, or distribution. Several companies, seeking to come to grips with the complexity of the Chinese market, have set up units to learn by providing after-sales service to machinery supplied by competitors, by leasing equipment, or by refurbishing existing plants.[8]

On the other hand, some sensing units may need to be engaged in a substantial amount of day-to day activity in order to perform their sensing role. It may not be possible to understand emerging market trends, for example, without a close involvement with sales and distribution. Dedicated sensors can also become isolated from the rest of the business. For example, by the time Cable & Wireless saw all the benefits it gained from C&W Innovations, a sensing unit it had set up in Silicon Valley to scout for Internet businesses in the early 1990s, the headquarters had already closed the unit for lack of results.

Clearly, dedicated sensing units have a potentially important role in unearthing new knowledge that lies outside the reach of a company's existing operational network (either because this knowledge exists in places where the firm doesn't operate or because prejudices within the established organization make it impossible to access). But before establishing a dedicated sensing, we need to be able to answer the following questions: What kind of people would be assigned to the new sensing unit? What would be their future in the organization? How would we measure their performance? How would we reward them?

Sensing from Existing Operations

Where a dedicated sensing unit was deemed ineffective, some companies have assigned a dual role to an existing operational unit, asking it to act as both sensor and an efficient local operation. This is a difficult double act because, as we saw in chapter 4, it often means trying to shoehorn a new and fundamentally different role into an existing organization. The mentality, structures, and rewards appropriate to "explorers" don't sit easily alongside those of "farmers." Still, some companies have been able to make this double-tasking work. Recall the example of Tatung, where the purchasing organization (charged with buying the right quality components from reliable suppliers at good prices) acted simultaneously as a sensor for new technologies. In our experience, however, successful double-tasking is quite rare.

At the same time, we need to recognize that important new knowledge often emerges as a by-product of day-to-day problem-solving, or it may be discovered fortuitously when operations people happen to stumble on a new technology or a salesperson meets a customer with a new market need. In this case, the management challenge is to encourage people to speak up and reveal what they have learned—and to listen and understand them when they do speak.

Regardless of whether sensing occurs through dedicated units or within existing operations, it must be actively managed. We now turn to the challenge of managing this process of learning from the world.

MANAGING THE SENSING PROCESS

It should be clear from the discussion so far that sensing is not just about scanning, observing, or benchmarking. It involves an active and sustained campaign to learn from the world. The most valuable knowledge will come from locations and sources that competitors haven't yet identified. It may be difficult to access because it is tacit and deeply embedded in a local context and culture. To obtain that kind of knowledge requires sustained interaction and, in many cases, substantial local investment in sensing probes, be they alliances with customers, distributors, suppliers, or universities, targeted acquisitions or other types of relationships.

This means consciously establishing a network to compete on what we termed in chapter 1 the "sensing plane"—the arena where companies try to preempt global sources of new knowledge. The sensing organization must excel in *prospecting* for, and *accessing*, distant pockets of new knowledge.

Top Management Roles

Top management needs to make a clear decision to augment the existing operating network with an effective sensing organization. Our research suggests that sensing activities require an annual budget of between 0.5 percent and 1 percent of corporate revenues. This budget will be higher for companies facing rapid technological or market change, or industry convergence, or where new ideas are emerging rapidly in locations that have been unimportant in the past. A lower budget will be sufficient in industries where much of the knowledge that the company requires is already scattered within the existing network of subsidiaries, where the pace of technological and market change is slow, or where a few industry capitals continue to maintain their dominance.

Equally important, senior management must shape the mindset that potentially valuable knowledge is available in far-flung pockets around the world rather than from headquarters or dominant, national subsidiaries. Perhaps the deepest challenge in sensing stems from the need to challenge, and reverse, home-country dominance— correcting the mindset that the home base is the natural leader and teacher. Reversing the knowledge flow, so that the periphery can lead the center, often requires a decisive move by top management—a corporate shock or discontinuity. For example, senior executives may set a high-profile goal of leapfrogging existing competition or entering new business areas. They may focus on emerging technological threats or personally champion projects based on new knowledge from the periphery.

As we noted at the beginning of this chapter, the CEO and other senior management play an important role in establishing and communicating, in broad terms, the company's sensing needs. They do so by identifying gaps in the firm's technological portfolio, by following market trends, and by bringing potential new hotbeds of knowledge to the attention of managers with a sensing role. A cosmopolitan top management team, whose senior executives create strong, informal networks as they operate in diverse locations, can be a powerful force in helping a company anticipate knowledge emerging from multiple sources.

At STMicroelectronics, for example, Andrea Cuomo—a restless executive in charge of the "strategic partners" global account program and the "Corporate Strategic Marketing" dispersed network of laboratories—provided a vantage point on sensing needs, fueled by constant travel and an entrepreneurial attitude. He gleaned countless ideas through his contacts with leading global customers across a variety of industries and linked them with the knowledge of new technologies and product architectures he came across in his strategic marketing role. Whenever he had the germ of an idea about new knowledge that ST might need, he involved a group of managers with different experiences to shape a sensing project and suggest possible prospecting locations.

Sensing, as we have already seen, needs to be purposeful, yet it must also provide space for serendipity. Senior management, therefore, needs to establish a structure, along with a set of roles and responsibilities, performance measures, and incentives, to achieve this balance for the sensing organization.

Structure

The structure of the sensing organization differs fundamentally from the structure of the traditional multinational's operating network. Rather than being closely integrated across locations, the sensing organization is a loose and flexible network. But each sensing unit is tightly plugged in to the local pocket of specialist knowledge that it is responsible for accessing. For example, the design centers that ST established close to lead customers in different locations were closely tied in with that customer site and the local environment. These sensing units needed to be tightly connected with other parts of the ST organization. But the direct links between the sensing units themselves were loose and informal. As we explain in chapter 7, many companies have mistakenly tried to connect pockets of knowledge scattered around the world directly with one another to form a kind of knowledge network. Our research suggests that this is more likely to result in the frustrations of a global debating society, rather than a powerful source of innovation.

The sensing organization needs a flat structure. There is no room for hierarchy: Each sensing unit has a unique potential contribution to make. Individual sensing units will often be temporary structures. Their lifetime should be determined by the value of new knowledge they can potentially access. Once a particular source dries up, the sensing unit should be disbanded or relocated.

We believe it is important for the sensing organization to have a direct reporting line to the top management team. It needs to be both nurtured and directed by those who set the company's long-term goals in the global competitive arena. There is a real danger that a specific function or individual (for example, global marketing, R&D, or a chief technology officer) hijacks the sensing function and focuses it too narrowly in perhaps idiosyncratic ways. Anticipating what new knowledge will be required, or which knowledge could be melded with existing knowledge to multiply its value, involves multiple inputs. That is why an externally oriented, cosmopolitan senior management team plays such an important part.

Staffing

The staff of the sensing organization are a special breed of people: explorers rather than farmers. Their prevailing motivation is discovery and reconnaissance. They need intellectual curiosity, empathy with locals, and sensitivity to their local context. They need to understand the difference between information and knowledge, to avoid the trap of underestimating knowledge complexity, as we discussed in chapter 5. They must be credible to people and partners in the local environment in which they operate. In a sensing role where the requirements and rewards are potentially large, but not clear-cut, they need a high tolerance for ambiguity. Finally, they need stamina, because finding and accessing complex knowledge that is deeply embedded in a local context is a demanding and time-consuming task.

Such a list makes it obvious to see why asking most managers who are already overloaded with day-to-day operations to act as sensor as well is doomed to fail. The logic of the operational tasks—scale, efficiency, and control—and the personal qualities they require could not be more different.

Performance Measures and Incentives

The job of the sensing organization is like basic R&D: It uncovers new pockets of knowledge and accesses them by turning over stones, knowing it won't necessarily find "pay-dirt" under every stone. Investments in sensing therefore represent a portfolio of small but risky ventures. The profits indirectly generated by the sensing organization will accrue elsewhere, when the resulting innovations are scaled up and leveraged by the day-to-day operations. Measuring the performance of sensing activities, therefore, is hardly compatible with discounted cash-flow analysis. The *ratio of learning over investment* is the appropriate performance measure for sensing investments, and it should be measured across the entire portfolio.

Such a performance measure can be implemented by using specific indicators such as the number of innovations to which a sensing unit contributes, the percentage of uptake of the technologies or market concepts it puts forward, or the estimated value of contributions to innovation from a particular sensing unit. The latter indicator requires the company to establish a family tree to track the birthplace of every capability or market insight that leads to a successful innovation.

The success of sensing activities needs to be judged over an extended period of time, measured in years, not months. Effective sensing cannot be activated at the flip of a switch. Sensing cannot easily be switched off without incurring cost to the organization. It is a slow process that involves a patient buildup of capabilities and relationships.

It is difficult to tie incentive structures tightly to the kinds of performance measures relevant for a sensing organization. The roles and responsibilities of those in the sensing organization are both important and challenging. Staff who accept these assignments need to be rewarded in line with their significant potential contribution to the future of the company. For people who are likely to excel at a sensing role, we found that recognition is sometimes even more important than financial reward.

It is therefore essential that senior management find ways to recognize and involve members of the sensing organization. Otherwise, disenchantment will follow, as described by a former ST manager who, for ten years, played a key role in sensing new technologies and market applications for the company: "I was tired of digging up things . . . and seeing others, at the center or in the divisions, being recognized for turning them into products and profits. I had no say in the future direction. . . . I only provided what I found out here."

BEYOND SENSING

An effective sensing capability will be an essential feature of the winners in the new global knowledge economy. This will require tomorrow's metanationals to build their capacity to identify critical sensing needs, prospect the world for new pockets of knowledge, and access that knowledge through a combination of local relationships and an internal sensing organization. Success in sensing provides the raw material for the innovation process.

But success in sensing is only the first step toward building metanational advantage. If the investments in sensing have done their job, the company will have a rich stock of knowledge at its disposal, but that knowledge will still remain scattered around the world where it was mined. Such dispersed knowledge will be of little value unless the company can find ways to mobilize it in the service of a focused innovation problem. Mobilizing dispersed knowledge is the subject of the next chapter.

Chapter 7

Mobilizing Dispersed Knowledge

METANATIONAL ADVANTAGE RESTS on the ability to mobilize and leverage pockets of specialized knowledge that are dispersed around the world. Learning from the world, by identifying and accessing these pockets of knowledge through a sensing strategy and organization, is the first step toward this goal.

The next step is to transform that knowledge into usable innovations. To accomplish this, an organization needs to address three related challenges:

- It needs to find a way of *focusing* dispersed and fragmented knowledge on a particular opportunity or problem.

- It needs to understand how and when to *move* particular knowledge (which, as we saw in chapter 5, can easily be misinterpreted when separated from its local context).

- It needs to find ways to *meld* different knowledge from different sources, because the true metanational breakthroughs are never based on any single knowledge source.

IDENTIFYING OPPORTUNITY: THE ENTREPRENEURIAL INSIGHT

Dispersed knowledge does not simply get together spontaneously. To ignite the innovation process, someone (an individual or a team) has to spot a value-creation opportunity in technological capabilities and market trends that are geographically dispersed. Spotting such an opportunity requires the following conditions:

- An individual or team inside the organization must be aware of the knowledge that exists in multiple locations (be it technology or market understanding).

- That individual or team must understand some of the possible combinations of those pieces of knowledge.

- That individual or team must recognize the potential strategic value of combining these pieces of knowledge in new ways.

We call this triple "AHA!" the *entrepreneurial insight.* Our metanational winners offer several examples: ARM's recognition of the opportunity to create a global standard for embedded RISC chips; PolyGram's insight into the profits to be reaped by bringing local artists to the global stage; STMicroelectronics spotting the value to its customers of developing a system-on-a-chip.

It is easy to see why entrepreneurial insights are a rarity in most traditional multinationals, where few people have a helicopter view of knowledge that might be valuably combined. In traditional multinationals, breakthroughs often occur within a local subsidiary (when country management uses local knowledge to create an innovative sales strategy, for example). Alternatively, they may take place at headquarters or within an R&D or marketing facility when the relevant knowledge happens to be together in one place. In the normal course of a multinational's operations, however, the three conditions for entrepreneurial insight generally exist only by coincidence. Obviously, tomorrow's metanational winners will have to improve the odds.

Fostering Insight: Senior Management's Role

In almost all the pioneering metanational companies that we studied, the CEO or the top management team shared extensive international experience—the outcome of long careers in one or several multinational corporations, including extensive periods as expatriates. This background created a cosmopolitan worldview and a broad knowledge base at the senior-most level. These executive teams were full of insights about where to find certain capabilities, where certain lead market needs might emerge, and how to get an inside track in key knowledge clusters.

Senior management also traveled extensively. Their entrepreneurial insights often took shape during trips to far-flung operations, or even during vacations. Of course, globetrotting itself is not a recipe for entrepreneurial insight. In general, the breakthrough ideas stem either from a problem in search of a solution, or a solution in search of a problem.

Problems in search of solutions can come from many sources—a CEO's sense of the next priority, a formal strategic analysis, an opportunity management team, and so on. Solutions in search of problems often arise when an individual develops a belief in the power of a particular technology, capability, or product design and begins to hawk it around an organization. The process can start at the top, or it can bubble up from the bottom.

It is senior management's responsibility to create a receptive environment for these bottom-up entrepreneurial insights. Our research suggests three ways to do so. All of these approaches try to re-create the kind of knowledge-sharing that happens naturally when people with different capabilities and insights are co-located, as we described in chapter 5.

Facilitate Chance Encounters. Chance encounters are one way that dispersed pieces of knowledge come together. The mechanisms that foster chance encounters may be as simple as holding meetings in unusual locations, where "traditional" knowledge and capabilities will collide with new needs or "fringe" capabilities. Assigning problems to subsidiaries that lack the complete complement of knowledge to solve them—thereby forcing them to look for help in other locations—can also facilitate chance encounters. Another approach is to manage "mismatches," thus promoting encounters between people who would not meet each other in the typical course of operations. Coordinate training sessions or meetings for diverse parts of the organization. Plan a social event combining two or three different project groups. Make sure people are aware when—as happens more and more frequently—colleagues from elsewhere in the corporation are meeting in the same hotel.

Define Challenging but Fuzzy Goals. The European Airbus project offers a good example. A group of senior managers and government representatives at France's Sud Aviation (later renamed Aerospatiale) set the audacious goal of challenging the incumbent American competitors, including the formidable global leader, Boeing, in the mainstream civil airframe market. Initially, the details of this objective were fuzzy: The project team had neither the market knowledge, beyond obvious routes in Europe, nor the full complement of technologies required. But the Airbus concept embodied an important entrepreneurial insight: that Boeing was missing the opportunity to serve the world market by drawing from specialized aerospace technologies and market understanding outside the United States. The result was a powerful platform able to mobilize technologies, capabilities, and an understanding of emerging market needs from around the world (including avionics that Airbus learned from the United States itself).

Create a Corporate Knowledge Map. A "knowledge map" that inventories different technologies, capabilities, and market knowledge within the global organization may help ideas for innovation based on dispersed knowledge to emerge more easily. "Knowledge yellow pages" or a "who's who" of in-house experts may play a supporting role.

With an explicit map of the knowledge terrain, we now "know what we know." Individuals or teams may use the map to find rough-cut combinations of problems and knowledge that are likely to create value if brought together. Or they may identify opportunities by noticing patterns in customer requests or complaints, in R&D projects at multiple locations, and so on.

Each of these initiatives can help to stimulate entrepreneurial insight about how knowledge scattered about the world could be used to provide an innovative solution to an existing problem or generate a new product, service, or business model. Clearly, however, an entrepreneurial insight alone is not enough to create tangible results.

FORMALIZING INNOVATION WITH METANATIONAL MAGNETS

As we saw in chapter 3, turning knowledge into innovation requires a mechanism that will attract the dispersed knowledge, direct it toward a common goal, and exert pressure to deliver new products or services. We use the term *magnet* to denote these activities and systems at the core of the metanational process. Looking at pioneers like Acer, ARM, Nestlé, PolyGram, and STMicroelectronics, we observed three kinds of magnets at work:

- A global lead customer.

- A global product (or service) platform.

- A global activity.

These magnets provide the focus and the energy required for innovation. But each type of magnet does this in a different way.

A Global Lead Customer as Magnet

The effective use of a few leading global customers as magnets proved critical to ST's rise during the 1990s. ST's entrepreneurial insight was to differentiate its offering by developing systems-on-a-chip. At first, ST created a structure—the Dedicated Products Group—to focus on this goal. But the new group faced a knowledge gap: ST understood *semiconductors*, but only its customers, like the HDD producers, had the necessary *systems* knowledge it would need to design the new, integrated chips. The knowledge architecture of the HDD and its controller was very complex, spanning the disciplines of physics, mechanics, electromechanics, electronics, manufacturing, quality assurance, HDD applications, and so on.

ST needed to work with a customer to access this complex knowledge about the HDDs. But not any customer would do. To be an effective magnet, the customer must be on the leading edge of its own industry. If the customer is an industry follower, the resulting innovation is unlikely to have widespread value. Potential lead customers also need an incentive to cooperate, as they will have to spend considerable resources and energy to guide the innovation by their metanational vendor. Ideal candidates, therefore, are customers seeking greater efficiency or new ways to differentiate their own products.

Typically it isn't clear at the start exactly what pieces of knowledge are necessary to fill the customer's unmet need. When ST began to serve Seagate in the late 1980s, it understood neither the architecture nor the exact technologies and capabilities involved in data storage systems. To overcome these gaps, it needed to assemble relevant knowledge from different sites and product divisions scattered around its own international network, from competitors, and from other customers, and meld this with Seagate's own complex knowledge about HDD architecture and the drivers of functionality, size, and cost.

The decision to create dedicated chips for Seagate eventually made it the magnet for new and distant pieces of knowledge. To design a single chip that would both power and control Seagate devices (dubbed the "star combo"), ST used its design skills and process technology drawn from Castelletto and Agrate, near Milan, and its design capabilities in Phoenix and Singapore. ST accessed other knowledge from Seagate by relocating designers from Singapore and Italy into Seagate facilities in Scotts Valley, California. It also tapped into its engineers who had earlier experience in developing specialized power chips for Conner and Western Digital.

The star combo project for Seagate was a success, and Seagate learned it could count on ST as a truly innovative global supplier whose resources and flexibility surpassed local vendors. As a result, Seagate asked ST to provide a read/write channel chip. When that was accomplished, Seagate wanted ST to work on the microprocessor subsystem of the HDD electronics. In each case, ST found and mobilized a complex array of knowledge—across its own network, throughout Seagate's, from large competitors, and from small specialized boutiques—to create a radically new design. The range of knowledge covered everything from sophisticated electronics to procurement, logistics, quality assurance, and after-sales service. (The resulting knowledge map is depicted in figure 1-2 in chapter 1.)

Through this series of innovation projects, ST eventually produced a set of system-on-a-chip products that replaced more than one hundred components in Seagate's HDD controller. ST had learned not just how to make controller chips that could eventually be sold to HDD producers. Even more important, it had learned how to use a customer as a magnet for mobilizing dispersed knowledge.

A Global Platform as Magnet

Perhaps the most obvious candidate for the role of magnet is a global product or service platform. By *platform* we mean the core architecture—of a product or service, of a process, or even of a business model—that may be adapted to serve different global customers or to compete in different global market segments.

Like the global lead customer, the global platform provides the magnet that mobilizes pieces of knowledge from around the world. Once the architecture of the platform is well-understood, the pieces of knowledge that are required become apparent. The pockets of relevant knowledge can be identified and accessed. It is an iterative process: As the platform is developed, it will become clear that new pieces of knowledge, possibly from additional locations, are required.

In our research we came across several cases in which the product platform played the role of magnet. The design concept of the Airbus A-300 series is a prime example. An ambitious but initially fuzzy entrepreneurial insight in France evolved to become the Airbus A-300 platform. It worked as a magnet for mobilizing technical capabilities that were spread across Europe to serve unique needs from different national carriers (such as Air France and Lufthansa, and later others). It integrated world-class British capabilities in wing design and manufacture, German expertise in metal structures, and French knowledge about cockpit/systems design and assembly processes as developed for the Concorde. The Airbus knowledge magnet was powerful enough to attract wing technology from Hawker-Siddeley (now British Aerospace), even though the British government failed to support the initial Airbus alliance.

Interestingly, the Airbus platform also drew in knowledge from American avionics companies—namely, the novel cockpit design and fly-by-wire technologies used in the popular Airbus A-320. These advanced technologies were actually developed for fighter planes by American vendors. Yet by setting up an innovation process—a magnet capable of mobilizing globally dispersed knowledge—Airbus was able to leverage these American avionics technologies before Boeing—a dramatic example of overcoming the tyranny of distance.

In a few outstanding cases (such as ARM's Bluetooth platform or the Airbus A-300), using a global platform as the magnet to mobilize dispersed knowledge proved to be a strategic turning point for the company. In most cases we observed, however, the impact of innovations from product platforms was more modest. Breakthrough innovations were more likely to emerge when a lead customer performed the role of magnet. This was largely because the platform architecture typically imposed limits on the extent of innovation. There were fewer such constraints when the starting point was an unmet customer need.

A Global Activity as Magnet

PolyGram's International Repertoire Centres (IRCs) demonstrate the potential of a global activity as the magnet for mobilizing dispersed knowledge in the service of innovation. In this case the innovation was a stream of global hit records, built around the distinctive sounds and personalities of local artists.

Nestlé also used a global activity—in this case R&D—to build a magnet for dispersed knowledge. Nestlé's equivalent of PolyGram's IRCs was Nestec, a separate company that would coordinate innovation by combining R&D capabilities with knowledge of emerging market needs from around the world.

Working inside Nestec, a twenty-person team headed by a very senior executive acted as knowledge brokers by putting "customers" (the operating units) in contact with the appropriate "suppliers" (drawn from Nestlé's Technological Development Centers in Switzerland, Germany, France, England, Sweden, Italy, Spain, the United States, Ecuador, Singapore, and the Ivory Coast) to serve specific R&D projects. Nestec took overall responsibility for the deliverables and charged a fee for its role as magnet and intermediary.[1]

All three types of magnet are viable. But, as these examples suggest, each has different strengths and weaknesses. To effectively mobilize globally dispersed knowledge for innovation, therefore, choosing the appropriate magnet is key.

CHOOSING THE RIGHT MAGNET

The right choice of magnet depends on three related considerations:

- How precisely can we define in advance what a successful innovation would look like? STMicroelectronics, for example, had only a broad notion that a system-on-a-chip could create value, whereas PolyGram could specify the characteristics of a global hit record quite precisely.

- How much of the innovation process that mobilizes dispersed knowledge can be replicated? Each innovation project in ST must be approached on a case-by-case basis, whereas PolyGram can use the same basic process repeatedly for each record release.

- How significant are the potential returns from any single innovation? How much can we afford to invest in creating it? A system chip that opens up a whole new area of application (like car navigation systems) obviously can justify more investment than any single record, even if it becomes a "greatest hit."

When to Use a Global Customer as the Magnet

When latent market needs are not yet well-understood, when the entrepreneurial insight yields only fuzzy goals, or when the goal is to discover a new solution, it is difficult to define a suitable global platform to act as a magnet for dispersed knowledge. Nor is it easy to specify a set of activities that will create an innovative product or service to satisfy that need.

Faced with these kinds of uncertainties, using a global lead customer as magnet has clear advantages. As we saw in the case of the ST–Seagate relationship, the customer provides valuable new knowledge and connections. But even more important, a customer can help refine our understanding of exactly what a successful innovation might look like.

On the other hand, learning with a leading global customer is often costly in time and resources. Considerable investment may be required either to access knowledge from the customer or to entice the customer to cooperate. Customer-led innovation may also require expensive, one-off customization. The process tends to be less predictable and more difficult to clone. ST, for example, has learned to use other global customers as magnets, but it cannot simply replicate what it did with Seagate. Each new project with another customer in another application has its own idiosyncrasies, including the particular history of interfirm relations, the personalities involved, and the economics and competitive environment of the particular application.

Having been developed in partnership with a specific customer, the resulting innovation may be more difficult to scale up and apply to other customers in the global market. Effective rollout is likely to involve a further round of investment in modifying the original innovation.

Recognizing these costs, it generally pays to use a global customer as magnet only for innovations that have a high potential impact on shareholder value. This was the case for ST's use of Seagate as a magnet, which paved the way for leadership in what is today a multibillion-dollar market.

Another major advantage of using a global lead customer as magnet is that the resulting innovation is more likely to match the market need. Where innovation around a global platform or a global activity as magnets can become isolated from the market, having a global leading customer constantly guiding the metanational innovation process keeps user needs at the fore.

A global customer must display several characteristics to be an effective magnet. It must see the potential value of the innovation to its own business. Ideally, it would also provide access to a diverse set of knowledge about technologies and market applications in different environments. This is most likely when the customer has a global network of R&D laboratories, engineering or design groups, manufacturing facilities, and sales and marketing subsidiaries spread across markets with different needs. Better still, the customer may have a vague sense of the value of mobilizing the knowledge imprisoned in these local pockets, but not know how to make this happen.

To be effective as a magnet, a global lead customer also needs an organization, strategy, and culture that will be receptive to a partnership that may last not months but years.

When to Use a Global Platform as the Magnet

When the entrepreneurial insight leads to a reasonably tight specification of future customers' requirements within an existing product category, rather than a vague notion of an unmet need or a fuzzy opportunity, a global platform can act as an effective magnet for mobilizing dispersed knowledge.

A global platform provides a more tangible magnet than a partnership with a lead customer. Early on, it is clearer what pieces of knowledge are required to further the innovation and how they might fit together. This, in turn, paves the way for a more predictable innovation process. It may also be easier to break down the innovation task into semi-independent modules of work.

When the global platform acts as the magnet, the resulting innovation will be easier to exploit on a broad scale. Rather than reflecting the idiosyncrasies of an individual customer, the innovation is designed for global applicability from the outset. ARM's global RISC chip architectures are a good example. They need to be integrated with particular applications, but the core technology is the same.

Using a global platform is less costly than innovating with a global lead customer. More of the process is under internal control and less dependent on external developments within the customer that might throw it off track. As a lower-cost type of magnet, global platforms can be used for projects with a more modest potential upside.

On the other hand, using a global platform as the magnet has a number of downsides. Because the basic platform architecture has to be specified in advance, using a global platform as the magnet can impose a straitjacket on the metanational innovation process and damage the quality of the final result. Breakthrough innovations are less likely to emerge when a global platform is adopted as the magnet.

Innovations based on a global platform may also be easier for competitors to copy, as the processes and sources of knowledge are likely to be more transparent than they are when the magnet is a global lead customer.

When to Use a Global Activity as the Magnet

Finally, in cases where many possible innovations can emerge from the same basic innovation process, but each has a relatively low impact on shareholder value (such as a new record for PolyGram), the global activity becomes the magnet of choice.

To use a global activity as the magnet, it must be possible to specify, in advance, the activities required to innovate. Where a global activity acts as the magnet, each small innovation, such as a new hit record, is different in content. But the basic innovation process is much the same.

The ability to spread the fixed costs of setting up metanational innovation processes and structures (such as PolyGram's IRCs) is an obvious advantage of using a global activity as the magnet. Using a global activity as the magnet makes it possible to mobilize dispersed knowledge even where the rewards to be reaped from the individual innovations are relatively small.

The disadvantages of using a global activity as the magnet are equally clear: The innovation process is tightly constrained on a single track. Large, breakthrough innovations are effectively excluded. And because the process is tightly specified in advance, it is generally unable to make use of newly discovered pockets of knowledge that don't fit into the standard process. Much of the potential for mobilizing and melding globally dispersed knowledge will therefore be lost.

Clearly, an important part of senior management's role in metanational innovation is choosing the right magnets. An inappropriate choice will either drown the innovation process in excessive cost, or sharply constrain the potential value that can be created. As we have seen, the choice must take into account how tightly the customers' requirements and the innovation process can be specified in advance, the downsides of imposing a straitjacket, and the potential value any single innovation could create. These choice criteria are summarized in table 7-1, which shows the choice of magnet under three common scenarios.

Table 7-1   Selecting Magnets

Innovation	Uncertainty (Uncertainty about how to satisfy or exceed customer requirements)	Process (Ability to specify the innovation process precisely in advance)	Impact (Potential value of the individual innovation)	*Selected Magnet*
Case 1	High	Low	High	*Global Lead Customer*
Case 2	Low	Medium	Medium	*Global Platform*
Case 3	Medium	High	Low	*Global Activity*

MANAGING MAGNETS

Put yourself in the shoes of a manager charged with coming up with an innovation by drawing on knowledge scattered around the world. You understand the potential for a new product or service, like a chip to power a car navigation system—what we called the entrepreneurial insight. You have chosen one of the three magnets—customer, platform, or activity—around which to build your innovation project. Your sensing organization has discovered and accessed a rich portfolio of knowledge that you may draw on, but this is still scattered around the world in documents, databases, and people's heads. You have a small team (we'll call it the "magnet team") and a limited budget.

So far, so good. But you now face three new challenges:

- How to identify and locate the knowledge you need to deploy.

- How to move the knowledge you need so that it can be shared by members of the magnet team.

- How to meld knowledge from different sources to create new insights and, from those new insights, develop innovative products and services.

Identifying the Dispersed Knowledge You Need

The first role of a magnet is to identify *what* pieces of knowledge are required by a particular metanational innovation. This transforms "not knowing what you don't know" into a different problem: prospecting for "what you know you don't know."

In some cases, the magnet guides the search to locate the missing pieces of knowledge (as when Seagate introduced ST to key external resources). In other instances, the location of the missing knowledge is in the public domain (such as Silicon Valley, Bangalore, or the other knowledge hotspots we described in chapter 2). Members of the magnet team may also use their previous experience to find missing knowledge (such as the experience the ST designers had gained with other partners).

The magnet will seek new knowledge from the sensing plane. Sometimes the missing piece of knowledge will require a search outside the company; sometimes it will be found inside existing operations. The activities in the sensing plane are therefore guided partially by an interactive and iterative dialogue between the magnets and the sensing units.

Moving Dispersed Knowledge

The next problem is figuring out how to move dispersed pieces of knowledge so that it can be shared by the magnet team responsible for creating innovative products and services. The burden of moving dispersed knowledge should rest on the magnet team, not on the sensing unit, which is dedicated to prospecting for new knowledge and accessing it. Therefore, the magnet team needs to include people who can act as brokers, facilitating the transfer of knowledge between the sensing unit and the magnet team.

The first step toward moving the pieces of knowledge is to understand the nature of that knowledge. Recall from chapter 5 the spectrum from simple to complex knowledge. Simple knowledge can be readily moved. Complex knowledge is often sticky and hard to transport.

Some knowledge can be simplified by making it explicit and then codifying it. Nokia engineers, for example, may not have written down the full performance specifications they need for the RISC chip inside a new mobile telephone. But by sitting down with an ARM engineer, they could codify the specifications in a set of algorithms that could then be emailed around the world.

As we saw in chapter 5, other types of knowledge cannot be easily simplified in these ways. If you emailed the customer requirements for a new car designed for the German autobahn to a Japanese engineer, much of what it takes would be lost in the translation. As Nissan discovered, to successfully share this knowledge, the Japanese engineer would have to experience the thrill of driving at 225 kilometers (around 150 miles) per hour down an autobahn. In this case, moving the knowledge means moving people, at least for a short period of time. Sharing even more complex knowledge, like an understanding of why a chip designer makes the tradeoffs that he or she does, requires personal interaction for months or even years.

Figure 7-1 sets out a framework for thinking about which bits of dispersed knowledge to move and how best to move them in the course of a metanational innovation project.

If both the required technology and the market understanding are simple, then sharing can take place at arm's length (the lower left quadrant of figure 7-1). Little content is lost by representing the knowledge as data and information. Thus, ICT can play an important role in moving the knowledge about so that it can be shared among the magnet team—over an Intranet or Extranet, for example.

When the success of the innovation depends on sharing complex market knowledge (such as an understanding of customer behavior that depends on a deep appreciation of the local context), then we should relocate our magnet team to where that knowledge sits. In this case, knowledge about technology should move to the market (the upper left quadrant of figure 7-1).

By contrast, if the technology is sticky (such as in the design of complex software involving large teams of engineers or in the case of biotechnology), then it makes sense to codify and move the market knowledge (such as customer needs or customer complaints) to the home of the complex technical knowledge (the lower right quadrant of figure 7-1).

Figure 7-1   How to Move Knowledge in the Metanational Innovation Process

	Low	High
High	Move information about the technology to where the market knowledge is	Connect and meld by rotating people and by temporary co-location
Low	Exchange information ("arm's-length," digital transfer sufficient)	Move information about the market to where the technology is

Complexity of Market Knowledge (vertical axis)

Complexity of Technology Knowledge (horizontal axis)

When both market and technical knowledge are inherently complex (the upper right quadrant of figure 7-1), as in understanding the drivers of functionality and cost in HDD electronic controllers, sharing knowledge will involve a succession of short periods of colocation (where members of the magnet team interact with the sensing unit to share the more sticky and fuzzy bits of knowledge). These interactions will need to be followed by extended periods of dispersed work assisted by regular videoconferencing (sort of a virtual colocation).

Unless absolutely necessary, the option of relocating people or bringing groups together so that they can be co-located for extended periods should be avoided. First, it is usually a very expensive approach. Second, a lot of subtle knowledge can be forgotten or lost when people are removed from their context to an unfamiliar one for long periods of time. Recall the failure of the Whirlpool design team (described in chapter 5) that tried to bring knowledge of the Asian markets with American technology by locating the entire team of Asian engineers and American engineers in Benton Harbor, Michigan.

Melding Knowledge

Knowledge melding is the third process that the magnet team needs to manage. The goal is to create new insights, and hence innovation, by melding knowledge that was previously separated by the tyranny of distance. Recall that we chose the expression *melding* because it shows we must *melt* and *weld* individual bits of knowledge into a coherent whole.

Melding is not simply juxtaposing pieces of knowledge as if they were the pieces of a puzzle or a Lego set. Melding is a process of transformation in which new knowledge is created by the interaction and integration of knowledge that was previously dispersed and diverse.

Think about the knowledge melding that needs to occur in creating a hit record. A member of PolyGram's IRC team takes a recording by a Venezuelan artist who may have global potential. The IRC professional sits down with his A&R counterparts who understand the tastes of consumers from the United States, the United Kingdom, and Japan. One suggests that the sound of the Spanish guitar is out of fashion and proposes replacing it with a synthesizer. Another says that will destroy the appeal of the work in Japan. After further discussion, they agree that inserting the sound of an electric guitar is the answer. A new rendition of the song is recorded. An innovation (albeit a small one), based on melding knowledge from dispersed locations, has emerged.

When we are all in the same room with a few pieces of knowledge and a relatively simple type of innovation, this melding process may seem trivial. Imagine, however, the melding challenges of producing a system chip or an Airbus—innovations based on millions of pieces of knowledge in the minds of hundreds of people in dozens of locations around the world.

A magnet team needs to attack these kinds of mammoth melding problems in bite-size pieces. One way to do this is to establish a *knowledge architecture*—the knowledge equivalent of a computer motherboard—that defines what pieces of knowledge need to be used where and how they interrelate with one another. Once this knowledge architecture has been agreed on, the magnet team can then alternate between working together, working in parallel, and working sequentially.

Some Guidelines

In the companies that we researched, we found that it was almost always necessary to bring key members of the magnet team together in one place to develop an initial knowledge architecture. In this early, "creative" phase, where most innovations remained uncertain and the respective knowledge required was unclear, melding by co-location of key individuals was required. As these meetings unfold, key members of the magnet team get to know one another personally, which enhances interpersonal trust and the effectiveness of technology-mediated communication later on. This process sometimes takes days, and sometimes weeks, of working together. Subjecting the innovation process to the tyranny of distance at this early stage was likely to end in failure.

Once an initial knowledge architecture has been agreed on, there are advantages in dividing tasks among the magnet team. First, those with complex knowledge that is deeply embedded in a local context are likely to be more effective if they work together back in that local environment. Second, dividing into subteams that can work in parallel has the advantage of minimizing the amount of knowledge to be transferred between geographically dispersed locations. This is because only the knowledge that pertains to the interface between the modules needs to be passed across the world between teams.

Where the magnet was a global lead customer, we observed that fairly continuous rounds of face-to-face interaction were required throughout the entire process. Travel costs were generally high.

Where the magnet was a global platform, the melding problem can be effectively simplified by dividing into subteams that focus on a particular module within the knowledge architecture (such as producing the GPS module for a car navigation system).

Where the magnet is a global activity, the melding problem is best divided into a sequence of steps, with different team members assigned to work on each step. Consistency through the entire innovation process then needs to be ensured by a single champion (such as the IRC representative at PolyGram) or by designing "rolling" teams in which some members join and others retire during the process.

Sometimes the melding of knowledge across subteams can be facilitated by the use of "scaffolding," which can take the form of a mockup, a set of preliminary specs, or a piece of software used by one part of the magnet team to simulate components that are being developed in parallel in another location.

A magnet team can take other steps to facilitate melding. Specifically, the team can:

- Modularize designs and explicitly specify interfaces.[2]

- Make all knowledge as explicit as possible.*

---

*Airbus, for example, puts enormous effort into codification during the design and development phase of its aircraft to facilitate melding of knowledge from different locations. The head of fleet maintenance at a major European airline noted that its MD11s were all slightly different, even though they were all the same model of aircraft. Each plane had its small idiosyncrasies: Some minor components were different, some cables were fitted in a different way, and so on. Airbuses, on the other hand, were all perfectly standard. They came with thorough documentation, including blueprints for all major subsystems and minor assemblies. This made

- Develop common design and engineering environments, providing a shared technical and procedural context (such as a technical/professional context that unites participants and transcends their local contexts).

- Provide mutual access and transparency across locations—including external partners.

- Exercise and enforce discipline in design changes and modifications and refrain from late design changes unless they are pre-planned or built into the knowledge architecture.

- Maintain and refresh local contacts with face-to-face interactions (as Charles Handy put it, "the more virtual is the organization, the more its people need to meet in person").[3]

THE MAGNET ORGANIZATION

Magnet teams will be the powerhouses of tomorrow's metanational organizations. Many such teams will operate simultaneously, each one charged with mobilizing knowledge scattered around the world to create innovative products, services, or processes. Together, this clutch of magnet teams will form a new suborganization that operates in the second of the three competitive arenas that we introduced in chapter 1.

The magnet organization will link the worlds of sensing and operations. The structure of the magnet organization is quite simple: Each magnet consists of a team of people—we called it the magnet team—that is itself dispersed, with subteams in several locations around the world, wherever the knowledge is complex and difficult to move. The

---

(continued) maintenance easier and cheaper. The needs of knowledge-sharing and melding between Airbus locations had resulted in added documentation and greater standardization. As a spin-off benefit, this had helped to reduce maintenance costs. Conversely, with most of its development, major component production, and assembly co-located, MD's planes could be produced with less documentation and standardization as variations were easily communicated and understood. The seamless knowledge combination and the simplicity of knowledge management under co-location, where no magnets are required, can have unexpected downsides.

vertical links—between each magnet and the sensing and operations planes—are very strong. The lateral links with other magnets are few and ad hoc. Remember that the sensing plane should be tightly plugged in to the outside world in local environments. By contrast, magnets are linked most closely to other parts of the organization and particularly to top management.

Top Management Roles

Magnets in the metanational require a lot of top management attention. Top management must play a role in making sure magnets get established, staffing the magnet organization, setting objectives and performance measures for magnet teams, and defining how they relate to the rest of the organization (the sensing and operations planes). Differentiation of organizational roles is key. A magnet might be physically housed in an existing R&D laboratory, for example, but its assignment must not be confused with other R&D work that uses only locally available technologies, or the role of which is to adapt a global platform to local conditions. Although these are legitimate R&D activities, they belong to the operations plane, not to the world of magnets and metanational innovation.

Setting Up Magnets. The CEO and the top management team can play an important, and direct, role in setting up magnets. But they should also create the conditions that allow for magnets to emerge spontaneously throughout the organization.

In some cases, a member of top management has the entrepreneurial insight about the potential for innovation by connecting dispersed pieces of knowledge. The obvious next step is to set up a magnet team, charged with realizing the potential from that insight.

Even if the entrepreneurial insight comes from elsewhere, senior management needs to be directly involved in setting up the magnet when it takes the form of a global activity (as in the case of Nestlé's Nestec or PolyGram's IRCs). This is because magnets based around an activity are generally long-lived (or even permanent) structures and often require the commitment of substantial resources.

Depending on the company's culture, incentive systems, and investment approval process, it may also be necessary for senior management to take an active role in setting up magnets around global lead customers and global platforms. In this case, the company needs a process to ensure that senior management receives a steady stream of requests for budget allocations to get new magnets started.

Promoting the Emergence and Effectiveness of Magnet Teams. Senior management can create an organizational context that promotes the emergence of magnets and facilitates their effectiveness. This means crafting an environment that recreates some of the dialogue and shared understanding that would happen naturally if people were co-located, rather than being dispersed around the world. It means building a climate in which dispersed individuals recognize that they can achieve more by working together than alone.

We observed four sets of initiatives that were important in promoting this goal:

1. **Promote mutual respect.** Most people are naturally unwilling to place their trust in those from far-away places and cultures that they neither know nor understand. Without a climate of trust and respect for what others can contribute, the "first date" between dispersed pieces of knowledge will probably also be the last. The development of trust is greatly enhanced by opportunities for frequent communication and socialization.

2. **Discourage knowledge hoarding.** Senior managers must demonstrate that knowledge hoarding is the route to a stalled career, not a means to promotion. Tournament cultures in which managerial rhetoric is full of defiance and secrecy, thus impeding the mobilization of knowledge, must not be tolerated. Simple things, like how knowledge is stored and communicated, can make a big difference. Several years ago at IBM, for instance, many documents were kept only as "foils" for use on overhead projectors. Managers shared them only as slide presentations in face-to-face encounters. The flow of knowledge was therefore reduced to a trickle.

   STMicroelectronics took proactive steps to discourage knowledge hoarding. The importance of working closely with lead customers was clearly spelled out. Progress was reviewed in regular meetings with the customer at senior, divisional, and business-unit levels. ST sites were always open to the customer's personnel. The relationship was often governed within an open-books framework, and each party was aware of its impact on the other.

3. **Create an appropriate language.** Even with the right climate, knowledge flows may be impeded by mutual incomprehension. Particular attention should be given to the language used to express common goals and common grounds. The use of metaphors can be tricky in an international setting, as they are often very context-dependent. For example, do you understand the expression "That's not cricket!" voiced by an executive in a business meeting? Or an American project manager who says to his team, "It's a third and long situation!"?[4]

   On the other hand, well-chosen metaphors can be powerful tools in the quest to mobilize complex knowledge from dispersed sources. Acer's CEO, Stan Shih, for example, constantly used a fast-food metaphor to convey the complex idea of a new type of supply chain.

4. **Build a rich information and communication infrastructure.** The flow of simple knowledge can be greatly improved by good information and communication systems. If a piece of knowledge can be codified, stored, and transferred as information, this will be much more efficient than using time and travel expenses to achieve the same goal. Beyond this, a broadband corporate intranet can support the work of magnet teams by providing a virtual space with electronic chat rooms and forums, posted news, or intelligent search agents capable of finding knowledge in the company's knowledge database. This potential can be further extended through extranets that connect the company to a selected number of suppliers and customers.

Staffing Magnets

Magnet teams need a special breed of individual: people who are comfortable working in the uncertain environment of innovation, people who can work in virtual teams with only infrequent face-to-face interactions, people who don't mind knowing that their current role may be temporary and transitory. Magnets also need a special kind of leadership.

Magnet Champions. Magnets need champions with the characteristics of internal entrepreneurs who will promote new initiatives and unprecedented knowledge combinations. These are people who create value by imagining how to combine dispersed knowledge in new ways in the service of innovation. Young, high-potential managers, who want the opportunity to prove themselves and advance their careers, are one fertile group in which to look for potential magnet champions.

Magnet champions need top management support as they face several distinct challenges. First, they need to obtain resources on the basis of innovation potential. In most companies, this means budget allocations that sidestep the usual approval process designed for investments in operations, not innovation. The magnets' budgets are actually like investments in R&D. A separate pool of internal funds (such as a venture fund) needs to be set aside to finance them.

At the same time, magnet champions will perform best when their goals stretch somewhat beyond the investment funding they have available. Scarcity will encourage the magnet champion to leverage all available knowledge, both inside and outside the company, in the service of innovation. "Hungry" champions have the incentive to mobilize knowledge and resources available from all over the world. The death knell for a magnet is having enough resources to become an isolated innovation project. This would defeat the very rationale for its existence.

Second, magnet champions need to see themselves as *process managers* in a virtual, global business. They must not view themselves as barons in charge of an organizational unit. They are subject to business performance objectives—to deliver an innovation that can be leveraged by the operations network. But they achieve these objectives by cooperating with others, and ultimately by making themselves redundant, not by building a permanent organization.

Magnet champions need the full entrepreneurial skill set, including personal leadership and charisma, tolerance for uncertainty, capabilities in problem formulation and synthesis, the ability to grasp the nature of the knowledge involved, and sensitivity to culture and context. They must be able to manage informal, temporary processes and teams inside large organizations. The best magnet champions will be rather cosmopolitan people, with several years of direct experience in national cultures distant from their own.

Other Members of the Magnet Team. The core members of the magnet team must be able to work across cultures and across organizational boundaries. They must be tolerant of ambiguity and must understand how to influence other people without the need for formal control. Interpersonal skills should be a prime consideration in composing magnet teams. Ideally, team members will have established their own informal, international networks within the company. They will be mature in their dealings with others, willing to travel, and have a broad technical competence as well as specific knowledge to contribute to the team.

As we mentioned earlier, some of the magnet team members will need to act as brokers between the sensing organization and their magnet. These people should be chosen for their knowledge of the main local contexts from which the magnet needs to draw local knowledge. They need to be empathetic, sensitive to diversity, and, perhaps above all, persistent.

Performance Measures and Incentives

The magnet team's dealings with internal and external parties cannot be treated as transactions. Magnets create innovations. As such, the work of the magnet team is ambiguous and uncertain. Like any creative process, it involves dead-ends and false dawns. It requires patience, partnership, and goodwill. The balance between team members' knowledge contributions and the benefits they reap must be calculated over the long term.

Recognizing these conditions, we believe that metanationals should institute "zero transfer prices" for knowledge (the value of which is naturally impossible to ascertain anyway), so that cash or profit credits do not change hands when knowledge is shared. This approach encourages the holders of knowledge to exchange it without worrying about the frictions of transactional accounting. Instead, knowledge sharing becomes an implicit, long-term contract in which successive favors are given with the broad expectation that at some stage they will be returned—all of which will be positive for the organization as a whole. This means that a metanational should link a significant proportion of total staff incentives to the overall performance of the company (say, stock price), as opposed to narrowly defined geographical or business-unit performance.

The magnet team is ultimately responsible for delivering an innovation that the operations network can exploit for global profit. Three main categories of reward are possible here:

- Offer the magnet champion and team members a share in the value of the innovation they create (either through shadow equity or royalties on the eventual sale of the innovation).

- Base bonuses on the successful adoption of the innovation by the operating units who must leverage it globally.

- Take note of successful magnet leadership, contributions to a magnet team, as a positive factor in future promotion. In tomorrow's metanational winners, successful participation in a magnet team may be a pathway to a senior management job.

Managing the Life Cycle of Magnets

Most magnets are, by their very nature, temporary structures: The day will come when diminishing returns set in, and the innovation capacity of that magnet is spent. Some magnets will be short-lived, and others may have a productive life of decades. Moreover, rather than simply being disbanded, many magnets will evolve into new roles. Smooth management of the life cycle of any magnet is key to maximizing its potential contribution to metanational advantage.

The optimal evolution of a magnet depends on whether its innovation process is replicable. In other words, how well can the existing magnet undertake a new cycle of innovation? Is the innovation process so case-specific that we need to create a new magnet each time we undertake a new innovation? Contrast PolyGram's IRC hit machine with STMicroelectronics' development of a specific system chip for every new application.

In PolyGram's IRC or Nestlé's Nestec, each innovation (a new record or a product improvement) adds incrementally to the company's performance. But the same innovation process and the same magnet can be replicated over and over again. Where the magnet is a global activity, it is likely to be a long-term structure that produces a continuous flow of small innovations. It needs to be managed and staffed as a permanent part of the organization.

By contrast, ST's relationship with Seagate as a magnet is hardly replicable. The magnet thrives for as long as Seagate remains a lead customer with the ability to guide the metanational innovation. When it can no longer bring together dispersed, leading-edge knowledge, the magnet should be disbanded. The customer relationship changes from an innovation partnership to a potentially very important source of sales and profits.

ST's relationship with Seagate has, in fact, undergone such a life-cycle evolution. Seagate acted as an effective magnet for over a decade. The life of Seagate's role as a magnet was long because of the key role it played in attracting knowledge to create successive waves of systems-on-a-chip for the HDD industry. As ST effectively learned HDD system know-how with Seagate, however, and as the HDD industry knowledge became better articulated over the years (published by university research laboratories, then taught in engineering schools, and so on), the effectiveness of Seagate as a magnet diminished. In some cases, magnets open up a new, wider domain of potential innovation. The original magnet recycles itself to reinvigorate its innovation potential. ST's car navigation system platform, for example, not only acted as a magnet for this application, but it also spawned new projects and products in car multimedia (such as digital radio, digital video, back-seat computer games for kids, mobile telephony speech-recognition, and Internet access inside the car).

Finally, one type of magnet (such as a global lead customer) may morph into another (such as a global platform). When a company gains sufficient understanding of a particular customer application, it can look at alternative ways of servicing that market. That may lead it to replace its original magnet—in this case the lead customer—with a global platform or even a global activity. Once ST gained a deep understanding of HDD systems, for example, it was able to initiate a new innovation project—this one based on a global platform for using HDD technology inside the TV set-top box that allows the user to record television programs for later viewing.

BEYOND MOBILIZING

An effective magnet organization is able to attract knowledge from the sensing organization, focus this knowledge on a clear innovation objective, and create innovative products and services by mobilizing knowledge that was locally imprisoned.

Magnets form the missing link between metanational learning and global operations. Building an effective magnet organization is essential to winning in the global knowledge economy.

To have an impact on the bottom line and create shareholder value, however, the innovations that magnets create must be handed over to managers and staff in the operations network—the people who know how to get from prototype to full-scale global rollout, who know how to drive down costs and how to build sales volume.

Separating the sensing and magnet organizations from operations has a massive advantage. It allows people to focus on their specific roles: prospecting for and accessing new knowledge and mobilizing that knowledge to create innovation. It means that top management involvement, structures, staffing, and performance measures and incentives can all be designed specifically to suit the needs of the separate sensing and magnet organizations.

The final step in metanational innovation entails passing the baton to the operating network, to create the conditions in which the day-to-day operations can leverage innovations to maximize the return on investment in a global market. In chapter 8, we address the challenges of relaying innovations into the operating network and leveraging them to create wealth.

Chapter 8

Harvesting Value from Metanational Innovation

I N   O R D E R   T O   create real shareholder value, metanational innovations must ultimately be deployed to enhance the bottom line. To achieve this, the successful metanational organization quickly passes its innovations to the operating network, where they can be leveraged and exploited for profit on a global scale. The process requires some new ways of thinking about the operating network and its relationships with the sensing and mobilizing organizations.

In this chapter, we explore three critical challenges that companies will face as they unlock the broad global potential of metanational innovations:

- How to conceive and manage an efficient metanational operations network.

- How to foster the interactions between the operations network and other parts of the organization (particularly within the "mobilizing plane" that we described in chapter 7).

- Creating and maintaining a corporate culture that induces and supports the global deployment of innovation.

DESIGNING AN EFFICIENT METANATIONAL
OPERATIONS NETWORK

The design of an efficient metanational operations network starts from its overarching goal: to leverage a stream of innovative products and services in markets across the globe, guided by the principles of operational efficiency, flexibility, and financial discipline.

The operations network in a metanational winner will share many familiar characteristics of today's multinationals. It will provide production, distribution, sales, marketing, and service capabilities. It will be able to balance global efficiency against local adaptation. This is hardly surprising—after all, the metanational operations network is fulfilling many of the same functions used to project and adapt a global corporate formula. There is a large body of managerial experience and literature on how to build and manage multinational operations.[1]

But the optimal operations network for a metanational differs fundamentally from that of a traditional multinational. The differences stem from the fact that, unlike traditional multinationals, the metanational looks beyond countries or nation-states as the basic building blocks of its strategy. As we have seen throughout this book, the metanational views its world as consisting of two canvases.

One global canvas is dotted with pockets of specialist knowledge that it can access and mobilize to fuel its innovation process. A second canvas is dotted with distinctive pockets of operational capability and capacity that it can use to exploit and leverage the innovations it creates. From this second canvas, dotted with distinctive pockets of operational capability, the metanational assembles its operations network.

As a result, the metanational operations network will differ from its traditional multinational cousins in three fundamental ways:

- It will be organized around sites (or locations) and their associated teams of people and capabilities, rather than around national subsidiaries.

- Its managers will "think local and act global," not the other way around.

- Influence, recognition, and reward will derive not from size, weight of assets, and people, or even from direct profitability, but rather from the unique contribution each site makes to the goal of leveraging metanational innovations globally.

Sites Are the Foundation

Because metanationals are looking for the best operating capabilities available anywhere in the world, they must think in terms of sites or specific locations. (We sometimes call them "capability sites" to emphasize this point.) It doesn't make sense, for example, to talk about drawing on capabilities for the large-scale production of software from "India," nor about accessing marketing capabilities from "America." The choice for software production might be between Seattle and Bangalore. For marketing capabilities, the alternatives might be New York or London.

The metanational seeks a distinctive set of operating capabilities that can help it squeeze maximum value out of its innovations or reduce its costs. Rather than location, it is the quality and depth of capability that counts. These qualities may reflect the accumulated experience (such as the carpet-making skills in Dalton, Georgia) or the natural geographical advantages of the site (such as the advantages of Rotterdam or Singapore as logistics centers). The country in which the site happens to be located is of subsidiary importance.

The primary operational unit in the metanational operations network, then, is a site and its mix of people and capabilities—not a national subsidiary. STMicroelectronics' site in Agrate, near Milan, for example, includes capabilities in marketing and product design, R&D in process technology, and front-end fabrication of mixed power circuits available to contribute to the global operations. Another site in Italy, Catania, represents a bundle of distinctive capabilities such as R&D in power transistors and RF devices and production of FLASH memories. Perhaps paradoxically, the global knowledge economy will distinguish individual sites for their preeminence in specific capabilities. This is a far cry from a homogenized global soup in which all local differences disappear.

Metanationals will think of each of their sites as a bundle of capabilities, including local suppliers and partners as well as the operations they own in any location. The historic distinctions between "internal" and "external" will become less and less relevant. The boundaries of the company will blur, as access takes precedence over ownership in a particular capability site.[2]

Given the costs of coordinating between sites, it will make sense for a metanational to select the minimum number of sites from which it can access all of the distinct bundles of capabilities it needs.

Assembling World-Class Capabilities. Each site wins a place in the operations network because of the unique bundle of operational capabilities it can contribute. These may be a mix of cost-competitive manufacturing, logistics or service capabilities, unique marketing skills, expertise in tailoring a global platform to a particular market, distribution capabilities, and so on. People working in the site will enjoy the benefits of co-location described in chapter 5. They will share a common context. Over time, they will come to share a common local culture and identity. This shared context and values, along with the possibilities for chance encounters and frequent, easy interaction, will enhance the exchange of knowledge and the integration of capabilities within a site. For these reasons, it will generally make sense for a metanational to concentrate its operations (but not its sensing units) in a particular location and a single site, rather than having them scattered around a city or local region.

An Interdependent Approach. Each site earns its continued place in the network by contributing unique services to the ongoing goal of leveraging innovations from the magnet organization. This has three important implications. First, it means that each site in the operations network accepts and values its interdependence with others. No single location will have all of the capabilities and activities necessary to run an independent operation, so there is no place for national fiefdoms in the metanational operations network.[3] This means that the site needs a mix of people who can interact smoothly with other parts of the operations network. Sites with only one type of highly specialized staff are likely to be less well-equipped for this kind of interaction. Most sites will therefore house a bundle of capabilities, consisting of the various technologies, functions, professions, and skills of the people at the site.

Openness and Flexibility. The second implication is that each site must be receptive and flexible enough to adjust to the flow of innovations it has a duty to help leverage and scale. It must communicate easily and freely with the magnet organization. There is no place for sites that try to avoid interference and disruption, as their raison d'être is to help every discontinuous and potentially disruptive innovation attain maximum success in the global market.

This is one reason why future metanationals will increasingly use subcontractor and partner sites as key components of their operations networks. A network of outsiders will often have greater receptivity and flexibility—because they will see other sites as their customer rather than as siblings. They provide a source of new capabilities. Outsiders may also reduce the capital that the metanational needs to invest. For example, ARM avoided the massive capital required to build a large-scale chip fabrication capacity and instead opted to rely entirely on partners that could turn its designs into final silicon chips. By licensing its designs and taking a royalty on each RISC chip that its partners produced and sold, ARM gained access to operational capabilities in manufacturing, physical distribution, and development tools and software to turn its designs into operational chips. The question ARM asked in designing this virtual operations network was, "How can we best leverage a stream of innovation on a global scale?" The answer, in ARM's case, was through its unique set of licensing and partnership agreements.

Continuous Local Learning. A third important implication is that, because each site sees its value in terms of a unique contribution to the network, it will constantly seek to deepen and renew its distinctive local capabilities. Unlike sites within traditional multinationals, whose secret aim is often to become a self-standing replica of the headquarters, sites in the metanational will recognize that their value comes from distinctiveness, not imitation. If a site no longer has a unique contribution to make, it will be closed, or—in the case of suppliers or alliance partners—the arrangement will be unwound.

Think Local, Act Global

Collectively, these characteristics create a new mentality for site managers in a metanational operations network. Their job is to think local and act global. This is not a misprint. Winners in the global knowledge economy will often have to *reverse* yesterday's "think global, act local" aphorism, popularized by Percy Barnevik, when he was CEO of ABB, and many other business leaders.

In a metanational, each site manager sees her role as maximizing the site's distinctive contribution to the overall goal of leveraging innovations globally. This means thinking local about how to develop unique, site-specific capabilities that can contribute to the global operations network. That might be, for example, the world's lowest-cost manufacturing capacity. It might be the most effective sales capability for a particular customer or market segment. Or it might be the R&D capability to turn a global platform into a successful local product to name just some of the possibilities.

Each site's role, and its long-term survival, depends on being able to contribute operational capabilities that are better or more efficient at leveraging metanational innovations than other sites around the world. Therefore, each site is likely to be strongly rooted in the strengths of its local cluster. Managers will continuously seek to improve their site's distinctive operational capabilities by harnessing the potential of customers, local authorities, suppliers, or other important stakeholders.

Take the example of PolyGram's local site managers, who were responsible for promoting, marketing, and distributing potential global hit records that came to them through the IRC organization. These site managers will be most effective if they have built strong relationships with local radio stations, if they have created efficient distribution arrangements to make sure the records are on retailers' shelves on the day the record is launched, and so on.

The site managers use the comparative advantage of their location to build and improve some unique operational competence. They contribute their site's specialized capabilities to the global network. They are responsible for ensuring the management of equipment, technologies, processes, and staff located at their site. Their jobs include the training and motivation of staff, day-to-day management of suppliers or partners working either on the site or at nearby locations, and maintaining facilities and infrastructure to support those working at the site.

Socially and professionally, site managers' most important ties are local. They take their pride and cues from the local community. In personal terms, site managers need frequent opportunities to interact with their colleagues from other sites, in a spirit of exchange and cooperation. But this is quite different from a traditional multinational, whose projection-adaptation formula requires a cadre of expatriates eager to cycle from job to job, from country to country, and between headquarters and subsidiaries.

The metanational wants site managers who, while ensuring what their own site can contribute to the whole, are experts at squeezing the greatest distinctiveness out of their local environment. Unlike those who work in the sensing or magnet organizations, site managers in the operations network may not aspire to cosmopolitan careers, but rather prefer to concentrate on building local capabilities. The performance of the manager of a differentiated site is likely to be site-specific. The same individual transferred to another site, with different competencies and in another context, may lose effectiveness.*

Reward Uniqueness and Interdependence

To perform this trick of thinking locally and acting globally, site managers and their staff need to be both proud of their local capabilities and committed to the global cause. This means that the incentive systems for site personnel must measure and reward both uniqueness and interdependence. Influence, recognition, and reward must come from the uniqueness of the contribution to leveraging innovative products and service globally. This means jettisoning the traditional scorecard by which many of today's multinational sub-

---

*Depending on local cultures, site managers may envision their future as an independent entrepreneur subcontracting work from a metanational company (Italy), as moving to public service (Singapore, France), or as moving to another, more thriving corporation (Spain). Relatively few nationalities will see site managers rotate across countries, as Indians do in Unilever. Indeed, the more uniquely differentiated and locally rooted the site, the less easily transferable the managers in the metanational.

sidiaries measure their success: local profits, size, weight of assets, and numbers of people.

The metanational must first be explicit about the unique contribution each site should make to the operations network. It then needs to measure and reward this unique contribution against the standard of world-class performance. Sites may be given targets for quality and productivity improvement, or for their ability to attract skilled and motivated employees from their local region. Assessing a site's contribution will also involve measuring the speed and cost at which the site absorbs innovations from the magnet organization.

Finally, sites must be measured on their share of value added in the total selling price of the metanational's product or service. This will be equal to their total costs (including costs for local suppliers and partners), less the cost of inputs they receive from other sites, all expressed as a percentage of the final selling price of the product or service to which they contribute. (Any tendency to bolster this figure by incurring unjustified costs will, of course, be countered by the need to meet benchmarks for world-class operating efficiency.)

Generally, it will not be possible to measure the direct profitability of a site. Any profit measure would depend on the artifice of transfer prices between sites within the metanational operations network. In most cases, these transfer prices would be highly arbitrary, as externally verifiable market values for a site's contribution will be impossible to find.

In the absence of a direct profit target, the site will find other ways to celebrate its winning contributions to the global network. These will include recognition for the local staff, as well as suppliers, partners, and other local stakeholders that have contributed to the site's success in furthering the metanational's global goals. The site's reputation for reliability and its willingness to contribute as a partner in the operations network will be important considerations in judging and rewarding a site manager's success.

MANAGING THE METANATIONAL
OPERATIONS NETWORK

Having abandoned the traditional structure of profit-oriented national subsidiaries, the metanational faces a new challenge: How do we manage an operations network comprising a set of individual sites, each offering a unique bundle of capabilities? How should these "dots on the capabilities canvas" be coordinated to form a network? What new measures will be required? How will the operations network interact with the rest of the metanational organization?

Promote Flexible Configurations

While sites form the basic operating units, the metanational's overarching goal is to create shareholder value by exploiting its innovations across global markets. This requires an operations network that can be flexibly reconfigured to squeeze the most leverage from any innovation in the shortest possible time. Actively managing the network's configuration is a key role for senior operating managers within the metanational.

When STMicroelectronics set out to leverage the innovative system chip it had originally designed for Seagate, it didn't use the traditional projector's approach of rolling out the new product sequentially across a set of national subsidiaries. Instead, it asked, "How can we use our existing operational capabilities, augmented by those of our potential partners, to leverage this innovation? Which specialist capabilities do we need? Where are these capabilities?" In answering these questions, ST assembled a unique configuration of operational capabilities specifically for the HDD chip innovation. A different operational configuration was assembled for the innovative chip used in ST's car navigation system.

Interestingly, this is similar to the approach used by construction companies when they put together a consortium of players with different capabilities and experience to bid on a large civil engineering project, or that an investment bank might deploy as it assembles a team for a complex M&A transaction. By contrast, traditional multinationals—especially those in manufacturing industries—seldom exhibit this degree of flexibility in reconfiguring their operations network according to the specific needs of each innovation.

This kind of flexibility in the operations network is obviously not easy to achieve. It is constrained by investments in fixed assets. But it is also limited by the way most managers think about their role, and by the organization's power politics. Senior managers need to work to remove these limitations.

Measure Success Globally

The test of success in leveraging a metanational innovation is global profitability, as measured by customer or market segment. Many customers, products, or business areas will require global strategies designed to win against multinational competitors. In these cases, the metanational will need a set of managers who are accountable for global results.

Profit and loss responsibility in the metanational will lie with these global units; they manage the bottom line. They will draw from the capability sites as required to deliver their sales and profit targets and to satisfy customers. They manage global integration of the metanational's operating capabilities.

In deciding whether to create a global unit, top management must assess the need for coordination across individual sites. Take the example of global customers who demand consistent service levels and pricing everywhere they operate in the world. If the metanational deals with customers of this type, it will need a global account management team. By contrast, if customers are only local, then each one can be handled by the local site.

In most metanational businesses, there are large flows of components or information between sites as they contribute their distinctive value-added to the global operation. It is therefore likely that the metanational will have a unit responsible for management of the global supply chain.

Managers in many of today's multinationals will be familiar with global profitability measures. They will also be aware of the age-old tension between maximizing global profitability today (which requires maximum efficiency) and ensuring long-term growth (which requires successive waves of innovation). This tension will be particularly acute for metanationals, as their continued competitive success depends on their ability to leverage a stream of metanational innovations—each of which is potentially disruptive to the operations network.

To counter the built-in resistance to innovations, metanationals will create global performance measures that demand specific contributions from each operations site. PolyGram, for example, set separate performance targets for the sales revenue and profits generated in local subsidiaries from metanational repertoire (from the IRCs), as distinct from local acts sold only in their local markets.

Create Global Support Functions

Other global units will look after services such as accounting, treasury, tax, and administration. Some financial and administrative functions may require national corporate entities to satisfy local legal and accounting regulations. But the financial, tax, and legal affairs of a metanational are optimized on a global basis.

Metanationals must also manage all-important relationships with governments and politicians at national, region, and international levels. They may, for example, have a "senior vice president, China" or a "deputy chairman for Europe." But these are not geographic management roles in the traditional multinational sense. They do not involve profit and loss responsibility. They are the metanational's equivalent of the U.S. State Department or the British Commonwealth and Foreign Office: high-level ambassadorial positions concerned with building and maintaining relationships with important stakeholders. Taken together, they comprise another team among the global operating units.

Managing Handoffs from the Mobilizing Plane

Even the best-designed metanational operations network will face a tension between promoting efficiency and operational stability, on the one hand, and absorbing a stream of valuable but probably disruptive metanational innovations on the other. When innovation needs to be transplanted into an organization whose lifeblood is operational efficiency, the equivalent of tissue rejection is likely to result. Our next task, therefore, is to help managers avoid this problem by adopting mechanisms that promote the smooth *transfer* (or *relaying,* a term we chose to capture the idea of a *handoff*) of innovations from the magnet organization into the operating network.

In many traditional multinationals, the operations network is accustomed to absorbing innovations that come from headquarters or large and powerful subsidiaries—parts of the organization they either respect or fear. In metanationals, the innovation is often stateless—it comes from a magnet organization that is often virtual and generally lacks the traditional weight that comes from large amounts of sales, assets, or people. More challenging still, the innovation may reflect technologies or market needs that were discovered in places that the operating network regards as peripheral to the business.

Consider the experience of Glaxo Wellcome (GW). As mentioned in chapter 6, GW acquired Affymax, which had set up and developed a drug discovery platform that combined specialized robotics and other advanced techniques. GW wanted to use this new process platform to enhance its mainstream drug discovery and development operations around the world. This required integrating the innovative Affymax approach into GW's highly developed procedures and routines for discovering, testing, and launching drugs on time and on budget.*

The new combinational chemistry platform could increase a lab's testing capabilities from one compound per chemist per week to thousands of compounds in a week. But relaying this new platform from Affymax in California to GW's laboratories in Europe was not just a matter of transferring a set of manuals and equipment. Instead, it required a complete change in the way the laboratory operated—a change comparable to the shift from a craft to automated mass production in manufacturing. In addition, it required biologists and chemists—two groups that use different techniques and approaches—to work much more closely together.

These transfer issues must be actively managed in a metanational. The key responsibilities lie in two places: at the senior corporate level and within the magnet organization.

Top Management Responsibilities

Top management can use a number of approaches to promote smooth handoffs of metanational innovations into the operations network:

---

*It is worth noting here that although drug development and testing is classified as R&D, it is actually part of GW's operations plane because it uses well-articulated routines repeated millions of time and leverages existing knowledge that is co-located. Despite common perceptions, therefore, the drug discovery process has more in common with a manufacturing line than it does with blue-sky research in the proverbial "garage."

- **Creating wider strategic context around the innovation.** GW's senior management, for example, positioned the need to embrace combinatorial chemistry as part of a wider effort to improve both the effectiveness and the efficiency of the drug development and testing processes. It became a cornerstone of the plan to rejuvenate the company following the expiry of key patents.

- **Signaling the value of the innovation.** GW had invested over $500 million in acquiring Affymax. That very large commitment—a huge sum of money, even by GW's standards—was a very powerful signal about how much value was expected from leveraging this innovation. When coupled with significant investment of senior management time, it sent a message that even reluctant scientists could not ignore.

  In the case of STMicroelectronics, CEO Pasquale Pistorio took every available opportunity to reinforce the potential value of metanational innovations created in partnership with "strategic customers"—all of his presentations included a slide on these initiatives. And he meets those partners regularly.

- **Creating a demonstration effect by nominating the most receptive sites as the "pioneers."** Not every site in the operations network will be equally receptive to a particular type of innovation. Verona was the most receptive site in GW because it was small, looking for opportunities to differentiate itself from larger sites, and ambitious for a bigger role in GW's network of drug development centers. On the other hand, the French center outside Paris was the least receptive. It had existing collaboration agreements with French partners in combinatorial chemistry and saw Affymax's technologies both as a threat to its differentiation and as a potential embarrassment in its relationships with local partners.

  Starting with a receptive site provides momentum for a metanational innovation and helps prove to doubters that it can be leveraged successfully. This can create a demonstration effect that gives confidence to more reluctant sites and pressures them to become involved in leveraging the innovation. It also provides a powerful argument against the classic not-invented-here syndrome, allowing senior management to drive home the question "If it works in the United States and Italy, why won't it work for you?"

- **Adjusting organizational structures and processes in the operating network.** It may be necessary to change the structure or processes of the operating network to increase the odds that innovations will be absorbed. Recall from chapter 5 that Ciba-Geigy asked already overloaded sponsors to incorporate innovative drug delivery technologies from Alza in California. The result depended largely on the sponsors' degree of personal interest. When sponsors saw delivery systems as important—for instance, for patches—strong commitment was forthcoming. When they failed to see the benefits or saw them as a disruptive challenge to their own efforts, commitment rapidly waned. By contrast, GW restructured its operating organization to aid the transfer of innovations in combinatorial chemistry. In its Verona laboratories, for example, the formerly separate chemistry and biology laboratories were combined (or "put under the same roof," as one senior manager termed it). This brought together different operational capabilities that were required to make use of the innovative combinatorial techniques and equipment. At its larger and more traditional Stevenage operation, located close to headquarters in the United Kingdom, GW created an almost perfect replica of the Affymax environment, with similar equipment and processes, but staffed with local GW scientists. This provided a test site that allowed local staff to explore the innovative combinatorial chemistry procedures and appreciate its value on their own turf, away from the hype of California—and effectively keeping small, entrepreneurial Affymax ring-fenced from the big, efficient GW.

  Absorbing an innovation generally requires not only mastering the new knowledge but also "unlearning" existing rules of thumb, mindsets, and operating processes. If the amount of unlearning is substantial, it may be beyond the capability and motivation of individuals who see it as destroying their life's work. As a consequence, some personnel changes may be necessary before an operation can absorb the innovation.

In some cases, the operating capabilities necessary to leverage the innovation may be so different, or the adjustments so disruptive, that it may make sense to create a separate unit or network. ST used this approach in leveraging its car navigation system innovations, in which, unlike HDD chips, the required operational capabilities were substantially new and different from existing operations (they included Japanese subcontractors for special chip packages, dedicated sales and customer services forces, a divisional advocate, and so on). Creating a new business unit also has the advantage of tying the success of operations firmly to the innovation. Such a new or separate organization may be temporary (until the innovation reaches critical mass), or it may represent the launch of a new and permanent structure.

- **Budgeting extra resources for full commercialization.** The operations network needs an explicit investment budget to cover the learning and setup costs it will incur. All too often, companies that are happy to allocate budgets for creating innovations fail to budget the right resources for leveraging them.

This may seem a heavy set of responsibilities for senior management to add to its existing burden. To put it in perspective, however, remember that major metanational innovations—particularly those coming from lead customer or global platform magnets—happen relatively infrequently. Even a large company may expect to handle no more than a dozen such significant innovations in a year.

The Magnet Organization's Responsibilities

The magnet organization, as the champion of a metanational innovation, also plays an important role in facilitating a smooth transfer to the operations plane. Specific initiatives that management and staff of the magnet organization can take include the following:

- **Selecting the right mix of carriers.** Recall, from chapter 5, that knowledge itself cannot move from place to place. What moves between two locations is a *carrier*: a document, a product, a person, or a piece of equipment, for example, which represents the knowledge. Relaying an innovation also involves a transfer of knowledge. If the carrier fails to transmit the bundle of knowledge needed to grasp the essence of an innovation, the operations network will misunderstand it. Sponsors from the magnet organization, therefore, must choose appropriate carriers to convey the knowledge inherent in their innovation.

Let's go back to the example of Affymax's innovative combinatorial chemistry techniques and processes. In relaying this innovation to its mainstream operations, it might have been tempting for GW simply to ship operating manuals and equipment straight from Affymax to the GW development and testing laboratories. Instead, GW sent young chemistry scientists from its various labs in Britain, Italy, and the United States to Affymax in California. There they spent a few months actually building the machines they would subsequently use back at home. These scientists then literally took "their" machines back to their mother laboratories. By pairing "man and machine" as the knowledge carrier, GW was able to transfer both the explicit knowledge (largely embodied in the machine and its manuals) and the tacit, complex knowledge about how to approach drug discovery using combinatorial chemistry techniques. In the process, GW also created a sense of buy-in among the scientists who would use the innovative technology.

At PolyGram, the carrier of a potential global hit to the operating network was not just a compact disc master but a complete package, including a promotional team made up of the IRC magnet champion plus marketing professionals and PR experts. Often the artists themselves participated by performing a concert tour.

- **Getting in tune.** There is considerable learning involved in relaying an innovation into the operations plane. While we can learn from a one-way barrage of wisdom, learning is more effective in a two-way dialogue. The sponsor from the magnet organization needs to recognize and respond to these considerations. This means fostering a two-way dialogue that helps the sponsor and the operations staff develop a shared understanding of the potential benefits and challenges involved in adopting and exploiting an innovation. This objective will be facilitated by rotating members of the magnet team through the operations network so that they get personally involved in the process of leveraging the innovation. Likewise, operations staff can be assigned to work within the magnet team on the final stages of developing the innovation, as GW did when it involved operational staff in the final phase of building the machines for combinatorial chemistry. Recall that at ARM, two-way licensing agreements with the chip manufacturers ensured constant interaction between the people designing a new global standard for RISC chips and those who would fabricate and distribute them.

• **Getting in synch.** The sponsor of an innovation needs to synchronize the transfer to the operations network so that it fits with other priorities and constraints. Monthly, quarterly, and annual cycles often loom large in the operating plane: the budget cycle, the recruitment cycle, seasonal peaks and troughs in demand, and so on. These cycles create "right" and "wrong" times to introduce an innovation into the operation. These rhythms differ substantially across the functions inside an organization. Absorption of metanational innovations will be improved if they are introduced at the right time in the activity cycle of the operation that must leverage them.

PolyGram again provides a case in point. Each of PolyGram's local sales operations has only a limited number of slots to launch new recordings because of the limitations on radio airtime, concert schedules, and advertising windows. Various festivals or seasonal releases have a strong claim on these slots. The IRCs (acting as magnets) had to be sensitive to these planning cycles: A potential global hit would fare better if introduced at times when it faced less competition from national repertoire. Nestlé had to adjust to similar timing constraints imposed by the fact that mass-market retailers only devote a certain number of shelf-space and promotional slots to the launch of new products each year. And in consumer electronics, for example, slots at the Hanover Fair or at Comdex force you to work back and time the innovations to suit. Time is, as always, of the essence.

• **Recruiting the customer as an ally.** Sponsors from the magnet organization can generate momentum in the operations network by announcing to customers that an innovative product or service will soon be available. This can be a powerful way to ensure that the operations network focuses on leveraging it efficiently. The customer can also help by letting the operations network know that, despite the possible disruption to existing operating routines, they value the new product or service.

Each of these initiatives reinforces of the magnet organization's efforts to turn its innovations into shareholder value.

BUILDING A METANATIONAL CULTURE

A metanational winner builds a shared culture that can act as a psychological glue to bind its sites together into a single network. But this does not mean suppressing local cultures; rather, it means recognizing their value-generating potential.[4] If you visit STMicroelectronics' site at Agrate, near Milan, for example, there can be little doubt that you are in Italy. The touch and feel of the site, and the behaviors there, are very local—we heard, for example, several conversations in the local dialect (let alone Italian). At the Paris site, however, ST is very French: The greetings are different, the tone in meetings is different, and even the layout and type of offices is different. In California, ST looks like an American company. Several elements, however, constitute common glue: Corporate identity symbols are omnipresent, total quality management (TQM) posters and charts decorate every wall, and it is rare to see a report of any kind ("reports" at ST are presentations, not documents). English is the official language, and at every site, we saw visitors from other sites. At every site, people are aware of the other sites—what they do, how they relate to each other, and so on.

Born as a government-owned organization representing two national cultures, France and Italy, ST worked hard at making the transition to a metanational culture. One way it made this change was by superimposing TQM throughout its organization. TQM provided a common language and a set of beliefs and values that were denationalized: TQM at ST was neither Italian, nor French, nor Asian. It was TQM, a shared context for the various peoples that make up ST, wherever they sit, wherever they come from. Importantly, ST did not impose a particular national culture over other local cultures. In its site in Casablanca, for example, TQM was interpreted within Islamic principles, allowing the corporate beliefs and values to be combined with local cultural values.[5] In this way, the distinctiveness of the site was able to coexist with a strong corporate culture.

The most effective corporate culture will obviously vary from company to company. But all successful metanationals will create a number of common beliefs and values that are fundamental to the way they compete. These powerful beliefs include the following:

- The belief that the corporate center is not the fount of knowledge but just one star in a galaxy of specialized technology, knowledge, and capabilities.

- The belief that no local cultures are superior or inferior; they are just different.

- The belief that innovation comes from harnessing diversity.

- The belief that winning in the global knowledge economy requires a combination of metanational innovation with operational efficiency.

The values at the core of a metanational's corporate culture include the following:

- Valuing difference over similarity.

- Valuing a site or location for its unique contribution to the global result, not for its stand-alone performance.

- Valuing the willingness to learn from others (and from the world).

- Valuing flexibility and willingness to embrace innovation.

GETTING THERE

The operations network in a metanational is managed with one overriding objective in mind: to efficiently leverage metanational innovations across global markets. To achieve this objective, the senior operations management (led by the COO) needs to assemble a set of world-class operational capabilities. These may be owned, provided by joint ventures or alliance partners, subcontracted, or in-sourced. The choice of these operating modes comes down to the tradeoffs between cost, flexibility, and control.

Having assembled a world-class set of capabilities, these must be deployed in a coordinated fashion that optimizes global efficiency, quality, and customer satisfaction. This is the job of the global operating units in a metanational. Each site—possibly a mix of a manufacturing facility, a distribution node, a marketing or R&D unit, a team, a joint venture or subcontractor relationship, and so on—must also be maintained and continuously improved to ensure that it remains world-class. In general, this is the role of the respective site managers.

The CEO and other top corporate managers in a metanational take overall responsibility for the sensing, magnet, and operations organizations and the interactions among them. As we saw in chapters 6 and 7, this means setting up and overseeing the sensing organization and the key innovation projects in the magnet organization. It means helping to ensure that innovations are smoothly relayed into the operating network. Top management also needs to concern itself with initiatives to improve the operations network's capacity to absorb potentially disruptive innovations. Senior managers need to visit various sites around the company and those of its partners, keeping abreast of changes in global markets and technologies, understanding what is being learned around the network, and keeping an eye open for potential metanational innovation projects. They need to reinforce the interdependence of all parts of the metanational and the common goal of contributing to global success. The CEO in a metanational is not the commander of mission control but more like a head of state who unifies three suborganizations (sensing, magnet, and operations) with a common interest.

Making such a metanational operations network effective requires a set of enabling structures and processes. These include global performance measures, global units charged with configuring and coordinating sites as an integrated network, and a supportive global culture.

Together, the three suborganizations discussed in chapters 6, 7, and 8—the sensing and magnet organizations and the operating network, and the links between them—provide a blueprint for the kind of company that will win in the global knowledge economy. Which road you take to this metanational ideal, however, depends on your starting point.

In our final chapter we explore these different roads and build a senior management agenda for competing in the new knowledge economy.

Chapter 9

From Global to Metanational

IN THIS FINAL CHAPTER we lay out the senior management agenda for winning in the global knowledge economy. For existing multinationals, this means launching a set of initiatives to take them beyond today's global company to become a metanational. It means exploiting the potential of learning from the world by unlocking and mobilizing knowledge that is imprisoned in local pockets scattered around the globe. For today's budding multinationals, it means leapfrogging their global cousins to build tomorrow's metanational companies, rather than emulating the internationalization strategies of the past.

We begin by assessing the relative strengths and weakness of global projectors, multidomestic firms, and newcomers to the global game in rising to the challenge of the knowledge economy. We outline three different blueprints to guide managers from each of these classes of company. These blueprints cover the key initiatives and priorities, and they include suggestions for practical projects to kick-start the transition.

We conclude with a call to arms for top management. Becoming a metanational means reshaping your company. But, as a senior executive, it also means changing what you do. For some, the starter's gun has already been fired. Others have the luxury of more gradual change. But those who doggedly ignore the metanational challenge will eventually be left stranded in obscurity as the global knowledge economy roars past.

219

Nokia, STMicroelectronics, PolyGram, Oerlikon Burhle, SAP, Alfa Laval, Acer, Shiseido, P&G, Hewlett-Packard, and many other companies we studied see a pressing need to extend the range of locations where they are finding and mobilizing knowledge. Metanational pioneers like ARM, PixTech, and PolyGram have already taken great strides in this direction. Even global stalwarts like General Electric and ABB have announced that they need to improve their ability to mobilize globally dispersed knowledge. We call this need to unlock the potential of globally dispersed knowledge *the metanational imperative.*

What follows is an outline of our three different paths to a metanational future. Most managers will find that their organization reflects some mixture of the three starting points. Many existing multinationals lie somewhere on the spectrum from global projector to multidomestic firm. Even within an established multinational, some business units may share characteristics of a startup or newly internationalizing company. Some young, new economy companies, meanwhile, will have rapidly put in place a global structure, but one without deep roots. Any one of our three blueprints, therefore, will probably need to be adapted with reference to the other two.

FROM GLOBAL PROJECTOR TO METANATIONAL

Centrally driven multinationals generally have a deeply ingrained mentality of global projection. They are much more comfortable teaching the world than learning from the world. The more successful a global projector has been in the past, the more difficult it will be to reverse this "teacher" mentality. People who spout the metanational doctrine in these organizations will undoubtedly elicit the retort, "What can we possibly learn from *them*?"

On the plus side, many global projectors share two potential sources of strength in a metanational world. First, they have an established mindset that defines success globally. Second, they have built a highly interdependent global organization despite the typically dominant headquarters and dependent subsidiaries.

The global definition of success encourages worldwide optimization of their operating network. These global companies are, therefore, culturally well-positioned to deploy a stream of innovations quickly and efficiently on a global scale. Tight global integration, which emphasizes the interdependence among subsidiaries, means that many of the mechanisms necessary to move products, systems, processes, and even knowledge around the network are already in place. But these channels tend to be designed for one-way flows: from a dominant home base to dependent overseas subsidiaries. Before they can use their existing operating networks to create metanational advantages, global projectors must learn to reverse the knowledge flow—in other words, to learn from the periphery as well as teaching it.

On the downside, a heritage of global projection creates a number of severe handicaps in the global knowledge economy.

First among these is the lack of a "prospecting" mentality. Rather than actively looking for new hotbeds of disruptive technology, skills, and market needs, most global companies are trying to find the most fertile ground to leverage their standard, existing competitive advantages. Global projectors are attracted by similarities to their home base that will provide maximum leverage with minimum adaptation. Metanational prospectors, by contrast, seek out environments and knowledge that are most differentiated from their home base, because differences provide the best raw material for innovation.

Second, global projectors lack the structures they need to access unique local knowledge. Their subsidiaries are tightly plugged in to the global corporate network—but not to the local, external environment. The subsidiary of a global projector is designed to deliver rather than to question and learn from the local environment. Subsidiaries on the geographic periphery tend to be seen, and to view themselves, as sales conduits or manufacturing outposts. They are certainly not designed to act as a source of innovation that overturns the company's tried-and-tested global formula.

These two key weaknesses mean that most global projectors lack the raw material required to fuel metanational innovation: They are not designed to find and access specialist, local knowledge dispersed around the world. If they could overcome this deficiency and seek out untapped pockets of knowledge scattered around the world, then setting up a magnet to use that knowledge would come quite naturally. These strengths and weaknesses of a centralized, global projector in a metanational world are summarized in table 9-1.

**Table 9-1 Strengths and Weaknesses of Centralized Global
Projectors in Becoming Metanational**

Metanational Capability	Strength/Weakness of a Global Projector	Rationale
Successfully *prospecting* for new pockets of knowledge	Weak	Emphasis is on finding new markets and low-cost production centers that are similar to the home-base environment to minimize adaptation.
Accessing new sources of dispersed and differentiated knowledge	Weak	Emphasis is on exploiting home-based advantages and home-grown technologies, systems, and processes.
Setting up *magnets* for innovation using dispersed knowledge	Moderate	Global products, platforms, and account management often play an important role, but as conduits for global transfer of home-based technologies, systems, and processes.
Moving and melding knowledge from dispersed and diverse sources	Weak	Melding of different types of knowledge tends to be confined to the home base, where it is managed through co-location.
Relaying metanational innovations	Moderate	Unwillingness to accept innovations that do not come from the center or from powerful subsidiaries.
Using global operations to *leverage* innovations	Strong	Global companies are experienced at exploiting their advantages globally and don't suffer from the legacy of autonomous national subsidiaries.

So how should the senior management of a global projector get started on the path toward metanational advantage? Our research suggests a two-pronged approach. First, they should create a few practical pilot projects that demonstrate the value of innovation based on learning from the world. Second, they must address the key deficiencies of a global projector in the knowledge economy: the lack of a sensing organization and a global prospecting mentality.

Set Up a Metanational Pilot Project

Select a potential innovation, a new business area, or a new product or service where the relevant knowledge does not all lie on home turf. Set it up to act as a metanational magnet, providing leadership and knowledge from the geographic periphery of your existing organization. The goal is to demonstrate the worth of innovation based on learning from distant and unfamiliar locations. In implementing this first pilot a number of guidelines are helpful to bear in mind:

- **Pick a pilot project of strategic importance that is largely outside the realm of existing operational experience.** By choosing such a project, the need to find and access knowledge from places and areas of expertise where the company is not currently strong will become obvious to all—such as the Swiss company Oerlikon entering the missile business. The project may fill a strategic gap (as was the case with Shiseido in fragrances), or it may seek potential substitutes for existing businesses or technologies that are under competitive attack.

- **Use the pilot project to get people involved in prospecting and sensing.** A good pilot project will create, and clearly demonstrate, the need to look outside the company and the home base for new knowledge. This reinforces the value of sensing activities.

- **Allow the periphery to lead.** Challenging a tradition of global projection requires that magnets for innovation be led from nontraditional locations. Entrusting leadership for a major project for the first time to a location away from the home base is a major step and a strong signal of the need to learn from the world.

- **Set up a magnet around a lead customer, global platform, or global activity—don't just project knowledge from a new place.** A true metanational magnet innovates by moving and melding knowledge from many different locations. Don't try to substitute a center of excellence that simply projects its own insights and prejudices.

- **Err on the side of excessive interaction and communications among members of the magnet team.** Until your company gains experience in moving and melding complex knowledge from different sources, use a variety of knowledge carriers, from data to people, with frequent interaction and many short periods of co-location.

- **As the innovation takes shape, forge a direct link between the magnet and the operating network.** In a centralized, global organization, the habit of looking to headquarters as the fount of innovation dies hard. When the innovation has an unknown pedigree, there are likely to be severe problems in relaying it to the operating network, as we described in chapter 8. It is therefore important to forge a direct link between the magnet team and a receptive part of the operations network that must leverage it.

Visible success in a few pilot projects will be far more effective than rhetoric or coercion in changing the mentality of global projection. These pilots will also establish a platform on which to build the kind of full-fledged magnet organization we described in chapter 7. To continue the transition, the global projector needs to remedy its lack of sensing capabilities.

Create a Sensing Organization and a Culture of Learning from the World

The next major step for global projectors is to establish a suborganization dedicated to sensing. As we discussed in chapter 6, the logic of discovery and reconnaissance must dominate this sensing organization. It needs to be capable of prospecting the world to identify and anticipate new hotbeds of technology and emerging customer needs and behaviors. It must be tightly plugged into local environments in ways that allow it to access complex knowledge, using everyone from customers and suppliers to universities and highly targeted acquisitions to further this task. It needs to be staffed by people who are more like explorers than farmers, whose performance measures and incentives reinforce their role as the eyes and ears of the corporation around the globe.

But even the best-designed sensing organization will fail if it is not adopted as a full and valuable partner by the rest of the corporation. This requires a further set of senior management initiatives to foster a culture of continuous global learning. These initiatives include the following:

- **Emphasizing throughout the organization that there are important things "it doesn't know that it doesn't know."** Remind people of the opportunities missed because of a failure to look outside the usual lead markets. Point out disruptive technologies that crept up unnoticed. Urge people to acknowledge that dominance doesn't last forever: Yesterday's capitals of innovation in an industry are often tomorrow's ghost towns.

- **Fostering a corporate culture that transcends the home culture.** This may sound like a wooly prescription, but it is not. Some very practical steps can be taken to achieve this goal. Recall the power of Acer's use of universal metaphors, or ST's decision to refer to sites, not countries, as the keepers of its core capabilities. Symbolism is all-important here. Choose carefully which national holidays to respect or where to hold pivotal meetings. Transcending local language identities ("Our official language is English . . . but, frankly, you really have to master French!") is another such critical signal.

- **Building a cosmopolitan management team.** Appointing people from outside the home country to top management jobs sends a strong signal that the center is no longer the sole fount of new and influential ideas. Of course, these appointments must not be seen as token gestures. Provide a global career path for young, high-potential managers—especially those from peripheral subsidiaries. But beware of fast-trackers who engage in country-hopping. They may be worldly but not deeply sensitive to, nor really familiar with, underlying local differences.

- **Dispersing headquarters' functions.** The most powerful symbol of global projection is the concentration of powerful, global functions at headquarters. Break the mold of projection. Distribute the global functional activities across different locations around the world.

Obviously, the appropriate initiatives and their implementation will vary from company to company. But the overriding goal for a centralized, global projector is to replace the global projection mentality with one of learning from the world.

FROM MULTIDOMESTIC COMPANY TO METANATIONAL

A geographically fragmented knowledge base is the enemy of the multidomestic company in the global knowledge economy. Multidomestic companies need to improve their sensing skills. But above all else, they need to fight fragmentation by creating magnets to mobilize knowledge that is scattered around the world. They should start with the knowledge so often imprisoned in their own local subsidiaries.

Multidomestic companies do have advantages that can help them build metanational capabilities ahead of their rivals.

First, a multidomestic firm already has a large stock of knowledge within its subsidiaries that can be leveraged to build global advantage. Second, because the multidomestic company is often already well–plugged-in to a set of local environments, it has an ongoing supply of new knowledge from those locations. Finally, if the company is skilled at establishing subsidiaries in new locations, then its people understand the process of accessing new sources of knowledge—they know how to go about it. Frequently, therefore, multidomestic companies have a head start in the race to identify and plug in to new and relevant sources of knowledge.

These are important capabilities for multidomestic firms as they enter the metanational game. At the same time, however, the multidomestic companies are handicapped by weaknesses that stem from their heritage. The concept of global knowledge magnets does not come naturally to multidomestic firms. "Local knowledge for local adaptation" is their implicit managerial mindset. As a result, they lack experience in establishing and running global knowledge magnets.

Multidomestic companies are good at melding diverse sources of local knowledge in a local context. In this sense, they have well-developed knowledge-melding skills, learned in the course of adapting their core formula to local conditions. However, they lack the experience of moving and melding knowledge from a global pool. As we saw in chapter 5, the problems of mobilizing knowledge—especially complex knowledge—from sources dispersed around the world are fundamentally different from those involved in melding local knowledge. When distance intervenes and knowledge is drawn from unfamiliar contexts, the challenge rises exponentially.

Multidomestic companies are also prone to the delusion that subsidiaries are in touch with all the specialist knowledge they need. In fact, subsidiaries' locations are largely determined by the pull of attractive markets or lower costs. The multidomestic firm focuses on places where it has decided to plant the corporate flag, rather than searching every corner of the globe for new sources of knowledge. Once a local subsidiary has been established, it embarks on the task of understanding the local environment to achieve the right balance between corporate dogma and local adaptation.

The multidomestic company often has employees with well-developed prospecting skills, but it tends to restrict the application of these skills to their immediate, local arena. These experienced individuals can be a source of strength in the quest for sensing new pockets of knowledge, but they need to be unshackled from their national subsidiaries.

Few multidomestic firms define their success globally. Each subsidiary's performance is judged by its own local results, as if it were an independent company, rather than by its contribution to the competitiveness of the system as a whole. Every tub stands on its own bottom—and local managers often prefer it this way. The corporation's performance is viewed as the simple summation of its parts.

The idea of small, possibly weak peripheral units leading the direction of innovation for the entire organization is anathema to the multidomestic company. Influence comes with size and strength. Knowledge is jealously guarded by the independent-minded subsidiaries: It is their source of power. Sales, assets, and employees are the decibels of a subsidiary's voice when the organization debates the future direction of its products, services, and strategies.

Table 9-2 summarizes the typical multidomestic company's strengths and weaknesses against the metanational capabilities it will need in the global knowledge economy.

Table 9-2 Strengths and Weaknesses of Multidomestic Companies in Becoming Metanational

Metanational Capability	Strength/Weakness of a Multidomestic	Rationale
Successfully *prospecting* for new pockets of knowledge	Moderate	Prospecting skills tend to be confined to local environments, where the multidomestic firm has well-established local subsidiaries.
Plugging in to new sources of dispersed and differentiated knowledge	Strong	Well-developed in local sub-sidiaries, sometimes to the point where local managers are said to be "better connected to their local environment than to the headquarters."
Setting up *magnets* for dispersed knowledge	Weak	Few structures or processes exist to move dispersed knowl-edge out of the local environ-ment where it is captured, leading to knowledge fragmentation.
Moving and melding knowledge from dis-persed and diverse sources	Strong locally, weak globally	Melding is a well-developed capability, but tends to occur on a "local for local" basis where local knowledge is melded to achieve local adaptations; melding of knowledge dis-persed around the globe is rare.
Relaying metanational innovations	Moderate	Experience in periodically absorbing and adapting innova-tions from elsewhere.
Using global opera-tions to *leverage* innovations	Weak	Lacks experience of global leveraging as each national subsidiary is a local imple-menter and adapter that jeal-ously guards its autonomy.

Given these strengths and weaknesses, how should the senior man-agement of a multidomestic company get started on the path toward metanational advantage? Again, our research suggests a two-pronged approach. First, they should set up a pilot magnet for a specific innovation that requires knowledge from all around the organization and its local environments. Second, they must create a magnet organization that promotes global interdependence as it mobilizes dispersed knowledge.

Set Up a Pilot Magnet

Select a lead customer, a global platform, or a global activity to act as a magnet for an innovation that is only possible by mobilizing knowledge scattered around the organization. To be effective, this magnet must transcend the boundaries of national subsidiaries. It must demonstrate the importance of magnets in unlocking global value from knowledge that is imprisoned in local subsidiaries or their environments. It must persuade skeptical country managers that they can benefit from embracing a metanational strategy. In implementing this pilot magnet, bear in mind the following guidelines:

- **Look for an innovation that depends on connecting knowledge from a number of locations**. Mobilizing dispersed knowledge must be critical to the success of the project. For example, a suitable project would leverage off the convergence of two technologies developed in different parts of the world.

- **Break the assumption that "voice equals weight."** It is easy to be seduced by the option of appointing a country manager from a large and profitable subsidiary—a trusted baron—as the magnet champion. But with this you incur the danger that, instead of championing the melding of dispersed knowledge, this individual may commandeer the project to create a self-styled "center of excellence" in her local subsidiary. To make sure the pilot acts as a true magnet for knowledge scattered around the world, appoint a champion without strong ties to a local subsidiary. Or choose dynamic managers from peripheral locations who demonstrably lack the necessary local resources and knowledge. They will be forced to involve other locations in fundamental ways. This will begin to break the traditional assumption that small or peripheral subsidiaries should have little voice in the innovation process.

- **Select a pilot magnet that encourages codification of local knowledge.** To move and meld local knowledge effectively, the multidomestic company must dramatically improve its ability to codify and articulate knowledge that has previously remained unarticulated. Choose a pilot that requires knowledge to be articulated so that it can be incorporated into a global innovation project.

- **Select a pilot magnet that develops skills in melding knowledge from different sources.** One of the chief weaknesses of multidomestic companies is the lack of experience in melding knowledge from different locations around the globe. The pilot magnet should help develop this capability by offering a chance to practice different ways of melding dispersed knowledge (such as alternating between large team meetings and separate, parallel work, as discussed in chapter 5).

- **Select a pilot magnet that encourages the sharing of existing knowledge, and also requires new knowledge.** These requirements will help kick-start the process of prospecting and accessing new knowledge, while better exploiting existing knowledge within the multidomestic company.

- **Actively manage the process of relaying the resulting innovation back into the operations network.** It is critical that the pilot magnet not only generates a metanational innovation, but also that this innovation is successfully leveraged to create value for the company. Ultimately, value creation is the way to win over skeptical managers who have grown up with the local freedom they enjoy in a multidomestic company. To ensure maximum impact of the pilot magnet, therefore, senior management must ensure that it is successfully adopted and leveraged globally by the operations network.

When the company begins to see the value created by successful pilot magnets, it is time to expand the concept into the kind of magnet organization we described in chapter 7. In parallel, the existing multidomestic operations network must be reshaped so that it is ready to deploy a new stream of metanational innovations.

Create a Magnet Organization and Reshape Your Operations Network

The next step for multidomestics is to start setting up a full-fledged magnet organization. As we discussed in chapter 7, the logic of entrepreneurship and mobilization must dominate this magnet organization. It needs to excel at moving and melding complex knowledge from the sensing organization. It should be structured around global lead customers, global platforms, or global activities. It needs enthusiastic people who are good at bootstrapping and cajoling contributions from people they don't control, people who are comfortable working in an ever-changing, uncertain environment. It needs to be backed by performance measures and incentives that reward entrepreneurship and innovation rather than efficiency and scale or empire-building.

But even the most entrepreneurial and innovative magnet organization will be irrelevant unless its innovations are deployed to generate sales and profit on a global scale. This requires a further set of senior management initiatives to reshape the traditional operations network into an efficient machine for exploiting metanational innovations across global markets. These initiatives include the following:

- **Emphasizing the opportunities wasted by the failure to leverage past innovations across the globe**. Remind people of competitive advantage squandered because most managers in the company dismissed a potential global innovation as a local peculiarity. In the early days of PolyGram's IRCs, for example, senior management at the firm was constantly reminding the local subsidiary managers of the profits they missed by failing to put as much effort behind potential global hits as they lavished on established local artists.

- **Fostering a culture in which operating managers think local but act global**. This means preserving the value of local capabilities, knowledge, and experience in adaptation. But "acting global" means asking what those distinctive local strengths can contribute to the global operating result, rather than asking "What's in this for my subsidiary's bottom line?" Operating managers need to become, as one senior executive put it, "globally generous." Senior management should continually reinforce the fact that, whatever wins an individual subsidiary may notch up, the game is ultimately won or lost on the *global* playing field.

- **Deemphasizing the national subsidiary as the basic building block of the operating network**. At one level this means increasing the importance of the site as an operating unit with a unique set of capabilities or capacity to offer to the global network. It also means creating global units, such as a global account management organization to serve major customers. The global operating units need seasoned managers with personal power and credibility. One option is to transfer former country managers of major subsidiaries to head these global units.

These initiatives will begin reshaping the structure, processes, culture, and mentality of the multidomestic operating network so that it can leverage metanational innovations across global markets. They are *not* intended to transform the multidomestic operations network into sensing or magnet organizations. Sensing, mobilizing, and leveraging need to remain distinct and differentiated roles.

FROM STARTUP TO METANATIONAL

Startup companies can leapfrog their competitors and go straight to a metanational structure rather than treading the well-worn path of internationalization we discussed in chapter 2. Surprisingly, many of today's high-technology startups such as Yahoo! and Sun Microsystems have followed an ultratraditional path to international expansion. But companies such as ARM and PixTech demonstrate the value of becoming metanational by mobilizing dispersed knowledge from the outset. The metanational route will position the new multinationals to prosper in the global knowledge economy. It turns the traditional problem of coping with global markets into a virtue, because the metanational strategy thrives on exploiting geographic diversity, rather than trying to suppress or ignore it.

A metanational strategy and structure will also help startups to internationalize more quickly than would be possible if they followed traditional routes to global expansion. The metanational alternative encourages startups to "borrow" international capabilities—as did ARM and PixTech—rather than trying to build them internally over years or decades. By leveraging partners' operational capabilities, metanational startups can attain global reach almost overnight.

Our research suggests a number of guidelines that managers of startups should follow in building a new metanational corporation:

- **Don't create a senior management ghetto in a single location**. Perhaps because startups often emerge from informal contacts among friends who share the same social networks, most startups used to be "born local." But this is no longer true. Companies such as ARM and PixTech, and many other successful ventures such as Logitech and Business Objects, have adopted a global perspective almost from Day 1. They did so because the founders or senior management team either had extensive experience of work in multinational organizations and traveled relentlessly, sensing new technologies and market developments, or because, like ARM, they posted senior managers in different places around the world at a very early stage in their development.

- **Seek out and leverage global diversity**. Recruit people from multiple nationalities and backgrounds from the start. Look for unity in a common corporate culture and value system, rather than shared nationality or business experience. Distribute key activities and functions across different locations; build the team through frequent and intensive communication rather than co-location in a single, headquarters site.

- **Assess each international foray according to the ratio of learning over investment**. Acer did this well. For new technologies and capabilities, it went to hotbeds like Silicon Valley, where a well-developed technology market offered quick and easy access. For market learning, however, it went to rapidly developing markets—forerunners of the explosion of PC and Internet use in developing countries. In these markets, Acer could sense customer needs that its competitors didn't understand. Because it provided direct competitive advantage, the value of this knowledge was huge, outweighing the high costs of learning about a complex and nascent market like small business users in Mexico. By ranking its internationalization options according to their attractiveness as sources of new knowledge, rather than by traditional measures such as market size or price levels, Acer maximized the value of learning for every dollar it invested.

- **Leverage partners to make yourself an "instant" metanational.** PixTech and ARM, with their massive partnership networks, are excellent examples. Their strategic use of alliances solved the intrinsic resource and location limitations of a startup and provided immediate global reach.

- **Carefully sequence your learning and capability development to avoid being spread too thinly.** Consider PixTech again. Rather than trying to access all of the knowledge and capabilities it needed at once, it focused first on small screens for particular applications. It accessed knowledge about manufacturing technology only when it was needed for the product design. This helped the company conserve its resources. It also let PixTech develop its partnering and accessing skills as it introduced new technologies and partners over time.

BEWARE THE SHOEHORNING TRAP

Many multinationals have recognized the limitations of their traditional approach. Global projectors such as McDonald's and Toyota have tried to grow sales and improve profits by better adapting their standard, global formula to different local conditions around the world. Meanwhile, companies from a multidomestic heritage, such as Unilever or Nestlé, have improved efficiency and created economies of scale and scope by integrating their subsidiaries and limiting unnecessary local variations in everything from branding to IT systems.

Both global projectors and multidomestic companies have begun to move toward an ideal that C. A. Bartlett and S. Ghoshal termed the "Transnational Solution" in *Managing across Borders*, their important book on the challenges of marrying global integration with national responsiveness. These are worthy initiatives. For many companies, they are essential to maintain and improve the global competitiveness of their operations.

But it would be foolhardy to imagine that such moves address the core issue of unlocking the potential of globally dispersed knowledge that we have raised in this book. In the global knowledge economy, misinterpreting the proper role of transnational integration is dangerous for two reasons.

First, it is likely to encourage senior managers to try to shoehorn the activities of sensing and magnet organizations into the operations network. As we explained in chapter 4, such a strategy is bound to fail because the operating network's mentality, structures, systems, and incentives are simply inappropriate for the activities of sensing and mobilizing globally dispersed knowledge. Moreover, the operating network is unlikely to be in all of the locations and have the right kinds of relationships to prospect for and access all of the knowledge required by tomorrow's metanationals. At worst, shoehorning the activities of sensing and mobilizing into a transnational operations network will undermine the network's efficiency. It will overload and distract operating managers who are ill equipped to take on these extra roles.

Second, the national subsidiaries' role as the basic building blocks of a transnational structure is fundamentally at odds with the way metanationals need to view the world. Placing national subsidiaries at the core of the organization constrains decisions about where and what to sense. It impedes the formation of magnets around global lead customers, global platforms, or global activities. It hinders the operating network's ability to exploit metanational innovation globally, because it causes managers to focus on the performance of the national subsidiary as a stand-alone business.

Transnational structures may help achieve the right balance between the global integration and national responsiveness within the network of day-to-day operations. But they should not obscure the important role of the sites and global operating units described in chapter 8. And a transnational operations network can never substitute for the sensing and magnet organizations that drive metanational innovation.

BECOMING METANATIONAL: THE CEO'S AGENDA

This book has painted a picture of the kind of company that we believe will win in the global knowledge economy. As we have seen, this new, metanational company can evolve from today's traditional multinationals. The transition requires a significant change of management mentality and a new organization culture, structure, and processes that can unlock the potential of knowledge scattered around the world. But success in the global knowledge economy also means new and different roles for the CEO and the senior (or top) management team. These new roles are demanding in their own right, so some existing activities will have to be delegated to others.

Don't hold your breath and expect a perfect metanational to emerge miraculously from your organization. The necessary changes are unlikely to bubble up from a group of activists, however smart and motivated. The CEO and senior management team need to take decisive action.

Even among your senior management colleagues, globalization probably still means penetrating foreign markets and reducing costs by deploying your company's products, services, and capabilities around the world. Your first task, therefore, is to lift your company's horizons about what it will take to win in the global knowledge economy. Your people need to understand, and embrace, the challenges of learning from the world, turning that new knowledge into innovative products and services and leveraging those innovations at the global scale.

Lift Your Company's Horizons

Some CEOs may try to do this by executive decree. They use the power of personality as, arguably, Jack Welch recently did in setting lofty learning goals for General Electric. The response, however, may well be disappointing. A radical message will require frequent reiteration and reinforcement, particularly when given to managers of an already successful (perhaps complacent?) multinational company. Will GE, a traditional multinational, become a true metanational, and at what speed? Or will it, instead, fall into the shoehorning trap as its existing operations try to commandeer the sensing and mobilizing activities of metanational innovation?

Other senior management teams may look to a major acquisition to break the mold of global projection and kick-start the process of learning from the world. Daimler's acquisition of the Chrysler Corporation offers great potential for learning a new set of capabilities and market behaviors in the mass-market segment. The danger, however, is that the desire to project the best of German engineering processes will overpower the opportunity to access and mobilize new knowledge from another part of the globe. Ultimately, senior management will set the tone.

In most of the successful cases we studied, the shift from global projection to metanational learning and innovation was driven by necessity. For successful global players or optimistic startups, the CEO's challenge is to create this same sense of urgency and determination to build metanational advantage before a crisis looms.

In selling the metanational blueprint for the future, CEOs should also emphasize the upside. The sensing and magnet organizations provide exciting new roles for ambitious managers. There is great opportunity in unlocking the potential of capabilities and knowledge that have been locally imprisoned.

Seize the Right Opportunity

The right timing can have a big impact on the probability of success. Seize the opportunity created by a discontinuity of some kind. This may take the form of a corporate discontinuity: a succession of mergers created an obvious need to integrate global expertise at Glaxo-SmithKline. Or take advantage of an industry discontinuity, such as the convergence of industries and technologies that have grown up in different locations, such as pharmacology, biotechnology, and combinatorial chemistry.

Move Outside Your Comfort Zone

A metanational's future competitiveness depends critically on the continued success of its sensing and magnet organizations in discovering new pockets of knowledge, accessing and mobilizing the newfound knowledge, and using it to create practical innovations. Yet these processes lack the stability and predictability of the world of operations. Nor are they susceptible to the precise and objective performance measures that can be used to drive and monitor operational efficiency. We cannot control what the sensing organization will discover tomorrow. Managing innovation in the magnet organization is not an exact science. These activities are more like basic R&D than incremental improvement.

Global projection, with its proven, home-grown formulas and its predictable rollout strategies, seems a safer route to success. It is certainly more controllable. In the global knowledge economy, however, the profitability of this strategy will erode rapidly as more and more companies master the art of projection. Senior management must therefore step out of their comfort zone and put their own reputations on the line to support investment in sensing and magnet organizations.

On the other hand, the cash risks of investment in the sensing and magnet organizations are generally not high. In the companies we researched, these activities could be sustained by an annual budget of 1 percent to 5 percent of total revenues.

Senior management must also place more power and put more faith in the periphery of their organizations. Proven core operations, backed by a depth of people and assets, will carry less weight in determining the company's future strategic direction. CEOs will also have to accept that their company's global performance will increasingly rely on an ability to manage relationships with internal and external partners over whom they have little formal control.

Get Some "Quick Wins"

Some people and organizations will inevitably lose power on the road from global to metanational. They are likely to become vocal skeptics. The power of quick wins in silencing these critics is obvious—hence our recommendations for pilot projects as detailed earlier. Global projectors should start with a project that extends their sensing net and reverses the traditional flow by allowing the geographic periphery to lead. Companies with a multidomestic heritage, meanwhile, should quickly establish an innovation magnet around a lead customer, global platform, or global activity to prove the value of mobilizing fragmented knowledge imprisoned in local subsidiaries.

Change What You Do and How You Allocate Your Time

Perhaps the most important leap of all is a change in your own behavior. First, CEOs need to extract themselves from direct management of the operating network.* This means appointing a COO with real authority and accountability for running an operating network that efficiently leverages products and services across global markets and continuously improves the distinctive capability of each site.

Second, it means maintaining a grueling travel schedule—but with a difference. You will no longer crisscross the world in order to manage and monitor the performance of subsidiaries or sites. Instead, your role is that of exploration and discovery: looking for the unique knowledge each location can contribute to a potential metanational innovation project, looking for weak signals of new technologies that might be relevant to your business, hearing the muffled calls of unmet customer needs. You will be an important source of entrepreneurial insights for your sensing and magnet teams to explore.

Third, the sensing and magnet organizations should report directly to you. Managing and motivating these organizations—not the operating network—is where you will allocate the bulk your time. The operating network, under the COO, is in the business of harvesting the fruits of past innovation and investment. Your role is to be continually planting the seeds and nurturing the seedlings of your company's metanational future. This means appointing the right people to the roles of sensing and magnet champions, removing roadblocks, making connections between people separated by geographic distance or organizational boundaries, and establishing ambitious goals in the sphere of metanational innovation.

---

*Clearly, it won't make sense for every CEO to delegate management of the operations network to a COO. Many companies will face performance issues or be in a sensitive stage in their development, such that shareholders rightly expect the CEO to continue to take personal charge of the ongoing operations. Our point is that the sensing and magnet organizations need to be led by a very senior executive who commands respect and can take a broad view of the company's future strategic direction. Rather than loading these additional burdens onto the CEO, companies may need to create a new role that is effectively the "chief innovation officer" (to be sharply distinguished from the chief scientist or head of R&D). Microsoft effectively took this route when Bill Gates became "chairman and chief software architect." In the latter of these roles, he effectively sets the future innovation roadmap for the company—an important task of the leader(s) of the sensing and magnet organizations in a metanational.

Fourth, you need to be constantly fighting the natural forces of reversion back to the comfort of global projection. Continually learning from the world is exhausting. The voice of the majority easily drowns out the voices of the periphery, especially when they are calling for the next round of disruptive change. The desire for scale and efficiency often leads to centralization and reliance on knowledge controlled by powerful decision-makers in larger operating units. Jorma Ollila, CEO of Nokia, refers to the constant energy required to keep the company open to new technologies and customer behaviors emerging around the world—something that he observes was a great deal easier when Nokia was building a new mobile telephony business from what was then seen as an isolated outpost rather than the home of a world leader.

A ROADMAP TO THE FUTURE

As the global knowledge economy becomes a reality, the sources of profit of traditional multinationals are under threat. The ability to move money, commodities, products, and information efficiently around the world is becoming a table stake in the global game. Complacent incumbents are being challenged by new competitors from unlikely birthplaces: Nokia from Finland, Acer from Taiwan, Shiseido from Japan, SAP from Germany. The old giants can no longer rely on the advantages of their home base to trump the competition. The advantage of coming from a charmed cluster like Silicon Valley is no match for a rival that can leverage knowledge from Silicon Valley *and* Cambridge, England, *and* Bangalore *and* Tel Aviv *and* Taipei *and* Tokyo. Learning from your backyard is no substitute for learning from the world. In the global knowledge economy, it's not *where you're from* that counts, its *who you are*.

The winners in this global knowledge economy will be companies that master the art of creating new sources of differentiation, companies that understand that you can't just shuffle a well-worn formula between existing markets. This means outinnovating the competition in products, services, and processes.

There are many ways to pursue innovation. Some companies try to nurture it in a skunk-works or acquire it from the proverbial startup in a garage. We have argued throughout this book that many companies are missing what is perhaps the biggest, untapped opportunity available to them: innovation that comes from connecting pockets of technology and market knowledge scattered around the world. Those who learn to tap and connect these pockets of locally imprisoned knowledge will find a powerful new source of innovation.

The untapped potential of globally dispersed knowledge is bigger today than ever, and it is growing. Industry convergence, technological complexity, solution selling, and the globalization of customers are increasing the breadth and dispersion of relevant new knowledge.

But much of this potential remains unexploited because today's multinationals lack the structures, processes, and incentives to leverage knowledge that is scattered in pockets around the world. Traditional multinationals know how to project what they have learned in the home market around the world. Increasingly, they can use their local knowledge to adapt a standard formula to the peculiarities of different national markets. But few traditional multinationals have the capacity to mobilize scattered knowledge to create world-beating innovations. Despite dramatic advances in information and communications technologies, the tyranny of distance still stands in the way. This is the metanational challenge.

In accepting this challenge, many companies risk falling into one of two traps. Some will attempt to get their existing international operations to innovate by learning from the world. This is using the wrong tool for the job—trying to shoehorn an existing organization into a role for which it wasn't designed. Other companies will try to overcome the tyranny of distance through heavy investment in ICT infrastructure. But the information these systems move will be a very incomplete representation of the knowledge their companies need to mobilize—a pale echo of the original complex know-how and insights they need to move and meld. Information and communications technologies can play an important supporting role. They cannot take the lead.

Companies that are serious about winning in the global knowledge economy will need to expand the net they cast for new knowledge: prospecting for interesting new technologies and consumer trends beyond those locations that dominate today, anticipating new hotbeds, and unlocking the potential of knowledge that lies underutilized in their local subsidiaries. Those who doubt this need to ask two basic questions: What share of all new knowledge relevant to my company's future am I capturing today? And am I convinced we are exploiting the full potential of what our far-flung network of local subsidiaries already knows?

Tomorrow's metanational companies will harness and exploit this hidden potential by building new structures, teams, and processes around global lead customers, global platforms, and global activities. They will form a new suborganization dedicated to entrepreneurship and innovation, with a unique set of roles, responsibilities, culture, and incentives. A flexible, efficient operating network, augmented by the capabilities of suppliers, subcontractors, and alliance partners, will turn these metanational innovations into global profits and shareholder value.

Winning in the global knowledge economy is not about choosing between innovation and operating efficiency, or between exploitation and entrepreneurship. It is about winning a global tournament played at three different levels: It is a race to identify and access new technologies and market trends ahead of the competition, a race to turn this dispersed knowledge into innovative products and services, and a race to scale and exploit these innovations in markets around the world.

The metanational pioneers discussed in this book are already showing the way forward. They have begun to leave behind the corporate world dominated by omnipotent headquarters and powerful national subsidiaries. To these companies, national boundaries are no longer a useful proxy for market segments or technology but little more than an administrative nuisance. Their world is a canvas dotted with specialized knowledge and operational capabilities that they connect and exploit to create new wealth. To thrive in this new environment, companies will have to become a new kind of metanational organization with new organizational structures, processes, and incentives, as well as a new set of roles for the CEO and senior management.

The road from global to metanational is a challenging and uncertain one. At the start of the twenty-first century, the challenge of globalization has changed. The race to penetrate world markets is being replaced by the race to learn from the world.

One question remains: Which race is your company equipped to win?

Notes

CHAPTER 1

1. See, for example, Unilever's 1998 Annual Report.
2. C. A. Bartlett and S. Ghoshal, *Managing across Borders* (Boston: Harvard Business School Press, 1989).
3. For example, M. E. Porter argues that "a firm must have a clear home base for competing in each strategically different business. The location for the home base is the location where strategy is set, core product and technology is created and maintained, and a critical mass of sophisticated production and service activities reside" (*On Competition* [Cambridge, MA: Harvard Business School Press, 1998], 332).
4. ST was referred to as being "the absolute leader in system-on-a-chip technology" in an article in *Business Week* (12 February 2001), with the significant title "From Niche to Goliath."
5. Y. Doz, P. S. Ring, S. Lenway, and T. Murtha, "PixTech, Inc. (A)," INSEAD Case Study (Fontainebleau: INSEAD, 1998).

CHAPTER 2

1. M. E. Porter, *The Competitive Advantage of Nations* (London: Macmillan, 1990).
2. W. M. Clarke, *How the City of London Works: An Introduction to Its Financial Markets* (London: Waterlow, 1988).
3. P. Krugman, *Geography and Trade* (Cambridge, MA: MIT Press, 1991).
4. For a fuller discussion of these processes, see G. M. P. Swann, M. Prevezer, and D. Stout, eds., *The Dynamics of Industrial Clustering* (Oxford: Oxford University Press, 1998).
5. See J. A. Mathews, "A Silicon Valley of the East: Creating Taiwan's Semiconductor Industry," *California Management Review* 39, no. 4 (1997): 26–54.
6. A. Marshall, *Principles of Economics*, 7th ed. (London: Macmillan, 1916).
7. For a deeper understanding on how traditional multinational firms leveraged their homegrown formulas abroad, see, for example, R. Vernon, "International Investment and International Trade in the Product Life Cycle," *Quarterly Journal of Economics* 80 (1966): 190–207; J. Johanssen and J. E. Vahlne, "The Internationalisation Process of the Firm—a Model of Knowledge Development and Increasing Foreign Market Commitments," *Journal of International Business Studies* 8, no. 1 (1977): 23–32.

8. Y.-S. Hu, "Global or Stateless Corporations Are National Firms with International Operations," *California Management Review* 34, no. 2 (1992): 107–126.
9. C. K. Prahalad, "The Strategic Process in a Multinational Corporation" (unpublished Ph.D. diss., Harvard Business School, 1975), and Y. Doz, *Government Control and Multinational Strategic Management* (New York: Praeger, 1979).
10. In this sense they are "multiple projectors."
11. R. Vernon, "The Product Life Cycle Hypothesis in a New International Environment," *Oxford Bulletin of Economics and Statistics* 41 (November 1979): 255–267.
12. "Silicon Envy," *Wired*, February 1998, 136–137.
13. "Taiwan: La plus grande usine de micro-ordinateurs du monde," *Les Echos*, 6 May 1998.
14. "It Was a Hit in Buenos Aires—So Why Not in Boise?," *Business Week*, 14 September 1998, 75.
15. A. L. Saxenian, *Regional Advantage* (Cambridge, MA: Harvard University Press, 1994).
16. J. Cantwell, "The Globalisation of Technology: What Remains of the Product Cycle Model?," in *The Dynamic Firm*, ed. A. Chandler, Jr. et al. (Oxford: Oxford University Press, 1998), chap. 12.
17. John H. Dunning, "The Geographical Sources of Competitiveness of Firms: Some Results from a New Survey," *Transnational Corporations* 5, no. 3 (1996).

CHAPTER 3

1. All the references, evidence, and propositions concerning global account/customer management, particularly those concerning STMicroelectronics, are drawn from the research work of one of the authors, José Santos, unless otherwise indicated.
2. P. Williamson and D. Clyde-Smith, "ACER—Building an Asian Multinational," INSEAD Case Study (Fontainebleau: INSEAD, 1998), and subsequent interviews with Chairman Stan Shih.
3. Y. Doz and K. Asakawa, "Shiseido," INSEAD Case Study (Fontainebleau: INSEAD, 2001).

CHAPTER 4

1. The data concerning ABB is also drawn from R. Simons and C. Bartlett, "Asea Brown Boveri," Case 9-192-139 (Boston: Harvard Business School, 1992); R. Simons, "ABB: Accountability Times Two," Case 9-192-141 (Boston: Harvard Business School, 1992); and M. F. R. Kets de Vries, "Percy Banevik and ABB," INSEAD Case Study (Fontainebleau: INSEAD, 1994).
2. General Electric Annual Report, 1998.
3. Both quotes are from an interview with the magazine *World Trade*, August 1996.
4. Examples of this phenomenon are discussed by J. M. Stopford, "Competing Globally for Resources," *Transnational Corporations* 4, no. 2 (1995).

CHAPTER 5

1. EuroDisney, which opened in 1992, is now Disneyland Paris.
2. For a detailed discussion of tacit knowledge, see M. Polanyi, *The Tacit Dimension* (New York: Doubleday, 1966), and, for example, P. Baumard, *Tacit Knowledge in Organizations* (London: Sage, 1999).

3. *Business Week*, June 1997.
4. A detailed discussion of know-how "stickiness" is available in B. Kogut, ed., *Country Competitiveness: Technology and the Organizing of Work* (New York: Oxford University Press, 1993).
5. The emergence of multinationals as a mechanism to overcome the "transactions costs" failures of the market has been thoroughly examined in the economic literature. See, for example, R. E. Caves, *Multinational Firms and Economic Analysis*, 2d ed. (Cambridge: Cambridge University Press, 1996). For a knowledge-based explanation of multinationals, see B. Kogut and U. Zander, "Knowledge of the Firm and the Evolutionary Theory of the Multinational Corporation," *Journal of International Business Studies* 24, no. 4 (1993): 625–646.
6. For a discussion of some of these problems, see, for example, G. Szulansky, "Exploring Internal Stickiness," *Strategic Management Journal*, Special Issue, 17 (1996): 27–44, and A. Bartmess and K. Cerny, "Seeding Plants for a Global Harvest," *McKinsey Quarterly*, no. 2 (1993): 107–132.
7. M. Cusumano and R. Selby, *Microsoft Secrets* (New York: Free Press, 1995).
8. M. Fruin, *Knowledge Works: Managing Intellectual Capital at Toshiba* (New York: Oxford University Press, 1997).
9. For a further understanding on how co-location, socialization, and facilities play a role in knowledge creation, see T. J. Allen, *Managing the Flow of Technology* (Cambridge, MA: MIT Press, 1977); and I. Nonaka and H. Takeuchi, *The Knowledge Creating Company* (New York: Oxford University Press, 1995). In "In Two Minds: Real versus 'Virtual' Co-location" (*Financial Times*, 10 November 1995, 10), C. Lorenz writes, "The principle of co-location is as old as the hills in small companies."
10. For a very interesting rendering of recontextualization of Disney in Europe and Japan, see M. Y. Brannen and J. M. Wilson III, "Recontextulization and Internationalization: Lessons in Transcultural Materialism from the Walt Disney Company," *CEMS Business Review* 1, nos. 1 and 2 (1996): 97–110.
11. N. S. Argyres, "The Impact of Information Technology on Coordination: Evidence from the B-2 'Stealth' Bomber," *Organization Science* 10, no. 2 (1999): 162–180.
12. See, for example, Argyres, "The Impact of Information Technology on Coordination"; R. Boutellier, O. Grassmann, H. Macho, and M. Roux, "Management of Dispersed Product Development Teams: The Role of Information Technologies," *R&D Management* 28, no. 1 (1998): 13–25; and A. De Meyer, "Tech Talk: How Managers Are Stimulating Global R&D Communication," *Sloan Management Review* (Spring 1991): 49–58.

CHAPTER 6

1. L. Kim, "The Dynamics of Samsung's Technological Learning in Semiconductors," *California Management Review* 39, no. 3 (Spring 1997): 86–100.
2. "Why Dell Is a Survivor," *Forbes*, 12 October 1992.
3. K. Asakawa, "The Multinational Tension in R&D Internationalization: Strategic Linkage Mechanisms of Distant Contextual Knowledge in Japanese Multinational Companies" (unpublished Ph.D. diss., INSEAD, 1996).
4. N. Griffin and K. Masters, *Hit & Run: How Jon Peters and Peter Guber Took Sony for a Ride in Hollywood* (New York: Simon & Schuster, 1996).
5. On the impact of lead users and other external parties in the innovation process, see E. von Hippel, *The Sources of Innovation* (New York: Oxford University Press, 1988).

6. D. V. Fites, "Make Your Dealers Your Partners," *Harvard Business Review* (March–April 1996): 90.

7. On home-base–augmenting vs. home-base–exploiting R&D labs, see W. Kuermmele, "Building Effective R&D Capabilities Abroad," *Harvard Business Review* (March–April 1997): 61–70.

8. See Chapter 2 in P. J. Williamson, *Managing the Global Frontier* (London: Financial Times Pitman, 1994).

CHAPTER 7

1. A. De Meyer, "Nestlé S.A.," INSEAD Case Study (Fontainebleau: INSEAD, 1993).

2. See C. Y. Baldwin and K. B. Clark, *Design Rules: The Power of Modularity* (Cambridge, MA: MIT Press, 2000), on how modularity (building complex products from smaller subsystems that can be designed independently yet function together as a whole) has implied high levels of innovation in the computer industry, for example.

3. C. Handy, "Trust and the Virtual Organization," *Harvard Business Review* (May–June 1995): 40–50.

4. Unless you have ties to England, you probably don't know that "That's not cricket!" means that a fair process or the proper rules are not being followed. And if you are not accustomed to American football, you will not know that "a third and long situation" means that we are behind, and this is the last chance to do it—or else we will have to give the "ball" (business) to the competition.

CHAPTER 8

1. See, for example, C. K. Prahalad and Y. Doz, *The Multinational Mission* (New York: Free Press, 1987); Bartlett and Ghoshal, *Managing across Borders*; C. A. Bartlett, Y. Doz, and G. Hedlund, eds., *Managing the Global Firm* (London: Routledge, 1990); J. H. Dunning, *Multinational Enterprises and the Global Economy* (New York: Addison-Wesley; 1993); S. Rangan and R. Z. Lawrence, *A Prism on Globalization: Corporate Responses to the Dollar* (Washington, D.C.: Brookings Institute, 1999); J. Birkinshaw, *Entrepreneurship in the Global Firm* (London: Sage, 2000); and J. R. Galbraith, *Designing the Global Corporation* (San Francisco: Jossey Bass, 2000).

2. The choice between owning a capability site versus leveraging it from a partner or subcontractor becomes an independent decision, based on the economics, risks, and potential need for proprietary learning.

3. In the field of international economics, D. Ricardo made an equivalent argument almost two centuries ago in *On the Principles of Political Economy and Taxation* (London: John Murray, 1817).

4. See S. Schneider and J.-L. Barsoux, *Managing across Cultures* (London: Prentice-Hall, 1997), on the impact of the various spheres of culture (national, industry, functional, and so on) on corporate culture. On the concept of "glue," see P. Evans, "Management Development as Glue Technology," *Human Resource Planning* 15, no. 1 (1992): 85–106.

5. P. D'Iribarne, "The Unexpected Resources of a Culture: An 'Excellent' Company in Casablanca," *Annales des Mines* [Paris], June 1997 (original in French).

Index

About the Authors

Yves Doz is the Timken Professor of Global Technology and Innovation at INSEAD in Fontainebleau, France. From 1987 to 1994, he was Director of INSEAD's Management of Technology and Innovation Programme, a multidisciplinary effort involving approximately twenty faculty members and researchers. From 1990 to 1995, he was Associate Dean for R&D. Since 1999, he has been Dean of Executive Education. He has also served on the faculty of Harvard Business School and held visiting appointments at Stanford University and Aoyama Gakuin University in Japan.

Professor Doz has worked on multinational aircraft programs and has consulted for many multinational corporations on global strategies, organization, strategic alliances, and competitive revitalization. His research on the strategy and organization of multinational companies, specifically in high-technology industries, has led to numerous publications, including four books. The most recent, *Alliance Advantage*, coauthored with Gary Hamel, was published in 1998 by Harvard Business School Press.

José Santos is Professor of International Management at INSEAD in Fontainebleau, France. He is also a guest Professor at the Catholic University at Porto, Portugal, and has held visiting appointments at Bocconi University, Italy; Bled School of Management, Slovenia; and Fundação Dom Cabral, Brazil.

Prior to joining INSEAD, Professor Santos had a twenty-year career in international business with responsibilities spanning international trade, licensing agreements, joint ventures, and cross-border M&A. His last appointment before returning to the academic world in 1995 was as a board member and Managing Director of Segafredo Zanetti, an Italian multinational. He continues to serve as a non-executive director of a number of corporations. His research focuses on the management of multinational firms, in particular on innovation, knowledge management, and global customer management. He is a frequent speaker at conferences in the United States and Europe.

Peter Williamson is Professor of International Management and Asian Business at INSEAD in Fontainebleau, France, and Singapore. He was formerly Dean of MBA Programmes at London Business School and Visiting Professor of Global Strategy and Management at Harvard Business School.

Professor Williamson's research and publications span globalization, strategy innovation, joint ventures and alliances, and competitive dynamics. His other books include *The Economics of Financial Markets* (1995); *Managing the Global Frontier* (1994); and *The Strategy Handbook* (1992). He has consulted on business strategy and international expansion for numerous multinational companies in Asia/Pacific, Europe, and North America. He is an adviser to governments on trade and investment and also serves as a non-executive director of several listed companies.